Better City Government

INNOVATION IN AMERICAN
URBAN POLITICS, 1850–1937

KENNETH FOX

Temple University Press

PHILADELPHIA

Temple University Press, Philadelphia 19122
© 1977 by Temple University. All rights reserved
Published 1977
Printed in the United States of America

International Standard Book Number: 0-87722-099-9
Library of Congress Catalog Card Number: 77-071957

To Diana, Kathe, James, Ellen and also Philip,
who was born only recently but must be included

Contents

Preface

This is a history book about how to improve the governing of American cities. I have used a historical analysis of urban political development in the United States between the 1850s and the 1930s to argue that the ability of reform-minded people to improve urban government depends upon how accurately they succeed in understanding the impact of national social and economic development upon city life. I have called the activity of analyzing the sources of urban political difficulties and devising governmental mechanisms for overcoming those difficulties "urban political innovation," and I have separated it from the larger topic of urban reform in the period so that it can be examined on its own merits. Clearly distinguishing the activities that constituted innovation in urban government in the late nineteenth and early twentieth centuries has facilitated comparison with the innovation process that has evolved since the 1930s, and the tentative formulation of generalizations applicable to both the present and the past.

The innovators of the 1890s were not reluctant about assuming that there were better and worse forms of urban government, nor were the academic social scientists among them uncomfortable about participating in a movement whose objective was "good city government." Today, urban social scientists take an equivocal stance on the uses and objectives of their work. The professional imperative to define one's activities in relation to the paradigm prevailing in a narrow field of theorizing and research has taken precedence over commitment to distinct trends of social reform. The gains this strategy has achieved in making social science more "scientific" may be of value, but the detrimental effects it is having on the everyday practice of municipal administration are considerable. City bureaucrats simply cannot effectively generate innovations in the structure and functioning of the administrative apparatus within which they work. They have neither the time, nor the energy, nor the expertise, nor the best analytic vantage point, nor the most advantageous political position to design and implement the changes that could improve the way their cities are governed. One of my hopes for this book is that it will encourage social scientists to re-evaluate their responsibilities for the practical tasks of improving urban government. If it accomplishes nothing else, a history of urban political innovation can at least remind modern social scientists that their turn-of-the-century predecessors regarded reform activism as an important professional responsibility.

Various people were indispensable, in diverse ways, to the final form this book has assumed and I want to acknowledge and thank each and all of them. Two historians, Seymour Mandelbaum and Thomas C. Cochran, both of the University of Pennsylvania, guided the original project as a doctoral dissertation. William Pollak, Richard Burton, Selma Mushkin, Harold Hochman, Ruth Kemper, and others on the staff of the Urban Institute introduced me to the practical work of modern urban social science. Without their example of how urban political and economic problem-solving is pursued today, it would have been impossible for me to develop the analysis of late nineteenth- and early twentieth-century innovation that is presented here. I also received important financial and technical support from the Urban Institute.

I want to thank Kenneth Jackson of Columbia University for reading the manuscript at a crucial stage and expressing his confidence in it. Alfred D. Chandler of the Harvard Graduate School of Business Administration, whose work on innovation in the structure and management of large industrial corporations inspired the original formulation of this project, provided particularly gratifying encouragement. Robert C. Wood of the University of Massachusetts shared with me insights from his experience in urban research and policy-making and offered useful comments on the manuscript. Harold Hyman of Rice University also contributed valuable assistance and support.

To Philip Brenner, who aided me first and foremost as a friend, I want to express special thanks. He has contributed to my work on this project with his concern, his criticism, and his unique ability to help me transform my ideas into straightforward propositions. His participation has been invaluable.

Several other people whom I consider my friends before anything else also made important contributions. Ira Katznelson provided crucial support and valuable comments. Marvin Swartz, Miriam Chrisman, Nancy Stepan, and Helen Swartz helped me through the difficult months of revising the original manuscript and finding a publisher. Alfred Stepan aided me with his advice and provided, in the form of one of his own books, a useful model of how a study of this kind can be presented. Fred Jackes, Graham Taylor, Cathi Rodriques, and Monique Cohen must also be mentioned for their friendship and support. I am grateful to Nonny Burack for typing the revised text.

The people at Temple University Press have been tremendously helpful in creating a book out of my manuscript. Kenneth Arnold has been particularly unsparing of his time and energy. Helen Swartz must be mentioned again for an excellent job of editing.

The people to whom the book is dedicated played a special role that they understand very well. They have seen me through the difficult periods and shared my belief that writing books can be useful in achieving a better life in the cities we all love.

Introduction

The years between the 1850s and the 1930s were a period of transformation in the development of the United States. During these years, an agricultural, extractive, and commercial nation became industrial, urban, and modern. Social science strives to differentiate separate processes of industrialization, urbanization, and modernization when analyzing present-day developing nations. In studying the United States during its era as a developing nation, however, such distinctions have not proved very useful. For the time being, it seems best to treat the transformation of the 1850–1940 period as a single national process, and to see the modern industrial cities of the early twentieth century as its most characteristic result.[1]

Urban historians of the United States have given considerable attention to the early twentieth-century industrial cities. While this research has not ignored the argument that urban development should be treated as an aspect of the national development of a modern urban-industrial society, American urban historians have tended to treat the cities as if they were themselves the crucial independent force in national urban development, and to treat individual cities, when one particular city was under examination, as if they were self-contained and self-determining social systems. This tendency has been particularly strong where the study of urban political development is concerned. Comprehensive overviews have necessarily acknowledged the similarities among cities during the industrial period, but not with sufficient strength to bring into question the assumption that forces generated *within* an individual city were the most important factors in its growth and development. Recent advances in the analysis of national economic development, however, have made this state of affairs increasingly untenable. From the perspective of the development of the national social system, especially during the transformation of the 1850–1940 period, cities have come to be seen much more as the products, and in some ways the victims, of national development, than as its engine or cause. Arguments that individual cities were the masters of their own fates have become difficult to sustain.[2]

The effects of the national transformation on the governments of late nineteenth-century cities were particularly devastating. City governments were not powerful institutions in the 1850s and the political manifestations of the new social and economic changes overwhelmed their formal mechanisms. The central problem of urban political development in the late nineteenth century became a matter of providing cities with a form of government that would enable them to confront and ameliorate the effects of the national industrialization, urbanization, and modernization process. Solving this problem involved generating innovations in city government structure and administration, and it is this aspect of the urban history of the years from the 1850s to the 1930s that I have tried to deal with in this book. This is a history of urban political innovation in the United States during the period of its transformation into an industrial, urban, and modern society.

The problem of providing an effective form of government for the late nineteenth-century city was resolved through the development of a systematic approach to generating innovations in urban government by a national coalition of elite reform activists, experts in municipal law, political scientists, progressive city officials, and a group of experts in urban statistics at the federal Bureau of the Census. The national coalition began to coalesce in 1894, and their approach to innovation assumed its finished form between 1909 and 1913. Three independent factors contributed

to the emergence of this resolution of the city government problem. The first was the failure of pragmatic innovations devised by
the cities between the 1850s and the 1890s. Cities contrived ingenious means of coping with the increasingly miserable conditions
produced by national social change. Various kinds of political
arrangements evolved, of which the "boss" and his ward "machine" have become the most familiar; some kinds of arrangements
came into use in many cities. But these indigenous innovations
were not effective in confronting the worsening state of city life
and politics. The second factor, operating quite separately from
the first, involved changes in the character of American law,
changes in the legal profession, and changes in the scholarly analysis of politics, that led to the creation of a field of municipal law,
to the rise of a political science profession, and to the creation of
municipal political science as a branch of the political science
enterprise. These changes were not initially stimulated by the
problems of the cities, but as the law and the analysis of politics
changed, their practitioners attributed more and more importance
to municipal questions. The third factor contributing to the emergence of a systematic approach to urban political innovation was
a shift in the primary focus of organized efforts to reform the
national political system from an intense concentration on obtaining federal civil service reform in the years leading up to the passage of the Pendleton act in 1882, to a similarly intense concentration on obtaining strong powers of self-government for cities in
the years from 1894 to 1899 and after. Elite reform activists
espoused strong city self-government as a means of reversing what
James Bryce had identified as the "one conspicuous failure" of
the national political system, the manner in which the cities were
governed.

Developing an effective form of government for the beleagured
late nineteenth-century American city would have been less difficult if the fundamental assumptions about state and city government inherited from earlier in the century had been different.
While the social and economic character of American cities of
the 1880s was similar to that of the cities of developing West

European countries, these assumptions contributed to producing political conditions in American cities that were shockingly backward. One European called them the worst governed cities "in the civilized world." The most problematic assumption was the axiom that responsibility for the governing of cities must reside primarily with their respective state governments. When city governments proved incapable or corrupt, state governments took back powers, reassumed delegated responsibilities, instituted direct supervision, and wrote special legislation covering specific problems of individual cities. The strategy that eventually resolved the "municipal problem" of the industrial city, strengthening the powers of city governments and increasing their responsibility for managing their own affairs, went against this principle and was rarely advocated. Few people of the 1850s believed that strengthening city government would produce improvement, and fewer still in the 1870s. The watchwords of reform were economy and honesty.

When state government supervision failed, and honest, economy-minded reform failed, the principles guiding improvement efforts were reevaluated. A national coalition of reformers, experts in municipal law, city officials, and political scientists undertook the formulation of a new conception of city government. Out of their reassessment of principles came a commitment to strong city self-government, insulated from state government interference and fully responsible for management of the city's environment and its social problems. In 1899, the National Municipal League, the organization founded to coordinate the efforts of this national coalition, published a declaration of the new principles in the form of a "Municipal Program."

Strong city self-government was a strategy for confronting the horrible conditions of late nineteenth-century city life. Its proponents attacked state government control of the governing of cities as an impediment to municipal improvement, and insisted that the people of the cities must have their own governmental means of overcoming their unique social and economic problems. Between 1899 and 1913, the new strategy grew into a comprehensive approach to urban political innovation. This comprehensive approach to innovation provided the substance of what has since become known as "Progressive" municipal reform. Yet for all that has been written about the mature character of early twentieth-century municipal reform, its origins and evolution remain only partially understood. While we know that reform movements in most cities, large and small, and in all parts of the country, derived the specific form of improved city government they advocated from one general model, we know very little about how this general model came into prominence and why it took the particular form that it did. I have called the strategy and content of these municipal reform movements the "functional" approach to innovation, and I have concentrated attention, in explaining its gestation, upon people who are better characterized as political "innovators" than as "reformers."

The objective of the municipal reformers was to provide American cities with effective government. The municipal "innovators," the lawyers, political scientists, federal statisticians, city officials, and elite activists who participated in developing the strategy and substance of municipal reform, devoted their energies to the narrower question of determining the form that an effective solution to the problem of governing American cities should take. They set about this task by a procedure that grounded their prescriptions for structural and administrative change in an analysis of the role of cities within the national social, economic, and political system. Out of the analytic determination that the social and economic conditions of city life were fundamentally different from conditions in towns, villages, and countryside, came the prescriptive argument that cities required a special kind of self-government strong enough to confront their unique difficulties. Further analysis of urban conditions proceded step-by-step with the elaboration of a general model of a strong city government. The model put in practice the principle that ameliorating urban social and economic conditions required the performance of certain essential "functions" by city governments. The model proposed a municipal government structure in which each essential function was the responsibility of a major administrative department. The other fundamental elements of the general model were a strong mayor at the head of the functionally departmentalized administrative structure, and a large, single-chamber, representative city council.

The principal formulators and advocates of the general model of "functional" city government were the urban statisticians at the federal Bureau of the Census. Building upon the principles put forward in the 1899 Municipal Program, the bureau developed an annual series of comparative statistics of expenditures and service performance for all cities of over 30,000 population that described the behavior of each city in terms of a centralized, functionally departmentalized structure. Field agents of the bureau, ignoring the peculiarities of each city's accounting procedures, aggregated expenditures and service activities into standardized functional categories. Where part of the responsibility for a functional activity resided with an independent commission, board, or agency, the bureau's agents lumped its expenditures with those of the city government, creating a centralized description of such a city's practices in spite of the fragmented nature of its governmental structure. The bureau coordinated its program closely with the National Municipal League's campaign for uniformity in municipal accounting. Both employed the same centralized, functionally departmentalized framework. The state uniform municipal accounting act promoted by the league mandated a state's cities to use an accounting format based on the League–Census Bureau model, and provided for state government auditing of city accounts. By 1907, Massachusetts, New York, Ohio, and Iowa had passed uniform municipal accounting laws, nineteen other cities had adopted the League-Census Bureau accounting system on their own initiative, and bureau field agents found that a majority of the remaining cities of over 30,000 had made at least minor reforms in their accounting methods. The Census Bureau also devised a method for evaluating city government performance by adapting the system of cost accounting evolved by business in the 1890s into a comparative measure of city productive efficiency.

As the general model acquired sophistication and importance, political scientists combined the principles of the Municipal Program with the centralized, functionally departmentalized model of city government structure in a prescriptive theory of American municipal government. The architects of the theory defined the city in terms of the unique "urban conditions" created by the dense settlement of a large population within a small geographic space. They cited industrialization as the force responsible for concentrating increasingly large and dense settlement around the city centers of the preindustrial period, and for the physical, economic, and social conditions prevailing within the turn-of-the-century city. The geographic extent of the dense conglomeration of population and activity around a center, they argued, defined the city as a community, and the problems arising from the physical, social, and economic conditions present in such communities necessitated the performance of a set of essential public "functions" by a municipal government. Formulations of the theory then provided a specific supporting argument for each of the major functional categories of the centralized, functionally departmentalized model. The appearance of four university textbook explications of the theory between 1909 and 1913, each by a prominent author, initiated its role as the standard framework for the political science of municipal government and politics.

By 1913, the elements of a comprehensive approach to urban political innovation had assumed their mature form, including a model of effective city government structure and administrative practice, a prescriptive theory of municipal government in the context of the American political system, a federal program of comparative statistical analysis and reporting, and of applied research in municipal administration, and an active national association of city and state municipal reform organizations. These developments are the subject of the first four chapters. Chapter 1 discusses the major types of indigenous responses to the impact of the process of industrialization, urbanization, and modernization on city politics in the 1860s, '70s, and '80s. Chapter 2 investigates early attempts to define the proper role of city government in the legal and political systems of the late nineteenth century. Chapter 3 describes the shift in the orientation of organized efforts to reform the national political system from a prevailing interest in federal civil service reform in the 1870s and early 1880s to a similarly intense focus upon municipal government reform by the mid-1890s. And Chapter 4 examines the construction of a general model of centralized, functionally departmentalized municipal government by the Census Bureau's urban statisticians, and its incorporation with the principles of the Municipal Program in a prescriptive theory of American municipal government.

Chapters 5, 6, and 7 deal with the "functional" mode of urban political innovation in its maturity, and with its decline. Chapter 5 is a statistical analysis of changes in the expenditure practices of all cities with populations over 30,000 between 1904 and 1930, using data from the Census Bureau's annual reports of city financial statistics. The changes are evaluated with respect to the prescriptive implications of the centralized, functionally departmentalized model and the theory of municipal government. Chapter 6 treats the major dilemma inherent in the functional theory: the potential conflict between "democracy" and "efficiency" that might arise from emphasis on making city government an effective provider of municipal services according to an intricately specified model. And Chapter 7 explains the difficulties that the "metropolitanization" of the nation's largest cities presented for the functional innovative mode, leading to its decline as an approach to innovation as a result of its inability to provide appropriate responses to the problems of metropolitan political development.

Since the 1930s, a new mode of innovation in urban political development has emerged. As with the evolution of the functional mode in the period of industrialization, urbanization, and modernization, 1850–1940, it was the emergence of new forces of national development, which generated new kinds of conditions in urban areas, that necessitated the formulation of a new approach to urban political innovation. Chapter 8 deals briefly with the characteristics of the new mode of innovation that has developed since the 1930s, compares the new mode with the functional mode, and uses both to derive some general statements about the relationship between national development and urban political innovation. I have coined the term "Keynesian pluralist" innovation to denote the manner in which improvements in urban government are devised today.

Finally, a word about purpose. This study deals with political innovation in a distinct period of national development. During the 1930s, a new era of development began, an era often designated by the term "post-industrial." This choice of words was inappropriate as far as I am concerned, for their intended meaning seems to be not that American society has ceased being "industrial," but simply that the industrialization, urbanization, and modernization of the previous era have concluded, and that we now live in a society that is fully industrial, urban, and modern. "Post-industrial" is also undesirable for its failure to convey the dynamic character of development in the present period. It is a description of where we aren't—that is, we are no longer experiencing the process of becoming industrialized—rather than of where we are and where development is taking us. One of the useful functions of the study of the past is to help us divide the complex flow of social change into meaningful periods. The brief present in which we live and make policy choices is also a period within the longer course of change. This book is an analysis of urban political development in the distinct period between the 1850's and the 1930's, but I hope that it will also contribute to our ability to understand current urban politics in the context of a distinct period of development. The present period runs from the 1930s to some presumably near point in the future. At the moment, the circumstances in which the current era of development can be said to have come to a conclusion, the greater and lesser importance of various forces of social change to the overall course of development in the period, and the appropriate innovative responses to social change over the next five or ten years, are all more vaguely understood than they have to be.

Better City Government

CHAPTER 1

The Municipal Problem of the Late Nineteenth-Century City

Our understanding of the impact of the industrialization, urbanization, and modernization process upon the American city of the latter half of the nineteenth century is still largely in the form of generalizations and hypotheses. We are acutely aware that cities experienced increasing difficulty in managing their physical environment and in coping with the social and economic condition of their populations between the 1850s and the mid-1890s. This inability of the city to govern itself effectively was what the political scientists of the 1890s meant by the term "the municipal problem." Cities responded as best they could to the changes in their physical, social, and economic character. The more effective responses were actually ingenious innovations in social and political organization, and in the management of city government. While none of these responses successfully overcame the municipal problem, almost every city experimented with its own version of at least one of the major types of innovative response. This chapter presents a typology of the various innovations, with representative examples of each type.

The failure of indigenous responses to mitigate the crisis of the cities in the 1860s, '70s, and '80s came as something of a shock to people who prided themselves on what James Bryce described in his analysis of the American political system in the 1880s as "that adaptability of the institutions to the people and their conditions, which judicious strangers admire in the United States."[1] When

Bryce called city government the "one conspicuous failure" of the American political system, he was referring not to the "municipal problem" itself, but to the failure of pragmatic innovation to resolve the problem. To illustrate what he, and increasing numbers of national political reform activists of the late 1880s, were concerned about, I have included in the description of each type of innovation a discussion of its chief inadequacies.

In treating the major developments of city politics in the period between 1850 and 1890 as innovative responses to a crisis of social and economic origin, I have diverged from the currently popular trend of historical analysis. At first, historians dichotomized the events of this period into a struggle between "bosses" and "reformers." Later, "bosses" and "reformers" and their characteristic political strategies became general types within a more complex analytic framework. In the 1950s, historians began to suggest that city political conflict could be characterized in terms of two major classes, the business class and the working class, and began to view reformers and bosses as the leaders of their respective sides in that struggle. Most recent research has been part of an effort to refine this approach by improving the characterization of the major classes and factions, in hopes of achieving a sophisticated social history of city politics.[2]

I have taken a different course. In accord with the premise that urban political development between the 1850s and the mid-1930s was largely a function of a *national* process of industrialization, urbanization, and modernization, I have approached city politics from a national, rather than a city, perspective. From this national perspective, struggles over the distribution of political power among classes and factions within cities continue to be important, but not as important as the power and ability of each city's political system *as a whole* to cope with the impact of the transformation of the national social system.[3] It is in this context that innovations in city government structure and administration, or the failure to evolve effective innovations as in the period between 1850 and 1890, become a central aspect of national urban political development. When no city possessed a dependable ability to put out fires, fight epidemics and disease, or master the perpetually intractable task of cleaning the streets, it mattered little which class or faction elected its leaders to the official positions of power in the city government. The failure of indigenous innovation was every city resident's municipal problem.

The Ward Machine

The most characteristic and widespread response to the changing nature of the city was the ward political machine. The appearance of the ward machine was related directly to the increase in municipal government activities, offices, and employment necessitated by the impact of national industrialization and urbanization. Its antecedents were the volunteer fire companies, gangs, social clubs, coteries of saloon frequenters, and other structures of status and prestige within the neighborhoods of the large preindustrial city. In the absence of an effective organizational structure for the new municipal activities, the social structures of the neighborhoods asserted their strength. The ward machine emerged as a social institution capable of organizing the municipal voting behavior of neighborhood residents on the one hand, and the distribution of offices, employment, and new municipal services on the other.[4]

The first true ward machines began to develop in New York City in the 1850s. New York had a long history of social organizations involved in politics, including the workingmen's organizations of the 1830s, and the Tammany Society, which began playing a role in the political life of the city soon after its founding in the 1780s. The first ward structures were organized by specific neighborhood leaders and tended to focus upon the leader's personality as a unifying principle. By 1868, recognizable "machines" had taken shape in numerous New York wards.[5]

New York City ward organization of the 1860s had two parallel aspects. On one side, the ward leader's followers occupied the offices and jobs of their ward's divisions of the city's geographically structured departmental bureaucracies and work forces. The ward leader had discretion over who would work for the departments of parks and public works within his ward, and who would be appointed to the ward's fire companies and police departments. He also had considerable influence over who would be hired to work for city contractors on projects within his ward. The ward leader and his machine provided a stable means of staffing the ward's branches of the city government. In addition, it is fairly certain that ward leaders determined how the work of city departments would be performed within their districts, deciding which streets would be well swept and which left mired in filth. With the police and their associated inspectors of buildings and sanitary conditions, ward leaders managed an intricate arrangement of petty payoffs and selective arrests or summonses. The Sunday closing law for saloons was selectively enforced with especially deft discretion. For practical purposes, the ward leader was the supervisor of city services for his district.[6]

The other, and more important, track of the ward organization was its fostering of neighborhood loyalty to assure electoral victories. The industrializing large city was socially and ethnically chaotic, but individual ward neighborhoods were considerably more homogeneous than the city as a whole. In the face of the whirl of conflicting interests rushing around them in the rest of the city, the shared concerns of life in the neighborhood bound the ward leader and his constituents together. Obtaining loyal support at the polling place under such circumstances was not overly difficult. Edward Banfield and James Q. Wilson have emphasized that modern ward machines succeed because an individual's votes for the city government positions in an election are not of particularly great value to him. When complicating factors do not enter in, the machine does not have to provide anything of great value in order to obtain such votes. Banfield and Wilson argue that the best currency to employ for this purpose is friendship, and they quote approvingly Jane Addams's recognition that the successful ward leader strove to stand before his voters as a "good neighbor and friend."[7]

Through an arrangement of subleaders, precinct captains, and all-purpose subordinates, the ward leader collected information on the loyalty of every voter in his district and issued specific instructions on the treatment of wavering or uncommitted individuals. On election day, the ward leader had to maneuver his following to the polls, provide each voter with a proper ballot, and see that his precinct workers kept strategic control of the ballot boxes and polling places. Where majorities were slim or non-existent, the ward leader brought in "repeaters" to vote in the names of deceased persons still on the registry lists or persons long since moved from the district. If necessary, "shoulder-pushers" and other ruffians could be called upon to stimulate disorder while the boxes were stuffed with excess ballots, or assorted tactics could be used to obtain a desirable result from the ballot-counting process.

Solid neighborhood loyalty, however, was always preferable to unorthodox electoral practices. Day in and day out, the ward leader and his organization strove to become a permanent social structure of the district. Ward leaders concentrated their activities on their personal political clubs, with the object of making the club the central social institution of the ward. Clubs coordinated the celebration of holidays, distributed Christmas turkeys and other scraps of assistance to the poor, and sustained the morale of the ward organization with camaraderie, liquor, and cigars. Precinct captains maintained daily contact with the people of their neighborhoods while the ward leader reserved his scarce and valuable time for major social milestones in the lives of his constituents, especially weddings, funerals, and wakes. Matthew Breen reports that a conscientious ward leader would attend the funeral of every man, woman, or child who died in his district, "not . . . as a tribute to the virtues of the dead, but as a diplomatic appeal for the votes of the living." In the era of Tammany chief Charles Murphy in the 1890s, ward leader George Washington Plunkitt divided a typical day between presiding over affairs at his clubhouse and rushing from an Italian funeral, to a Jewish funeral, and then to a Jewish wedding where he had conscientiously arranged for an expensive gift for the bride to precede his appearance.[8]

By the 1890s, the ward machine, and the role of "boss," had become institutional forms that could be imposed upon a politically unorganized city neighborhood. The artificiality of the resulting social ties between the machine and its constituents does not seem to have impaired the machine's effectiveness. A striking example is William Lorimer, an ambitious young man who perceived the potential advantages of organizing Republican ward machines to compete with the dominant coalition of Democratic ward machines in Chicago in the late 1880s. As the son of a Scottish Presbyterian minister, Lorimer was a Republican by natural family inheritance. But since Catholicism was an almost indispensable prerequisite for working-class leadership in Chicago, Lorimer took an Irish Catholic wife, converted to the Church himself, and raised his eight children as Catholics. These and other efforts bore fruit, and when a split in the Democratic coalition led to a Republican victory, Lorimer obtained the patronage needed to consolidate his machine structure. Personal political skill was the crucial attribute of a successful boss, and if Lorimer had possessed greater innate ability he might have accomplished even more. Lincoln Steffens wrote of him in 1903 that he "does not make the impression, either as a man or as a politician," that bosses such as Richard Croker of Tammany made. This judgment foreshadowed Lorimer's eventual political demise when the revelation of a bribe paid to an Illinois state legislator led to his expulsion from the U.S. Senate.[9]

The great failing of the proliferation of ward machines in a city was that they exacerbated the antagonism already endemic between neighborhoods, races, and religious and ethnic groups. For the politics of the city as a whole, ward machines increased the discord and conflict. The most typical situation of the 1870s and 1880s was that of Boston. Harold Zink, writing in the 1930s on the machine as a city political institution, explained that Martin Lomasney was known as the "Czar" of Boston in this period, but that in fact he functioned effectively only in his own Eighth Ward. "Boston has given birth to a sizable band of powerful ward and local leaders," Zink wrote, "who have warred so vigorously and yet survived so stubbornly as to render impossible the emergence of a single all-powerful boss." According to Moorfield Storey, a reform activist of the 1890s, the inability of Boston ward leaders to cooperate with each other led them to develop an impartial system of dividing the city's public resources:

each member of the Common Council received a certain number of tickets corresponding to his share of the total number of men in the employ of the city. No man could receive employment from the city unless he presented one of these tickets, and workmen were discharged as fast as it was necessary to find places for those who bore these credentials.

By building his political strength on the social cohesiveness of his own neighborhood, the ward boss was increasing the fragmentation of the city rather than uniting diverse classes, nationalities, and groups in a common attempt at governing.[10]

State Legislative Supervision

The second major type of innovation, state legislative supervision of the governing of the city, was in part a direct response to the impact of industrialization, urbanization, and modernization, and in part a reaction to the appearance of ward machines and city-wide coalitions of ward bosses. The ideological spirit of early state legislative action in the 1850s was an intense concern over the threat to the moral order of city communities posed by immigrants and alcohol. This danger was usually most strongly perceived by state legislators from rural districts. The thrust of several different political movements in the 1850s, from elite reform at one extreme to the nativist Know-Nothing movement at the other, was that enforcement of the law and preservation of the peace in cities could only be assured by transferring responsibility from the municipality to state government commissions.

In 1855, a combination of Know-Nothings and Republicans in the New York state legislature passed a prohibition law that banned all sales of alcohol (except for "mechanical," "chemical," "medicinal," or "sacramental" purposes), in the belief that its enforcement would prevent "intemperance, pauperism and crime." New York City Mayor Fernando Wood announced that the law would be enforced, pending its testing before the courts, but in practice he employed technicalities to assure its nonenforcement. The Know-Nothing and Republican forces countered with investigations of the New York City police. In 1857 their struggle with Wood and his city following culminated in a choice between increasing the mayor's control over the police department, or placing control in the hands of a commission chosen by the governor and approved by the legislature. The legislature won. The mayor was reduced to the position of being one of seven members of a "Metropolitan Board of Police," the others being the mayor of Brooklyn and five members appointed by the governor, only three of whom could be from New York City. When Wood openly opposed the act, the existing police department split into supporters of Wood and supporters of the new metropolitan police force. The split quickly led to open rioting between the two factions. Eventually the courts ruled in favor of the Metropolitan Board, but by 1860 the state legislature was so disgusted with the behavior of the Mayors of New York and Brooklyn on the board that it amended the original act to remove them entirely from the higher administration of police functions in their cities.[11]

Other states quickly imitated this use of independent state-government commissions to administer city police forces. Maryland established a state commission for the Baltimore police in 1860, and state commissions for St. Louis and Kansas City (1861), Detroit (1865), Cleveland (1866), and New Orleans (1868) were all modelled on New York's example. Similar factions in the Massachusetts Commonwealth government fought to enforce their prohibition law in Boston, and tried twice, in 1861 and again in 1869, to place the city's police under a state-controlled commission. Boston's failure to control crime and vice, combined with corruption in the police department, invited attempts to institute state control, but the unexpected effectiveness of the force in dealing with the draft riot of 1863 slowed the momentum of the legislature's campaign. Finally, fear of electoral retaliation by Boston voters produced a sound defeat of the 1869 bill. In most of these situations, moral concern was amplified by Republican opposition to the increasing power of Democrats based in the cities, and nativist hatred for Catholics and immigrants.[12]

A genuine desire to mitigate the impact of industrialization and urbanization also played a part in the state legislatures' attempts at supervision. State legislatures tended to believe that independent commissions would be able to act with greater effectiveness than city government departments. Impending crisis often provided the incentive to form state commissions to perform new municipal functions. Their experiences in 1832 and 1849 led New Yorkers to believe that a third cholera epidemic would arrive from Europe in the spring and summer of 1866. The state legislature had been considering the establishment of a Metropolitan Board of Health for New York City and the cholera scare galvanized them into action. They made the board responsible for averting the expected disaster and gave it unprecedented powers. The police, under the control of the state-appointed Metropolitan Board of Police discussed above, provided the health board with office space and a system for collecting complaints about sanitary conditions by means of the police telegraph and messenger service. The board was able to assign a physician as sanitary inspector in every one of its ten-block-square sanitary districts, and when the work proved overwhelming, they were able to provide each physician-inspector with an assistant.

The state legislature's efforts to supervise the prevention of a cholera epidemic accomplished little of practical value, however. Contemporary medical theory of the 1860s prescribed that cleanliness could prevent the spread of the disease, so the board resolved to clean the streets of New York. They failed. Many tons of refuse, dust, dirt, and dead animals were removed, but the streets remained only temporarily clean. The board could order a vacant lot cleared, and see that the lot was cleared, but the courts denied them the power to erect fences around vacant lots. Without the protection of fencing, cleared lots soon returned to their original filthy state. As for the streets themselves, the contract system of cleaning proved intractable. Jackson Schultz, president of the board, met with the contractors and pleaded with them to fulfill their obligations. He offered to forgive them if their work had to be done over again. Neither tactic succeeded. When the epidemic failed to materialize, the board became famous for saving the city through its efforts, but good fortune played the major part in averting disaster because the streets were never more than temporarily clean. By the 1870s the city was busy concocting new arrangements of inspectors, police enforcement, and contracts in the hope that trial-and-error would hit upon some effective system of street cleaning.[13]

City-Wide Machines

Try as they might to accomplish their tasks, the single-function independent commissions failed because each municipal problem was entangled in all the other parts of the city's physical and social system. New York City had five state-initiated commissions at the time of the 1866 cholera crisis and they cooperated with each other relatively well, but their ability to clean the streets and perform other basic tasks was not impressive. Better city-wide coordination of municipal activities came not from elaborations of state government supervision, but from further developments of the ward machines. Soon after the establishment of strong organizations in numerous wards, coalitions of ward leaders formed what became known as city-wide machines. These took two forms. First came the decentralized, weak-centered, city machine structure, and later, in the 1870s, came attempts to forge centralized city-wide structures. The distinction between a decentralized and a centralized structure is extremely important.

The first conversion of a group of ward organizations into a true city-wide machine occurred in New York City during the election of 1868. This "Tammany" machine was the first comprehensive indigenous response to the problem of governing the late nineteenth-century city. Assembling the machine was primarily the accomplishment of William Marcy Tweed, New York State Senator and boss of Manhattan's Seventh Ward, as well as chairman of the General Committee and "Grand Sachem" of the

Tammany Society. The heart of the machine's structure was the Tammany General Committee, made up of the leaders of the city's Democratic ward machines. The traditional image of the Tammany machine is that this committee was in turn personally dominated by Tweed, who made the structure function by virtue of his personal political "power." This was not the case, however.[14] Tweed's Tammany machine was a decentralized organization. Its central committee of ward bosses was weak and chronically prone to disintegration. With each ward leader pledged to fight for his neighborhood's interests against those of all other wards, any suggestion that a committee of ward leaders could combine with each other to form a strongly centralized and unified organization would have been inherently contradictory. Such a contradiction was avoided by allowing the city-wide organization to be a decentralized coalition of ward leaders, bound together primarily by their common interest in winning city elections and obtaining the spoils of electoral victory.

As a cohesive and relatively stable institution, the city-wide Tammany machine was much more social and economic in character than it was political. Its working structure was a set of social relationships among the ward leaders and the members of the society's upper hierarchy. Although loyalty and deference to Tweed were important, the chairman of the General Committee could not have dominated or "bossed" his fellow ward leaders. In fact, he never attempted to dominate them. Instead, he managed the coalition of leaders through his control over City Hall patronage, through direct cash contributions to their ward organizations, and through an intricate hierarchy of status distinctions.[15]

At the top of the status hierarchy sat the one hundred members of the Americus Club, a resplendent yachting and country club at Indian Harbor in Greenwich, Connecticut. The middle ranks of status were designated by the privilege of dressing and behaving in increasingly flamboyant ways. A system of diamond pins developed in which power and importance were signified by the size and brilliance of the diamond a ward leader or other functionary wore. There was also a hierarchy of generosity, in which leaders rivalled each other in the size of their contributions to the poor of their districts. Tweed solidified his position at the very top by making large contributions to the poor of each and every ward, and excessive donations in his own Seventh Ward. In the cruel winter of 1870, he distributed $1,000 to each ward leader for Christmas dinners for his poor constituents, while contributing $50,000 to the poor of his own ward. The ritualistic function of this procedure was consummated by a ceremony on Christmas night at which the ward leaders acknowledged the unbounded generosity of their beloved "Boss" by presenting him with a diamond valued at $16,000. The splendor and complexity of the hierarchy teetered to a breathtaking climax in May and June of 1871 with the $700,000 wedding of Tweed's daughter, and the formal opening of the extravagant new clubhouse of the Americus Club. Six months later the entire structure was in ruins and Tweed was in jail.

Ultimately, both the cooperativeness of the ward leaders on the Tammany General Committee, and the smooth functioning of the status hierarchy, depended upon obtaining increased powers for the city from the state legislature, and upon vast amounts of money. The key to both was a new city charter, for which Tweed is reputed to have paid $600,000 to obtain the votes of Republican legislators. The new charter established a Board of Special Audit, which could issue city bonds and approve the payment of city bills on its own authority. This board simplified a process that was already under way through more intricate channels. Seymour Mandelbaum has estimated that between 1867 and 1871 Tweed and his close associates increased the city's bonded indebtedness from approximately $30 million to about $90 million. When the secret operations of the Board of Special Audit were exposed, it was revealed that New York State savings banks held approximately $50 million of the $90 million total; the bond markets of Paris, Frankfort, London, and Berlin had absorbed about $20 million; and the remainder had gone to New York and other American bond holders. On the expenditure side, where only very rough estimates are possible, it appears that between $10 and $15 million of the $60 million increase in the debt went towards real capital building projects and improvements, and between $45 and $50 million were used to smooth the workings of the coalition of ward leaders.[16]

The great failing of Tweed's Tammany machine as a means of governing the city was its instability. Its underpinnings were weak, its glory was brief, its collapse was disastrous and complete, and once its secrets became known it could not be attempted again. Only the great monetary expansion necessitated by the Civil War, combined with hundreds of millions of dollars of European investment in American stocks and bonds, made a capital manipulation such as Tweed's possible. The period during which the city-wide machine was able to operate with full effectiveness lasted little more than a year, from the initiation of the Board of Special Audit in April, 1870, to the revelation of its secret operations in the *New York Times* in July, 1871. New Yorkers learned a bitter lesson about inadequate oversight of bond financing and debt. As late as 1896, New York's municipal debt was "considerably" larger than that of any other city, and very little of the $60 million issued under Tweed's auspices had been permanently liquidated.[17]

The immediate sequel to the demise of the first Tammany machine was an attempt to replace it with a centralized machine structure. "Honest" John Kelly, Tammany's "reform" replacement for the ignominious Tweed (after July, 1871), announced that the central Tammany Committee would be used to control and discipline individual ward leaders and their organizations. The new arrangement was never tested, however, because the attempts to institute it generated immediate dissension.

The opposition mobilized behind the flamboyant gambler and ex-prizefighter John Morrissey. Kelly countered by expelling Morrissey from the Democratic party and reorganizing the leadership of the rebellious wards. He explained to the newspapers that Morrissey's notorious past made his presence in the party leadership obnoxious to respectable Democrats and prevented their wholehearted commitment to Tammany's efforts at unifying all the city's Democrats within one organization. Morrissey retaliated by forming a working coalition with the Republicans and the Tilden Democrats (a "reform" group led by the ambitious Governor Samuel J. Tilden) and together they administered a sound thrashing to Kelly and Tammany in the November election of 1875.[18]

Until the structure of New York City's government became more centralized, beginning in 1894, Tammany continued to be a decentralized machine. The applicability of even the decentralized machine structure to the politics of other cities was minimal. Most cities came to have ward machines and ward bosses, but the only organizations worthy of being considered city-wide machines were the "Gas Ring" in Philadelphia and the operations of "Boss" Alexander Shepard in Washington, D.C. The Gas Ring flourished only because circumstances in Pennsylvania Commonwealth politics guaranteed Republican majorities in Philadelphia city elections. Alexander Shepard's accomplishments were largely a function of his dominance over the Congressional commission responsible for governing the District of Columbia. When irregularities came to light, Shepard fled to Mexico to avoid arrest and his organization collapsed. In all, the city-wide machine was a brilliant but inadequate innovation, whose importance as a mechanism for controlling city politics in the period between 1860 and 1890 has been greatly exaggerated.[19]

The Weak Charismatic Mayor

Analysis of the "boss" and the machine in late nineteenth century city politics has made far too little of the fact that bosses almost never attempted to manage their organizations by assuming the office of mayor. They avoided the mayoralty because it was a position of little power, but great responsibility, especially as the focus of discontent with the functioning of city government. Fernando Wood tried to assemble a city-wide machine from the New York City mayor's office in the 1850s. He failed for several reasons, the most important of which was that he sparked the movement toward state legislative supervision discussed above. The legislature crippled the already modest powers of the office, largely to prevent anyone from using it again as Wood had tried to do. The first even moderately successful attempt to use a weak mayor's office as a position from which to assemble a viable city-wide organization was made by Carter Henry Harrison, mayor of Chicago for four-and-a-portion of eight two-year terms between 1879 and 1895.

Analysts of Harrison's political career have avoided calling him a "boss." Charles Merriam called him "a novel type of a powerful leader" because he was "neither a boss on the one hand nor a demagogue on the other." The term "charismatic" describes this distinction very well. A former slave-owning Kentucky planter who regularly galloped in and around the city on a white horse, Harrison forged an alliance between the real estate and commercial business classes (of which he was a prominent leader), and the immigrant and working classes, that was unbeatable in city elections in all but exceptional circumstances. His travels in Europe, where he dined with the prominent leaders of the cities from which Chicago's immigrants came, helped him to touch the hearts of German- and Bohemian-born voters in a way that won their loyalty to the city Democracy. Despite his aristocratic seventeenth-century Virginia ancestry, Harrison was so effective in appealing to home-country memories of Norwegian, German, Irish, Bohemian, and recent English immigrants, that the Republican Chicago *Tribune* sneeringly remarked in the campaign of 1893 that he was American "only through an accident of birth." He was even able to win over a majority of Chicago's black voters by playing on the fact that both he and they had been raised in the Old South, and by promoting an image as "Marse Catah" who could provide them with city jobs.[20]

Where cultural mores conflicted, Harrison appealed strongly to the "ritualistic" elements, groups that approached individual morality with a spirit of forgiveness such as Irish, Bohemian, and German Catholics, and German Lutherans. This strategy necessarily earned him the undying enmity of groups with a "pietistic" or "evangelical" orientation, such as Swedish Lutherans, Scotch-

Irish Protestants, and American evangelicals of all kinds, who believed that government should forcefully assist in individual salvation, especially through alcohol prohibition. Alcohol and drinking were part of the way of life of "ritualistic" working-class groups and Harrison insisted that "puritanical" nativist middle-class groups must tolerate the "intemperance" of their German, Bohemian, and Irish neighbors. Such rhetoric outraged much of Chicago's middle class and made Harrison the bane of most Protestant ministers, but the gains outweighed the losses on election day.[21]

Harrison's ability to win elections made it possible for him to obtain the cooperation of the Democratic leaders in the city's wards, and to overcome inter-ward feuding within the city's Democratic party. The "bosses" of the Harrison era, such as "Bathhouse John" Coughlin and "Hinky Dink" Kenna, joint leaders of the First Ward, worked diligently for Democratic victories in general elections, but limited their personal ambitions to their wards. When Charles Yerkes, the streetcar magnate, threatened to upset the city's politics for the sake of his franchises, Coughlin and Kenna provided the crucial city council votes to defeat him. Coughlin later explained his idiosyncratic opposition to graft on a city-wide scale by remarking "I never take the big stuff." As long as Harrison's personal popularity maintained the stability of politics on a city-wide basis, ward leaders were content to represent their half of his coalition between the business classes and the working and immigrant classes. After Harrison's death, his son, Carter Harrison II, was elected mayor as a thirty-seven-year-old neophyte. The younger Harrison proved equally competent at managing the business class—working and immigrant class coalition, and eventually also won the mayoralty five times.[22]

If it could have been applied to other cities, Harrison's weak-but-charismatic mayor system would have been an excellent model for stabilizing city politics in the 1880s. But Carter Harrison's success seems to have been in considerable measure a function of factors unique to Chicago. One factor that was probably important was the separation of Chicago city elections from state and national elections. Chicago held its city elections in April, and its mayoral elections in odd-numbered years. This practice seems to have increased the ability of a charismatic mayor to capture attention and votes. Chicago's fantastic rate of growth in this period also seems to have facilitated the kind of coalition that Harrison organized, rapid growth being desirable to employers, workers, and real estate owners alike.

But the accomplishments of the Harrison system should not be exaggerated. It did nothing to mitigate the violence arising from industrial class conflict. During the infamous Haymarket Affair in May, 1886, Harrison refused to take repressive police measures and defended the right of anarchists to free speech and assembly. Later, he publicly stated that he did not believe those convicted in the subsequent trial had been involved in the crucial bomb-throwing incident. For his pains, he was accused of "leniency with the disorderly classes" and forced to retire from politics for five years. He recovered his popularity, however, and was elected mayor a fifth time, only to be assassinated on the closing day of the great World's Columbian Exposition by an insane disappointed office seeker. If he had survived the assassination attempt, he would still have been mayor when the Pullman Strike, a nation-wide working class upheaval in which the crucial events and most of the violence transpired in Chicago, occurred in the spring and summer of 1894.[23]

Harrison's management of the city administrative structure and of the coalition of Democratic ward leaders was also not notably more successful at cleaning the streets than the methods of other large city governments. Under the charter of 1875, the city council had reorganized the health department and distributed its field workers according to a decentralized plan of assigning one general inspector to each ward. This practice gave the ward leaders an opportunity to coordinate street cleaning and health department administration with the social and political activities of their wards' political organizations. The ward structure of organization was not altered when health department practices became more sophisticated. Special inspectors were simply added to each ward inspection unit to deal with meat, milk, tenements, and burials. Carter Harrison's political coordination of the ward leaders did little to facilitate interward coordination of administration and work activities, however. As a result, the worst problem confronting the health commissioner was the dumping of waste collected by the street sweepers of one ward into the vacant lots and low-lying areas of neighboring wards. In 1893, health department supervision was abandoned, and a Bureau of Street and Alley Cleaning was created in the hope that it would find a solution to the problem of cleaning the streets.[24]

The Strong Mayor

The final major type of indigenous response was the "strong mayor" structure. The first experiment with concentrating the majority of a city's administrative powers and responsibilities in the hands of the mayor occurred in Brooklyn. A new city charter, passed by the New York state legislature in 1880, provided the necessary structural arrangements, and Seth Low became the first mayor to serve under the new charter. He enjoyed mixed success. Most of the ward leaders were Democrats, Low was a Republican. He therefore could not assume the kind of joint leadership of both the official administrative structure and a coalition of ward machine bosses that Carter Harrison had enjoyed. Where Harrison suffered because his official powers were weak, Low's effectiveness suffered from the opposition of the Democratic ward leaders. His participation in the "Mugwump" revolt during the 1884 presidential campaign (which will be discussed in Chapter 3), disrupted his relations with his fellow Brooklyn Republicans. After two terms of two years, Low declined to run again, fearing the strong possibility that he would be defeated. The Democrats took possession of the mayor's office and conflict shifted to attacks by the Republican "reform" forces upon the "corrupt" manner in which the mayor's powers were being employed in the interests of the Democratic ward leaders and their machines rather than in the interests of the "people" of Brooklyn.[25]

Low's administrative accomplishments were considerable, but even his experience suffered from inherent drawbacks of the strong mayor structure. Too much depended upon the initiative and skill of the occupant of the mayor's chair. The rest of the administrative structure could not function effectively without the mayor's constant coordination of the activities of the departments. Discord between department heads would immediately frustrate his efforts. In addition, public discontent with any aspect of the administration became concentrated almost entirely upon the mayor. The necessity of making appropriate responses consumed the mayor's time and distracted him from maintaining the necessary momentum to keep the administrative machinery turning efficiently. Under an incompetent, venal, or dishonest mayor, the system lost all advantages over other structural arrangements. Although the strong mayor system became quite popular as a reform model, it was far from an adequate solution to the municipal problem.

Conclusion

I have called the developments of the period between 1850 and 1890 "indigenous" innovations in order to distinguish them from the national, social scientific, and statistical mode of innovation in city government structure and administration that will be our central concern. Robert Wiebe laid the groundwork for distinctions of this kind by suggesting that between 1890 and 1920 institutional change of all kinds in the United States came under the influence of what he calls a "bureaucratic orientation." "The ideas which moved in and took the fort," Wiebe argues, "were bureaucratic ones . . . peculiarly suited to the fluidity and impersonality of an urban-industrial world." Wiebe's approach is a social historian's version of the more analytic concept "bureaucratization," pioneered by Max Weber, that plays a crucial role in the political modernization process currently being investigated by political scientists and political sociologists.[26]

Although the shift from the indigenous to the national, social scientific, and statistical mode of innovation in city politics began rather suddenly around the year 1890, the emergence of the new mode was not sudden, and indigenous innovation did not suddenly disappear. The "commission-manager" system of city government, for which great significance has been claimed, was an indigenous type of innovation that emerged independently in the cities of Galveston, Texas and Staunton, Virginia between 1900 and 1910. What did begin to occur rather suddenly around 1890 was the application of a national "bureaucratic" mode of innovation to the municipal problem.

As we shall see in the next two chapters, the first premise of the new municipal analysis was that cities lacked the necessary powers for adequate self-government. Innovation, and "reform" in the 1870s and 1880s failed because the tasks that a city government had to perform were more complex than those confronting any business firm of the time, while its administrative structure lacked the authority to reorganize itself, lacked the power to assume new responsibilities, was subject to state legislative interference in all aspects of its activities, and was expected to soothe public dissatisfaction with poor performance by keeping real estate taxes and assessments as low as possible. Even if indigenous solutions could have been devised under such circumstances, the incentive for men of high administrative ability to expend their energies on city government, rather than on business and finance, or state or national politics, was essentially nonexistent.

CHAPTER 2

Municipal Law and Municipal Political Science

Neither the law nor the analysis of politics offered much guidance concerning how a city should be governed in the mid-1860s. Francis Lieber, professor of constitutional history and public law in the Columbia College Law School, conceded as much in an essay written in 1867 on the revision of the New York State Constitution. "The problem how to harmonize dense and large city populations with the highest demands of political liberty—with universal suffrage, for instance—has nowhere been solved," Lieber wrote, "and the least approach to a solution has probably been made with us," meaning the people of New York State, "especially so in the city in which these pages are now writing," that is, New York City on the eve of the Tammany victory of 1868.[1]

The best Lieber could do was to offer suggestions derived from his general knowledge of politics. The experience of city democracies in ancient and medieval times, for example, showed that the people of cities "are far more subject to demagoguism than the rural population." Lieber's implied explanation was that city dwellers enjoyed more liberty. This "evil" (the tendency toward demagoguism) was being cultivated and encouraged in American cities by granting foreigners the franchise on easy terms, and by proposals to resolve every problem by means of universal suffrage and more frequent elections of ever more city officials. City government, Lieber, proclaimed, "is not and ought not to be like a general, legislating government;" it should be "chiefly a police government" to oversee safety and health, public morality, common education, and public charity, the "legitimate ends" of city government supervision. Suffrage should be restricted to taxpayers where fiscal matters were involved, the city comptroller should be selected and watched over by the state government, and expenditures should be rigorously limited to "city objects of public necessity—no dinners, no medals, no receptions." Perhaps, Lieber concluded, after twenty years experience under such stern austerity, cities might be granted more powers of self-government, but not before.[2]

By 1872, however, the detached critical method of legal and political commentary employed by Lieber had become obsolete. Processes of standardization, professionalization, and specialization, already under way in 1867, soon transformed the law and the analysis of politics into highly structured bodies of knowledge from which solutions to such practical problems as the relationship of industrial workers to their employers, the obligations of businesses engaged in interstate commerce, or the governing of cities, could be derived. Four developments of particular importance are considered here: the standardization of state law through a system of generally applicable common law principles; the development of municipal law as a special field within the new standardized system of law; the separation of the analysis of politics from the law; and the beginnings of the specialized field of municipal political science.

The impact of the larger social processes of standardization, specialization, and professionalization upon the law and the analysis of politics was the second of three major factors contributing to the emergence of a new mode of urban political innovation in the 1890s. I have concentrated upon the significance of these changes for the one issue in which we are interested, city government, rather than upon their general significance as part of the social transformation of the late nineteenth and early twentieth centuries. That significance was considerable. The treatment of municipal law under the newly standardized system of law, and the treatment of city government in the new field of political science, were both largely determined by rules of reasoning unrelated to the specific problems of governing cities. What is described in this chapter is not a "better" approach to municipal innovation than the attempts of indigenous pragmatism described in Chapter 1, but simply the effects that the larger forces of specialization, standardization, and professionalization produced as they exerted an increasingly strong influence upon how the question of city government was addressed. When the focus of organized efforts to reform the national political system shifted to the cities in the late 1880s (the topic of Chapter 3), the formulations of the new law and the new political science became the framework for a new mode of urban political innovation.

Thomas Cooley Standardizes State Law

The conversion of the law into an effective mechanism for dealing with the problem of governing American cities began with the publication of Thomas M. Cooley's definitive treatise on state law and government in 1868.[3] Cooley's treatise, familiarly known as *Constitutional Limitations*, provided the framework within which the legal knowledge and scholarship of the succeeding generation were organized. This was due not to Cooley's personal genius and influence so much as to his foresight concerning the direction in which legal reasoning and theorizing would probably progress. Where Lieber, writing in 1867, felt compelled to apologize for his inability to specify how cities should be governed, Cooley, writing in *Constitutional Limitations* in the very next year, felt able to devote a large section of the book to a specification of the law of municipal corporations. The chapter published in 1868 was reprinted in expanded but fundamentally unrevised form in editions published at various times into the twentieth century, years after Cooley's own death.[4]

Cooley's treatise was a uniform theory of state constitutionalism built upon a foundation of common-law principles. Cooley brought consistency to the organic law of the states by establishing abstract limits to the constitutional powers of state government, and to the law-making powers of state legislatures. While

state constitutional conventions might presume to mould governmental power without restraint, Cooley used the common law and
associated general principles to postulate that state constitutions
going beyond the limits of appropriate power were, in effect,
"unconstitutional." By defining limits to the powers of state legislatures, Cooley's treatise provided a basis for judicial review of
state law by state courts, something that was almost unknown
before the 1850s. John Marshall's principles of judicial review had
made the voice of the Supreme Court the "law of the land" with
regard to the federal constitution, but the state courts were much
slower to assert their right to final judgment over the acts of state
legislatures. Cooley provided the first comprehensive body of
principles for interpreting state constitutional powers. Since the
incorporation and chartering of municipal governments was one
of the powers of state legislatures, Cooley included in his treatise
an application of the principles of constitutional limitation to municipal corporations. He defined the circumstances in which legislatures might create a municipal government, and the grounds
for determining what powers the legislature might allow municipal governments to exercise. As in his treatment of all the specific
topics of the treatise, Cooley tried his best to generalize the common practices of the states, to ground every statement in an existing facet of the common law, and to maintain the internal
coherence of his theory of limitations on state power from one
topic to the next.[5]

We find then in Cooley's *Constitutional Limitations* a fully ex-
plicated legal theory of city government. Americans take great
care, Cooley wrote, "to bring the agencies by which the power
is to be exercised as near as possible to the subjects upon which
the power is to operate." American government was a system of
"complete *decentralization*," local affairs being managed by local
authorities, and the "central authority" being concerned only with
"general affairs."[6] This statement can serve as a good illustration
of the significance of Cooley's method as opposed to the persua-
siveness of the actual substance of his claims. By his manner of
stating it, he elevated a simple descriptive generalization to the
status of a fixed principle of state and local government.

This principle of decentralization and proximity of power to its subjects had, in the course of American development, "impel[led]" the states, "as if by common agreement . . . to incorporate cities, boroughs, and villages wherever a dense population renders different rules important from those which are needful for the rural districts." The same practice had been followed in England since time immemorial, Cooley reported, and "almost seems a part of the very nature of the race to which we belong." The colonists put it into practice "as if instinctively," and since colonial times no alternate arrangement had ever been advocated. "Towns, villages, boroughs, cities, and counties" should exercise "the powers of local government," while the state governments exercised the more general powers. In addition, this arrangement was desirable because it conformed to Cooley's principle that the powers of government should be "carefully" distributed, "with a view to being easily, cheaply, and intelligently exercised, and as far as possible by the persons more immediately interested."[7]

But although the powers of local government properly belonged in the possession of local entities, they had to be granted to the local government by the state legislature in a formal charter. Cooley acknowledged that the common law did not define the "rights, privileges and powers" of a municipality, but that did not deny the citizens of local governments the "right to expect that these charters will be granted with a recognition of the general principles with which we are familiar." Here Cooley asserted that state legislatures must adhere to uniform principles of government and of the making of law. This being a treatise on the limitations upon state legislatures however, he did not feel compelled to specify the powers that municipal governments ought to be granted. If the state legislature failed to adhere to the "familiar" positive principles of municipal chartering, Cooley stipulated that the courts had no power to interfere, and that responsibility fell upon the people to "right through the ballot-box all these wrongs."[8]

Cooley laid down two guiding principles concerning the powers of municipal corporations that he hoped to establish as the axioms of the future body of case law and scholarly commentary.

First, municipal by-laws had to be "reasonable."[9] And second, in accordance with the principle that every governmental agent must confine its powers to its "proper functions," the powers of municipal corporations must be limited to "the object of their creation," which was to serve as "agencies of the State in local government."[10]

Reasonableness was to be a matter of judicial discretion. Cooley's rule about reasonableness was that by-laws "should tend in some degree to the accomplishment of the objects for which the corporation was created and its powers conferred."[11] If a by-law purported to be a "police regulation," intended for preserving the public health, but in fact had the effect of depriving someone of the use of his property without generating any purposeful benefit to public health, such a by-law could "be set aside as a clear and direct infringement of the right of property without any compensating advantages." As an example, Cooley cited a Charlestown, Massachusetts by-law prohibiting the burial anywhere within the town limits of dead bodies brought from outside the town. Another unreasonable by-law was the attempt by the city of Detroit to use a law requiring that slaughterhouses be clean as a pretext for prohibiting all slaughtering of animals in certain parts of the city.[12]

The second principle, which can be called the principle of "proper municipal functions," advised the courts to strike down grants of powers made to municipalities by state legislatures if they could conclude that the power granted was not "within the proper province of local self-government." In other words, Cooley established that the courts, rather than the state legislatures or the municipalities themselves, should have the power to decide what was the "object" of creating municipal corporations, what should constitute "the exercise of their proper functions," and what territory fell within the "proper province" of a city government. As an example of this principle, Cooley offered the case of the provision of "an entertainment and ball for its citizens and certain expected guests on the 4th of July" by the city of Buffalo, under the power in its charter to spend money "to defray the contingent and other expenses of the city." Approving the reasoning that led the court to rule this expenditure improper, Cooley commented: "Providing an entertainment for its citizens is no part of municipal self-government, and it has never been considered, where the common law has prevailed, that the power to do so pertained to the government in any of its departments." Such entertainments were "not within the province of the city government."[13]

John F. Dillon Standardizes Municipal Law

Cooley's theory of the law made the courts, and the lawyers arguing before them, more important agents for defining the law of municipal government than the state legislatures and the city councils. The cities could pass presumably reasonable by-laws, and the states could grant powers of local administration, but the acceptable body of law had to be tested and proven in the adversary process. Cooley's discussion of municipal corporations was quite general, however, serving more as an illustration of his mode of interpretation than as a complete explication of municipal law. The definitive application of Cooley's method to municipal questions came with the publication of John F. Dillon's *Treatise on the Law of Municipal Corporations*, in 1872.[14]

Most of Dillon's *Treatise* involved application of the common law to the special circumstances and problems of municipal corporations. Dillon arranged the various aspects of municipal government according to the legal practices involved, such as the law of property or of liability, and then accumulated, in frequent new editions, the growing body of argument and decision generated by the courts. Since common-law principles applied in almost every state, a body of municipal government law grounded in common law precedent and reasoning could be relevant and useful to practically every city. On the one hand, Dillon's approach harnessed the thinking and decisions of judges and lawyers throughout the country to the problems of municipal government, and on the other hand, it forced state legislatures to conform to the emerging tone of the new body of law, or else have their municipal charters and special legislation for cities controverted by their own state judiciary.

Dillon's approach offered the possibility that as the case law of municipal corporations evolved, it would slowly but surely develop ways of dealing with all the complexities of governing a city. Case law would supply cities with innovations and procedures from all over the country. It would provide solutions that could be implemented by city ordinances and through the courts, thereby freeing the cities from dependence upon state constitutional changes, charter revisions, and legislation as the means of improving their ability to govern. Rather than resolving the problem of governing a city by constructing fantastic new relationships between mayors and councils, state legislatures and city comptrollers, gubernatorial commissions and city departments, Dillon approached the city government as a corporation whose proper management was a matter of using the correct legal procedure in dealing with each minute aspect of day-to-day affairs. Other legal commentators soon joined in this effort. The new approach was parallel and complementary to developments in the law of private corporations, where it was also assumed as a fundamental axiom that as the law became properly specified and elaborated, the difficulties of corporate management, and the dangers to the public arising from the actions of corporations, would be alleviated.[15]

Dillon's Rule and Its Implications

Unfortunately city governments did not flourish and prosper under the influence of the theory of constitutional limitations in the way that industrial corporations did. Being "public" as opposed to "private" corporations, city governments felt the ultimate impact of the doctrine of limited public power in a way exactly opposite to its effect on the business corporation. The first major effect for both kinds of corporation was the general institution of simple, standardized procedures for their creation under general incorporation laws. During the 1870s and 1880s, the tradition of rigidly regulating either kind of corporation through the specific terms of individual charters was abandoned. For private corporations, this was followed by increasing restraints upon the power of the states to control and regulate, leading by the 1890s to the philosophy that the true function of the law of private corporations was to provide for businessmen the maximum of freedom and utility in pursuing production and commerce. Assuring that business ultimately served the general public interest became the responsibility of regulatory institutions administering a new body of law that was kept separate and distinct from state law for corporations. As Willard Hurst has described this new attitude of the state governments and state courts:

The new style of corporation statutes in effect judged that corporate status had no social relevance save as a device legitimized by its utility to promote business. The obverse of this judgment was that regulation of business activity was no longer to be deemed a proper function of the law of corporate organization. The function of corporation law was to enable businessmen to act, not to police their action.[16]

Because the distinction between public and private power was fundamental to the new legal philosophy, however, the impact of the theory of constitutional limitations in the case of the municipal corporation fell upon the corporation itself, rather than upon the state government. The "public" power of the municipality became directly subject to limitation. For example, the doctrine of *ultra vires*, meaning "beyond the powers," had been traditionally used to rule that an activity of a corporation was illegal if it involved a power not literally specified in its charter. Corporations received charters for specific types of manufacturing, for example, and were prevented, under the *ultra vires* doctrine, from engaging in other kinds of activities. With the introduction of the theory of constitutional limitations upon public power, the impact of the *ultra vires* doctrine upon private corporations dissipated almost entirely. For public corporations, however, the theory of limitations inspired a very stringent application of the *ultra vires* doctrine. Strict interpretation came originally in the form of Cooley's rule of proper municipal functions. It acquired its definitive formulation from Dillon in what became known as "Dillon's rule":

It is a general and undisputed proposition of law that *a municipal corporation possesses and can exercise the following powers, and no others*: First, those granted in *express words*; second, those *necessarily or fairly implied* in or *incident* to the powers expressly granted; third, those *essential* to the declared objects and purposes of the corporation,—not simply convenient, but indispensable. Any fair, reasonable doubt concerning the existence of power is resolved by the courts against the corporation, and the power is denied. . . . All acts beyond the scope of the powers granted are void.[17]

The rule set forth the central principle of Dillon's delineation of the new municipal law. The courts, and the lawyers arguing before them, should pursue the narrowest available interpretation of the words employed in municipal charters, and of their implications. The purpose of this principle was not, however, to limit the powers of municipalities to a narrow compass, nor did it have that effect. While the rule limited the *interpretation* of granted powers, it did not limit the state legislature in the powers it might choose to grant. The actual effect of the rule was to liberalize the implications of Cooley's principle of "the proper province of local self-government." Where Cooley prescribed that the courts should bear responsibility for determining whether a particular function fell within the "proper province," Dillon transferred this responsibility entirely to the state legislature. Under Dillon's rule, the courts were to base their interpretation not upon their conception of the "proper province of local self-government," but rather upon the "declared objects and purposes of the corporation"; that is, the literal statements of municipal powers and functions made by the legislature in writing the municipal charter.

This innovative aspect of Dillon's rule had two very important effects. First, it greatly simplified the role of municipal law in the governing of the city by giving the courts, and commentators on the implications of evolving judicial reasoning (such as Dillion himself), explicit statements of municipal powers upon which to ground their interpretations. And second, it moved the controversy over what the "proper" character of municipal self-government should be out of the realm of the law and into the political arena. While the courts and the legal commentators would continue to evolve standardized conceptions of municipal objects and purposes, Dillon's rule transferred primary responsibility for innovation, change, and adaptation of municipal powers to the state legislatures, and to experts in the *political* as opposed to the legal character of municipal government.

The New Political Science

The effect of Dillon's rule on municipal law was part of a larger process of specialization that was producing a general division of the undifferentiated consideration of legal and political questions into the separate fields of law and political science. Institutionally, this process took the form of the establishment of law schools, the founding of graduate programs and schools of political science, and the separation of academic professionals into two distinct groups: professors of law and professors of political science. For example, when Francis Lieber first came to Columbia College, he taught history, political science, natural and international law, and civil and common law. In 1865, the trustees transferred him to the Columbia College Law School, an undergraduate institution, where he taught constitutional history and public law. When Lieber died in 1872, John W. Burgess replaced him. Burgess persuaded the trustees to start a graduate School of Political Science in 1880. Burgess transferred his popular courses in public law and political science from the Law School to the new graduate program, and many of the students entering the School of Political Science came directly from completing the two-year undergraduate law curriculum.[18]

The numerous law schools founded in the 1860s and 1870s taught both the old body of legal and political commentary and the new system of law initiated by Cooley. This left to the entirely new field of political science the difficulty of articulating a distinct second body of knowledge and system of reasoning.

Progress came slowly. Cooley's *General Principles of Constitutional Law*, published in 1880 for use in law schools, immediately became one of the most popular texts in courses and programs that were nominally supposed to be "political science." The only important new political analysis of municipal government was the search for the origins of American institutional forms in the distant English, German, and Anglo-Saxon past under the direction of Herbert Baxter Adams at Johns Hopkins University. Unfortunately, the historical approach was not ideal for investigating the current status and processes of political institutions. Despite its age, Tocqueville's *Democracy in America* did considerable service as a basic text in political science until it was supplanted by another comprehensive analysis of the American political system by a foreign observer.[19]

The new analysis was James Bryce's *The American Commonwealth*, first published in 1888. It immediately became the overwhelming favorite as a foundation for the political science curriculum.[20] As far as the division of labor defined by Dillon's rule was concerned, Bryce did not entirely resolve the question of what should constitute the political science of municipal government. *The American Commonwealth* dealt with politics in America as a single system, of which municipal government formed one branch. As the analysis of the system proceeded from part to part, however, Bryce narrowed his conclusions about the failings of the national system to the point where he concentrated them in the well-known judgment that the governing of the cities was the "one conspicuous failure" of the American political system. The analysis that led to this conclusion about the failings of the system also suggested an approach to resolving the difficulty that was crucial to the initiation of municipal political science by followers of Bryce.

The crux of Bryce's theory of American politics was that the United States was a democracy in which public opinion ruled. While "orthodox democratic theory" assumed that all voters thought matters out for themselves, and that their amassed opinions, in the form of "public" opinion, determined how their polity would be governed, Bryce argued that in America any group of twenty persons had to be divided into the nineteen whose opinions were "passive" and the one person who functioned as a leader or moulder of opinion. This did not mean that 95 percent of the population contributed nothing to the governing of the country, however. Bryce meant that the leaders of opinion acted upon those with "passive" opinions, and "public opinion" was the result.[21]

Passive opinion consisted of the opinion "of those who have no special interest in politics," which included several groups. Bryce classified the opinion of the working classes, the uneducated, and the unpropertied as "sentiment" rather than "thought"; however:

the soundness and elevation of their sentiment will have more to do with their taking their stand on the side of justice, honour, and peace, than any reasoning they can apply to the sifting of the multifarious facts thrown before them, and to the drawing of the legitimate inferences therefrom.

For different reasons, Bryce also classified the opinion of the educated, propertied, commercial, and professional classes, the remainder of the nineteen persons out of twenty, as "passive." The opinion of these people consisted, according to Bryce, not of sentiment, but of narrow conceptions of their own self-interest. These conceptions were "often erroneous."

Having something to lose, they are more apt to imagine dangers to their property or their class ascendancy. Moving in a more artificial society, their sympathies are less readily excited, and they more frequently indulge the tendency to cynicism natural to those who lead a life full of unreality and conventionalisms.

Consequently, these people were no better suited than the humble classes to formulate the kind of opinion that would make for good public policy.[22]

Responsibility for leading and moulding public opinion fell upon the one man in twenty with very special political skills and intellectual abilities.

The man who tries to lead public opinion, be he statesman, journalist, or lecturer, finds in himself, when he has to form a judgment upon any current event, a larger measure of individual prepossession, and of what may be called political theory and doctrine, than belongs to the average citizen.

The function of this leader was to convince the masses that their interest, regardless of class or other distinctions among them, was in good government, what Bryce sometimes called "the realities of good administration." Bryce rejected the proposition that class distinctions were important to American politics. Unlike European countries, where "suspicion, jealousy and arrogance" characterized class relationships, in America "good feeling and kindliness reign." The poor did not struggle with the rich in America because they already possessed the things that the humbler classes hope to obtain from political class conflict: "political power," "equal civil rights," careers "open to all citizens alike," and "gratuitous higher as well as elementary education."[23]

The fundamental conflicts of politics having been resolved in America, narrow self-interest need not dominate anyone's political opinion. No more should the property owner's interest in his property define his political interests than should the interest of the man without property be defined by his lack of material holdings. The interest of both, where politics was concerned, Bryce argued, was in good government.

As for the failings of the American system, Bryce claimed that it was partisan politics, rather than class conflict, that was preventing the attainment of better public management. The professional politicians were in control, and the natural leaders of public opinion, the men of talent and distinction, were "amateurs" and outsiders. In his chapter on the "true faults" of American democracy, Bryce singled out as the most dangerous fault: "the prominence of inferior men in politics and the absence of distinguished figures. The people are good, but not good enough to be able to dispense with efficient service by capable representatives and officials, wise guidance by strong and enlightened leaders." "Perhaps no form of government needs great leaders so much as democracy," he warned. In the mid-1880s, "neither the political arrangements nor the social and economical conditions" prevailing were eliciting the participation of the country's "best intellects and loftiest individuals," the 5 percent who should be leading public opinion.[24] Nowhere was this failing more visible than in the great cities. Although Bryce discussed the findings of the Tilden Commission, a blue-ribbon New York State panel that had investigated the larger implications of Tweed's brief ascendancy in New York City, and gave them some approval, his own analysis of the failings of democracy in the cities and his proposed remedies were quite different from the structural reforms recommended by the Tilden Commission. Bryce identified five major difficulties:

A vast population of ignorant immigrants.

The leading men all intensely occupied with business.

Communities so large that people know little of one another, and that the interest of each individual in good government is comparatively small.

The existence of a Spoils System (= paid offices given and taken away for party reasons).

Opportunities for illicit gains arising out of the possession of office.

Because immigrants were ignorant, especially of the habits of self-government, they failed to recognize the evils of the "Boss" and his machine, and they failed to rally around well-qualified men attempting to remove bosses. But much more serious was the reluctance of well-qualified men to campaign for office and occupy positions of power. In addition to being preoccupied with business, the city's natural leaders were apathetic, short-sighted, and, being "cultivated citizens," "unusually sensitive to the vulgarities of practical politics." The humbler classes and immigrants might be ignorant and reckless, but they were "generally ready to follow when they are wisely and patriotically led." Rather it was the apathy and reluctance of those with leadership abilities, when combined with the ignorance and manageability of the immigrants and lower classes in the presence of a spoils system and the opportunities for graft, that resulted in the domination of city government by Rings and Bosses.[25]

"Even now," in 1888, when the grip of Rings and Bosses was so strong, Bryce believed they could be excised, "were the better citizens to maintain unbroken through a series of elections that unity and vigour of action of which they have at rare moments, and under the impulse of urgent duty, shown themselves capable." The "best citizens" of the Eastern cities and "in many of the smaller towns, especially in the Eastern and Middle States," constituted "a reserve fund of wisdom and strength" and their opinion, if impressed upon the masses, could be the means of controlling the professional politicians and obtaining the good government that was everyone's true self-interest.

The fatalistic habit of mind perceptible among the Americans needs to be corrected by the spectacle of courage and independence taking their own path, and not looking to see whither the mass are moving. Those whose material prosperity tends to lap them in self-complacency and dull the edge of aspiration, need to be thrilled by the emotions which great men can excite, stimulated by the ideals they present, stirred to a loftier sense of what national life may attain.

Bryce placed the responsibility for initiating this political revitalization entirely upon the one man in twenty capable of leading the opinion of the remaining nineteen.[26]

The Municipal Political Science of City Self-Government

Bryce's approach to American politics made no distinctions between the practice of political leadership and the academic study of political institutions. He presented a model of professional activity similar to that of the law. Lawyers moved without hesitation from the bar, to the bench, to the academic lecture hall, or to the legislature, never fearing that one activity might conflict with another. As political science took shape as an independent discipline, there was some tendency for university professors to specialize in writing and teaching, but they remained as strongly committed to guiding and influencing the course of political change as they were to analyzing political structures and processes. Bryce himself not only encouraged both activities in his treatment of American politics, but engaged in both during the course of his own career in England, moving from a teaching position at Oxford to the House of Commons and finally, as a viscount, to the House of Lords. The people with whom Bryce worked in the United States also tended to be both analysts and activists. They included E. L. Godkin, editor of the *Nation* and prominent reformer, Seth Low, twice mayor of Brooklyn, president of Columbia University, and author of the major chapter on city government in *The American Commonwealth*, Theodore Roosevelt, who provided Bryce with comments on the page proofs of several chapters of *The American Commonwealth*, and Woodrow Wilson, who was a student in Herbert Baxter Adams's graduate seminar at Johns Hopkins in 1883 when Bryce assumed part of the responsibility for the teaching.[27]

Following Bryce's formulation of the appropriate concerns of political science, municipal political science concentrated upon developing a form of city government, and a process of municipal administration, that would unite all city residents on the basis of their common interest in "good government." Early writers on municipal political science assumed their share of the division of responsibility defined by Dillon's rule and began formulating principles for the *political* determination of the powers of municipal self-government.

We find Frank Goodnow engaged in this task in *Municipal Home Rule*, published in 1895, one of the earliest texts in municipal political science. Having started his career as a professor of administrative law, Goodnow was acutely conscious of the work of Cooley and Dillon. In *Municipal Home Rule* he reviewed both Cooley's arguments concerning the proper functions of municipal government, and Dillon's rule, and found Dillon's rule superior because of the narrowness of its criteria for legal interpretation. Goodnow then went on to devote the bulk of the book to developing a political basis for defining the nature and powers of municipal government. He solved the chief problems involved by generating the principle of city self-government, what he called "municipal home rule." When a municipality was acting "as an organization for the satisfaction of local needs," Goodnow argued, it should not suffer interference from either the courts or the state legislature. It should hold all legislative power to deal with local affairs in its own hands. The city alone should have the power to determine the "necessity" for satisfying local needs, and the city should be "the sole uncontrolled judge of the manner in which it shall provide for the satisfaction of the needs which it has determined exist." Cities should have the "freedom necessary for their good government and healthy development."[28]

Goodnow's strategy in *Municipal Home Rule* involved a decision about specialization that was crucial both to him and to law and political science. One alternative was to generate a major municipal field within the new political science. The other was to resolve the division of responsibility created by Dillon's rule by specifying the proper character and functions of municipal government on the basis of another branch of the law. The chief candidate for this alternative was Goodnow's own legal specialty, administrative law. The solution offered by administrative law would have been to consider municipal government as an administrative arm of state government. Goodnow considered this alternative fairly seriously in *Municipal Home Rule* and concluded that there were some aspects of city government in which it acted, and should continue to act, as an administrative arm of the state government. Administrative law would continue to be important in dealing with those aspects. If the majority of municipal activities could be subsumed under the city government's role as an administrative arm of the state, however, there would be little necessity for political determinations of the proper character of city government, or for the development of an important specialty of municipal political science. Unless city governments were more like real governments, and less like corporations, they would provide little for a municipal political science to analyze or influence.[29]

Ultimately, the value of municipal political science depended upon which trend in the development of city government became dominant in the 1890s: continued control of city affairs by the state government, or increasingly independent power for cities to manage their own affairs. By 1895, when Goodnow published *Municipal Home Rule*, he could be fairly certain that city self-government was going to be the prevailing trend. As a result of a major change in the character of elite reform activism in the late 1880s and early 1890s, Goodnow knew that the thrust of reform movements, in the near future, would be in the direction of more city government independence. Whether city political development would follow the same course remained to be seen. It is to this shift in the focus of national reform activism that we must now turn.

CHAPTER 3

City Self-Government Becomes an Objective of National Political Reform

The third major factor contributing to the emergence of a new mode of urban political innovation, along with the failure of indigenous pragmatism, and the development of municipal law and municipal political science, was the dramatic rise of enthusiasm for strong city self-government as an objective of efforts to reform the national political system. Rather suddenly, between 1889 and 1895, municipal reform came into national prominence. Obtaining strong city self-government became the objective of a generation of elite reform activists who were too young to be prominent in the federal civil service reform movement of the 1870s and 1880s. Their search for an appropriate substitute led them first to independent city reform organizing, and then to a national movement to pressure state governments to grant cities strong powers of self-government.

The chief concern of the preceding generation of elite reformers had been federal civil service reform. The typical leader of the civil service reform movement first came into political prominence at the time of the Civil War. Organized activity began in the late 1860s and gathered momentum through the 1870s. In 1881, the movement's efforts came to a sudden and unexpected climax as a result of the assassination of President James A. Garfield by a man who was mistakenly believed to have been a disappointed office-seeker. In 1882, Congress stopped obstructing reform and passed the Pendleton Act, establishing an effective merit system for the federal bureaucracy. To the leaders of the move-

ment, the Pendleton Act was only the first step towards changing the character of the civil service, and many of them maintained their enthusiasm for civil service reform for the remainder of their public careers. The overall range of elite national reform efforts, however, became increasingly diffuse after the passage of the Pendleton Act. Interstate commerce and federal trust regulation were important issues, but neither was the focus of broadly organized elite activism. Finally, beginning around 1890, aspirants to national prominence as reformers sparked a rapid proliferation of city reform organizations. By 1894, municipal reform was the major objective of efforts to reform the national political system, serving the younger generation of reform leaders as federal civil service reform had served the elite reformers of 1865–1882. As the cities became the object of national reform efforts, the opportunity arose to overcome the obstacles to strong city self-government and begin to initiate an effective response to the unpleasant consequences of industrial urbanization.

National Political Reform After the Pendleton Act

The leaders of the federal civil service reform movement were a group of older men when in 1883 President Chester Arthur signed the Pendleton Act. They had first risen to prominence in the 1850s and during the Civil War, and by the 1880s they were in the latter part of their public careers. Ari Hoogenboom's analysis of New York civil service reform leaders has shown that, by 1883, they were a group of older, backward-looking, and socially conservative merchant businessmen and professionals. Civil service reform had been progressive and forward-looking in the late 1860s, but a young man hoping to make a promising start toward a career as a prominent national reform activist in 1883 could see that civil service reform would not serve his purposes. Once responsibility for reforming the federal bureaucracy passed to the president, the Congress, and the Civil Service Commission, reform activists needed new concerns on which to focus.[1]

Younger aspirants to national political prominence began experimenting with organized municipal reform even before the 1883 victory of civil service reform. The City Reform Club of

New York, an elite organization founded by Theodore Roosevelt (born in 1858) and his friends in 1882, typified the efforts of these vigorous young gentlemen. Membership was small. Respectability, social prominence, education, Protestant beliefs, and native American ancestry were virtually indispensable prerequisites for admission. Very quickly, the club voted to admit only men of wealth involved in commerce and the professions. Meetings were occasions for full formal dress. A newspaper satire of an early meeting reported that a speaker dressed slightly less formally than the others present was greeted with scowls and "taken for a Democrat." Despite its exclusiveness, membership grew to more than three hundred and fifty by the end of 1883. Its characteristics as a social club overshadowed its political purposes and frustrated the ambitions of the founders. After three years of minimal political effectiveness, the club resolved to create a central body of twenty-five "active" members, and relegate all others to the status of supporting "subscribers" to the club's activities. Reorganization freed the leadership to undertake an expensive and very intense secret investigation of corruption in the New York City police department. Their efforts eventually led to the formation of the famous Lexow Committee, whose report on police corruption played a crucial role in the reform victory over the Tammany Democrats in the mayoral election of 1894. J. Pierpont Morgan was one of the largest contributors to the underwriting of the club's investigation.[2]

Young elite activists in Baltimore experimented with a similar organization. The perpetration of electoral frauds in the Baltimore city election of November 1885, leading to the narrow defeat of a respectable "Independent Democrat" who was also endorsed by the Republicans, incited the formation of a "Reform League." Its stated purposes were "to secure fair elections, promote honest government, and to expose and bring to punishment official misconduct in the State of Maryland and especially in the city of Baltimore." A full membership of close to three hundred provided support for an executive committee of fifteen. Charles J. Bonaparte, a patrician lawyer who had aided in founding the Na-

tional Civil Service Reform League in 1881, undertook most of the league's practical work with the aid of two or three other executive committee members. James B. Crook's investigation of sixty-five active members of the league as of 1895 has revealed that two-thirds of them appeared in Baltimore's exclusive Social Register, one-half were lawyers, one-third businessmen, and one-sixth from other professions. Two-thirds of those whose education could be determined were college graduates, and two-thirds came from colonial American families. Charles Bonaparte was a grandson of the Emperor Napoleon Bonaparte's youngest brother. Of twenty-four very active participants in the work of the Reform League, sixteen were younger than forty years of age in 1895.[3]

The city reform organizations of the 1880s represented a new kind of elite activism. Unlike the committees of notables that often formed in the 1870s to fight specific campaigns against municipal corruption, the purpose of these new organizations was to lay foundations for major political movements of the future. The New York City "Committee of Seventy," formed in 1871 to officiate over the demise of Boss Tweed, disbanded once its work was completed. So did the "Committee of Seventy" formed in Chicago to aid Mayor Joseph Medill in encouraging the police to enforce the fire laws and the Sunday closing law for saloons in 1872 and 1873. The Cincinnati "Committee of One Hundred," assembled in 1885 to "purify the city and county government" by righting electoral abuses and rooting out police department corruption, was also short-lived, but it spawned the more formal Citizens' Club of Cincinnati, officially founded in 1893. Similarly, the Citizens' Municipal Association of Philadelphia, founded in April 1886, was the successor to a "Committee of One Hundred" that had disbanded several months before. The association carried on the committee's aim of obtaining strict compliance to agreed standards of work and service from recipients of city contracts.[4]

During the 1880s, ad hoc committees became less popular; reform effort went increasingly into founding permanent organizations. The role that these early city organizations played in solidifying groups of gentleman reformers and elevating them to prominence was more important than the practical reform work that the organizations managed to accomplish. The most important function of the Baltimore Reform League, for example, was to designate a small group of men on its executive committee as a nucleus of reform leadership. The general membership paid annual dues of one dollar, and attended infrequent meetings. One man, John C. Rose, conducted the league's work of investigating election frauds and reforming Maryland's election laws almost singlehandedly. The Massachusetts Society for Promoting Good Citizenship was another organization founded to support the efforts of a small elite group. Its purposes, according to the proclamation of the twelve gentlemen who founded it in 1887, were to protect "the stability of our republican institutions" from the "indifference" of American citizens to their "duties," from the "greater or less ignorance" of those duties on the part of the foreign-born, and from the "avowed, deliberate purpose of a large number of citizens, and of residents who are not citizens, to change our present time-honored form of citizenship for other and experimental forms." In practice the society had annual dues of one dollar and its activities consisted of sponsoring series of public lectures supervised by an executive committee of seven members. Edward Everett Hale served as honorary president. An additional indication that unification of elite groups was the real purpose of these city reform organizations of the 1880s was their almost total exclusion of women, despite the fact that numerous middle- and upper-class women were anxious to participate in reform work. The Baltimore League expressly excluded women from membership. Other groups obtained the same result by letting it be known that women were not welcome to join. Including women in an organization pursuing political influence and power would have openly invited the derisive label of "man-milliners" that had been pinned on the civil service reformers in the 1870s.[5]

The advantages for the younger generation of promoting a movement away from civil service reform carried with them the danger that the momentum of reform might falter and dissipate before a compelling new cause could be found. It was fortuitous therefore that the events of the presidential election of 1884 brought together both older and younger activists in a great spontaneous outpouring of reform sentiment. The passage of the Pendleton Act supposedly represented a victory for the basic principles of civil service reform. Both Republicans and Democrats had promised sincerely that they would phase out the "spoils system" of patronage and graft. Then, less than two years later, the Republican presidential convention of 1884 gave indications of blatant hypocrisy. The convention nominated for president James G. Blaine, a man who had been one of the most notorious practitioners of the politics of spoilsmanship. His Republican backers fondly referred to him as the "Plumed Knight," but the Democrats succeeded in shackling him with the unfortunate two-line epigram:

> Blaine, Blaine, James G. Blaine,
> The Continental Liar from the State of Maine.

To the prominent Republicans committed to civil service reform, Blaine was anathema, despite all protestations that he had changed his political ways. His selection as the presidential candidate, the reformers charged, amounted to an open declaration that the Pendleton Act would not be enforced if the Republicans captured the White House.

To the cry of "traitor" to the party, a considerable group of prominent Republicans bolted the party's ranks and organized a strenuous campaign of Republican support for the Democratic candidate, Grover Cleveland. Republican regulars saddled them with the name "Mugwumps," an Algonquian Indian word connoting a man who is excessively proud of himself. Cleveland's reputation as a reform mayor of Buffalo and a reform governor of New York provided an additional reason for reform-minded Republicans to prefer him to the all-too-recently repentant Blaine. In New York State, where the Mugwump campaign was especially effective, defecting Republicans gave Cleveland an advantage of one thousand more votes than Blaine out of a total of almost 1,200,000 votes cast. The resulting award of all of New York's electoral votes to the Democrats put Cleveland in the White House and gave "Mugwumpery" a significance it otherwise would not have achieved.[6]

In many ways, the Mugwump revolt was simply an extension of the civil service reform movement. Republican civil service reformers felt that Blaine's nomination demanded a forceful defense of their ideals. They had been working to prevent Blaine's nomination during the course of the convention and undertook the Mugwump revolt when their efforts failed. Party identification was closely akin to religious affiliation in the 1880s, and renouncing one's party was a deadly serious business. Horace Deming, a leading New York Mugwump, explained the gravity of joining the revolt to a banquet of urban reformers in 1897 by recounting how the members of his church had convened prayer meetings for his sake in the hope of encouraging him to return to the Republican fold:

when in 1884 thousands upon thousands of what were considered Black Republicans abandoned their party because they felt it was a question of common honesty, it was like being separated from your church and from your dearest friends. You were ostracised for it.

When Mugwump efforts produced a victory for Cleveland, the revolt turned into a successful movement without a unifying purpose. Many Mugwumps tried to convert themselves into true Democrats, but Cleveland did little to make a permanent place for them in the party. The implications of the revolt for the future of national political reform were unclear. The ambitious young men searching for new causes were greatly encouraged by the success of the revolt. Their search for a new reform objective had to continue, however.[7]

City Reform Organizing Becomes the Rage, 1890–1894

Many of those involved in founding the more formal city organizations of the late 1880s had been participants in the Mugwump revolt. The Mugwump victory heightened enthusiasm for the prospects of well-organized reform movements, for it demonstrated what a dedicated group of prominent men with a clear-cut objective could accomplish. It would be incorrect, however, to suggest that there was a smooth transition of reform activism from the civil service movement of 1882 to the Mugwump campaign of 1884 and then to city-based reform movements that expanded and merged together in a national municipal reform movement by 1895. Between 1884 and 1890 national reform activism was diffuse and uncoordinated; no distinct direction or purpose prevailed. It was only after 1890 that leaders of municipal reform claimed to perceive the origins of their movement in the Mugwump enthusiasm of the mid-1880s. "Some ten years ago," James C. Carter told the members of the National Municipal League in his presidential address to the 1896 National Conference for Good City Government, conditions in cities "began to excite, to a much greater degree than . . . theretofore, the public attention." But even Carter, who had been a prominent leader of the New York Mugwump campaign, did not attempt to explain *how* Mugwump enthusiasm became transformed into excitement about improving conditions in cities.[8]

As the number of city reform organizations suddenly mushroomed from approximately twenty in 1890 to more than eighty by the end of 1894, the diffuseness of elite reform activity resolved into a clear commitment to the reconstruction of the institution of municipal government. The new clubs and leagues had large memberships, sound organizational structure, and a dedication to achievement rather than to elite organizing for its own sake. Prominent among the spirited new groups was the City Club of New York, successor to the more cautious City Reform Club of the 1880s. Its aims were specific and its membership was large. Annual dues of fifty dollars supported a magnificent clubhouse on Fifth Avenue, large enough to accommodate meetings of all several hundred members. The club intended:

To promote social intercourse among persons specially interested in promoting good government of the city of New York, in securing honesty and efficiency in the administration of city affairs, in severing municipal from national politics; and to take such action as may tend to the honest, efficient, and independent government of the city of New York.

To further its aims, the club backed the formation of "Good Government Clubs" in each of the city's election districts. Edmond Kelly, who initiated the founding of more than twenty clubs by 1895, originally conceived of them as working-class drinking and social clubs that would use conviviality in the same way that the City Club did among the elite to mobilize reform strength. The stated aims of the Good Government Clubs were extremely specific: their function was to organize the majority of citizens who desired "good municipal government,"

which means clean streets, a plentiful supply of pure water, a vigilant Health Board, unbiased by political proclivities, reasonably low taxes and rents, protection of property, life and limb, proper rapid transit accommodations, and that rigorous enforcement of city ordinances which is indispensable to the general comfort.

Dues consisted of a one dollar initiation fee and then fifty cents a month. The clubs tended to attract middle-class business and professional people rather than the workingmen for whom they were designed, but the effort was a remarkable success in any case. By the time of the great electoral battle against Tammany in November, 1894, there were twenty-four clubs with a minimum of fifty members each. On election day, the clubs turned out more than two thousand poll watchers to guard against fraud and irregularities, an unprecedented accomplishment that was probably crucial in assuring the election of reform candidate William L. Strong.[9]

The leading new organization of elite reformers in Philadelphia was the Municipal League, organized in 1891. Employing a network of election district associations similar to the Good Government Clubs organized by the City Club, the Municipal League assembled a nominal membership of more than three thousand behind the proposition that "the highest principles of municipal self-government in the United States will be materially promoted by the absolute separation of Municipal politics from National and State politics." In addition, the league undertook to conduct "a thorough and scientific investigation of the correct principles of local self-government, especially as adapted to this municipality," a project that produced such pamphlets as "Duties of Citizens in Reference to Municipal Government" (1892), "The Proper Standard of Municipal Affairs" (1894), and "Municipal Politics—The Old System and the New" (1894).[10]

A third outstanding new organization was the Municipal League of Milwaukee. The league formed in the early months of 1893 in the aftermath of the discovery that the city's public librarian had embezzled more than $9,000 of library funds. The incident convinced numerous Milwaukeeans with vague but well-intentioned sympathies that putting good men in public office was not a sufficient guarantee of good government. The league committed itself to reforming the *system* of city government in Milwaukee, and proved so effective as a working organization that it catalyzed a state-wide municipal reform movement throughout Wisconsin between 1894 and 1897.[11]

Good City Government as a National Reform Cause

Late in 1893, the leaders of the Philadelphia Municipal League conferred with their counterparts from the City Club of New York about holding a conference to publicize the emergence of municipal reform as the leading concern of national political reform activism. The City Club leaders were enthusiastic and on December 29, 1893, the two groups issued a call for a "National Conference For Good City Government" in Philadelphia at the end of January 1894, which stated in part:

The Principal objects of the Conference will be to determine, so far as is possible by inquiry and debate, the best means for stimulating and increasing the rapidly growing demand for honest and intelligent government in American cities, and to discuss the best methods for combining and organizing the friends of Reform so that their united strength may be made effective.

Signatories, in addition to leaders of new city reform organizations, included elder statesmen from the civil service reform movement such as Dorman B. Eaton and Carl Schurz, leaders of the Mugwump revolt of 1884 such as Richard Watson Gilder, Franklin MacVeagh, Richard Henry Dana, Moorfield Storey, Gamaliel Bradford, Charles Francis Adams, Jr., Edwin L. Godkin, and R. Fulton Cutting, and prominent university presidents and social scientists such as Charles W. Eliot (president of Harvard), Daniel Coit Gilman (president of Johns Hopkins), Richard T. Ely (economist), Francis A. Walker (economist), E. P. Allinson (political scientist), Herbert Baxter Adams, and Albert Shaw (political scientist and editor). Four of the signers, Eliot, Gilman, Godkin, and H. B. Adams, had been intimate confidants of Bryce's while he was writing *The American Commonwealth.*[12]

The characteristics of the participants invited to the conference, and the plan of its agenda, were both crucial facets of an attempt to implement the strategy for national political reform outlined by Bryce in 1888: to get the prominent leaders of reform in the large cities to unite in a campaign to make the improvement of municipal government the chief concern of informed political opinion. If (as both Bryce and the organizers of the conference believed) "reformers" constituted potentially the most influential group of leaders of national public opinion, and if these reformers could be mobilized behind the problem of municipal government, then a national movement could well result that would meet Bryce's requirements for reversing the political failings of the great cities. John A. Butler of the Milwaukee Municipal League told the conference participants that there was "no doubt that the active work of any and all [municipal] leagues will have to be done by a small circle of men," backed by "a larger numerical body of pledged followers." By coordinating the efforts of the leaders of reform opinion in the large cities, the conference would produce, it was hoped, a dramatic new orientation of national reform sentiment. "After this convention," Butler predicted:

it will be felt everywhere that municipal reform is an assured and well accredited national movement, and men of first rate ability and character will everywhere find it an honor to be associated with a cause which certainly stands in the fore-front of American political regeneration and progress.[13]

The conference efficiently completed three major tasks: a survey of existing conditions and the current status of reform efforts in the nation's leading cities, an examination of various means of influencing public opinion in favor of municipal reform, and preparation for the founding of a "National Municipal League" to serve as a clearing house for municipal reform information and as secretariat for an annual series of "National Conferences For Good City Government". The cities covered in the survey included Boston, Brooklyn, Chicago, Baltimore, Philadelphia, and New York, the cities from which most of the conference delegates came. Then, after Leo S. Rowe gave a presentation of current political science views on municipal improvement entitled "Municipal Government As It Should Be And May Become," and Carl Schurz defined the relationship between civil service reform and municipal reform, the conference considered papers on influencing public opinion grouped under two broad headings: "How To Arouse Public Sentiment In Favor Of Good City Government," and "How To Bring Public Sentiment To Bear Upon The Choice Of Good Public Officials." On the second day of the conference, the chairman of the Committee on Arrangements submitted a resolution for the organization of a "National Municipal League," which carried unanimously. Five months later, on May 28 and 29, 1894, the first meeting of the Board of Delegates of the National Municipal League (at the clubhouse of the City Club of New York) approved a constitution and initiated the life of the organization.[14]

Preparing a Municipal Program

Once a successful first conference had been held and the National Municipal League had begun to find its legs, the small circle of key leaders began to arrange for the preparation of a very prominent statement of the principles held in common by reform movements in diverse cities and states. Three men undertook the greater part of this work: Clinton Rogers Woodruff of the Municipal League of Philadelphia, who became the first secretary of the National Municipal League and eventually served continuously as secretary until 1920; James C. Carter, president of the City Club of New York, who served as the league's first president from 1894 to 1903; Horace E. Deming of the City Club and the People's Municipal League of New York, who chaired the committee delegated to write the "Municipal Program." Deming began promoting the development of a program of common principles as early as the banquet of the first conference. He explained that a recent national conference of educators had appointed a committee to pool information about educational principles from all over the country. When the findings were examined, the committee discovered that a consensus existed concerning the "philosophical principles" underlying education, which could be condensed into a "practical program" for the future of education. Municipal reformers, Deming suggested, should do likewise.

Before there was this national organization [of educators] which fused and combined all these various experiences, the different educational reformers were working by themselves, and working in the dark. Cannot we do something like that for municipal reform? The Chairman of this Conference can easily nominate a committee to ask these questions. These questions can be sent to men all over the country familiar with the local conditions. The answers to these questions will give us a practical program.[15]

University professors of political and social science figured prominently in the work of the second Good City Government Conference and strengthened the National Municipal League's character as a coalition in which elite reformers and professional social scientists assumed fairly equal roles. Edward W. Bemis of the University of Chicago, Jeremiah W. Jenks of Cornell, and Edmund J. James of the University of Pennsylvania gave major addresses. James spoke on the question of a "model charter for American cities," emphasizing what was to become the dominant theme of the municipal reform enterprise: that democratic self-government of American cities had yet to be attempted.

It is not fair and will not be fair to say that democracy has broken down in American cities until democracy shall have had a fair chance at self-government in our American cities, and that chance has nowhere been given to the extent to which it is desirable. In other words, a city charter should give to the people of the city the largest degree of self-determination, both as to the form of government and as to the things which the government shall do.

From the side of the reform participants in the emerging coalition, Herbert Welsh of Philadelphia voiced a desire for the guidance that a broadly approved theory of municipal reform could provide:

The movement for good city government which is now spreading over the United States, which has produced a ferment of thought in a thousand active minds, stirred a thousand brave men and women to courageous action and has fought its first great effective fight in New York, presses at once the question: "What is the sound theory which should guide the work? What the reliable, practical methods in which that theory finds its safe channel, its guarantee of growing life and achievement?"[16]

At the fifth National Conference in Louisville in 1897, the league completed its "preliminary descriptive work" and embarked on a "policy of concrete, definite work,": composing a "Municipal Program." Prominent on the conference agenda were addresses by Horace Deming, Leo S. Rowe, and Frank Goodnow that together fully summarized the current state of municipal political science.

Deming led off the new business of the conference with a resolution calling for the appointment of a committee to investigate and report on the feasibility of a Municipal Program which shall embody the essential principles that must underlie successful municipal government and which shall also set forth a working plan or system, consistent with American political institutions and adapted to American industrial and political conditions, for putting such principles into practical operation.

"The theory of the city under our American form of government," Deming proclaimed in support of his resolution, "is identical in every state in the Union." The "municipal reformers of Illinois and of Georgia and of Pennsylvania and of New York" were in agreement about principles. They disagreed only about methods for putting those principles into practice. However, Deming continued:

if the men familiar with conditions in the States where the municipal problem is most important should put their heads together for the precise purpose of endeavoring to devise a system which fits into our scheme of government, in my judgment they would succeed; with slight local variations, the system applicable in New York is applicable in Kentucky.[17]

The Municipal Program Advocates Strong City Self-Government

The aim of the Municipal Program strategy was to produce a document that would serve the purposes of both reform activists and political, economic, and legal writers. Thus an attempt was made to obtain roughly equal representation of both elements of the league coalition on the Municipal Program Committee. Deming served as chairman. The body of the committee consisted of three political scientists: Frank Goodnow, Leo S. Rowe, and Albert Shaw; two prominent reformers: George W. Guthrie of Pittsburgh and Charles Richardson of Philadelphia; and C. R. Woodruff representing the league. Among the alternate members named to the committee were Louis Brandeis and John F. Dillon. This attempt to involve both the leading municipal political scientist, Frank Goodnow, and the leading municipal legal theorist, John Dillon, in the committee's work, indicates a desire on Deming's part to make the final document the most significant possible statement of fundamental principles of American municipal government.[18]

Although its tone was modest and it did not hold great "truths" to be "self-evident," the document produced by Deming's committee was intended to serve as a declaration of municipal independence. By exaggerating the harmful effects of interference by state legislatures, the committee heightened the sense of urgency surrounding their conclusion that what the cities needed were sufficient powers of self-government to resolve their own problems. Of the "fundamental propositions" summarized by Deming in his commentary on the Program, the second was the best statement of the intent of the document as a whole:

The citizens of the municipality under general laws should be free to make and amend their own form of municipal government, provided it be based upon democratic-republican principles, and to determine their own methods of administration of the local governmental powers, according to their own ideas of what will best satisfy their local needs.

When combined with the first proposition, that "the municipal corporation should be invested with the governmental powers requisite to determine all questions of local public policy," the statement advocated a strong brand of "municipal home rule." The function of casting the issues in terms of a compelling necessity for municipal independence and self-government was to rally the reform elements associated with the National Municipal League around a very clearly defined cause, and to identify exactly where their efforts would have to be directed in order to achieve their aims. The only way to secure municipal independence was to revise the state constitutions and rewrite the state laws relating to municipal government.[19]

The body of the Program consisted of five model state constitutional amendments and a model state municipal corporations act. Although the Program has forever after been casually referred to as a "model city charter," the committee did its best to convince reform activists that charter reform was not the proper strategy for obtaining improved municipal government.

The constitutional amendments defined the relationship between municipal governments and state government, defined the powers of municipal governments, delineated the general methods for municipal administration, specified the nature of the municipal franchise, mandated the use of a "merit" system for the administrative service, and guaranteed to every city of over 25,000 population the right to "adopt its own charter and frame of government." The municipal corporations act, the most important element of the program, was a model state law for the establishment and structuring of city governments. As a model of what reform activists should strive to obtain from state legislatures, the municipal corporations act called for a mayor-council system, concentration of administrative power and responsibility in the hands of the mayor, a merit system for the administrative service, and clear specification of the major powers possessed by the municipal corporation. Cities of over 25,000 were guaranteed again, as in the constitutional amendments, the right to frame their own structure, even to the point of allowing them to controvert provisions mandated by the act for smaller cities. The Program Committee indicated that it considered efforts to convince state legislatures to pass some version of the model municipal corporations act the best use of reform energies. The function of the constitutional amendments was to provide absolute protection against subsequent legislative interference with the elements of the municipal corporations act after its passage, such as contradictory special legislation or outright repeal. The corporations act could stand on its own, however, as long as the legislature maintained its will to see the act properly implemented.[20]

The Municipal Program set out an excellent strategy for elite reformers. By insulating the cities from the meddling of state legislatures, and providing them with strong powers of self-government, the Program attempted to increase the potential effectiveness of reform activism. A reform electoral victory in a city with strong powers of self-government could lead to impressive municipal improvements. Furthermore, calls for strong city self-government helped to set the cities in their own special political arena, where the issues of municipal reform could be clearly defined. Unique characteristics of state politics in New York, as compared with Illinois or Maryland, would be set aside, and the commonality of the dilemmas of municipal improvement in New York, Chicago, and Baltimore would become obvious. On this common basis, reform activism could mobilize public opinion in all the cities around common issues. Above all, the Program rested upon the belief that municipal improvement could only come about through the forceful assertion of massed public opinion, guided by skillful elite leadership. The Program insisted that cities could not act upon the demands of organized public opinion unless they were in a position to organize their own structure, formulate their own policies, and implement those policies with strong powers. As L. S. Rowe explained in his "Summary" of the Program:

Civic advance in general and municipal efficiency in particular are the result of a combination of forces, of which higher standards of public opinion and lofty civic ideals are the most important. The form of governmental organization is to be judged by the ease and readiness with which it gives expression to these forces. In the Constitutional Amendments and Municipal Corporations Act the endeavor has been made to give to the city such a position in the political system of the State and to provide it with such a framework of government as will give the widest possible freedom of action to every city in formulating the details of its own organization and in the determination of its local policy.[21]

The Municipal Program as a Basis for a
New Mode of Innovation

Following the promulgation of the Municipal Program, new arrangements of legal, social scientific, and activist efforts began to take shape. The Program was of greatest value to those who formulated it: reform activists and legal and political science experts interested in the city as an element of the national political system. For them, the Program constituted a legitimating statement of the fundamental assumptions and principles upon which they hoped to ground a systematic mode of urban political innovation. The Program's legitimacy for this purpose derived from the city reform organizations in numerous states that participated in authorizing its formulation at the annual Good City Government Conferences of 1894–1899. Of the several municipal reform strategies competing for prominence in 1894, obtaining strong powers of self-government from the state legislature had become predominant by December 1899.

The importance of the Municipal Program for specific reform efforts in individual cities and states was not very great. The Program was never intended to be the platform for a unified reform campaign and was not used in that way once it was publicized. Its strength as an implement in reform campaigns could be no greater than the influence that similar efforts in other cities and states might have upon a particular city council or state legislature. At best, it helped to make officials and politicians who were the objects of reform campaigns aware that they were confronting a set of assumptions, principles, and strategies common to almost all the elite municipal reform campaigns in the country. While this kind of influence could be considerable, it was not a product of the Municipal Program per se.

The Program was most useful for the division of labor that it made possible. Reform activists and experts in analysis who were primarily interested in municipal reform as a means to national political improvement could now regard their link with state and city reform campaigns as permanently forged. The mutually approved Program left those with a national orientation free to pursue their own campaign of analysis and innovation. As long as they based their efforts on the tenets of the Program, they had good assurance that city and state reform organizations and campaigns would accept, and make use of, the products of those efforts as elaborations of the basic Municipal Program approach. The Program was a statement of purposes held in common by groups of people intent upon pursuing their common objectives by diverse but complementary means. Such a common statement was particularly important to those intending to pursue analysis and innovation on a national scale, for their efforts would be worth little without the acceptance and support of city- and state-oriented groups.

Three aspects of the Program were of importance to attempts to approach municipal structural and administrative innovation from a national perspective. First, the Program interpreted Dillon's rule in such a way as to shift the responsibility for clearly defining the powers of city government from the state legislatures to the cities themselves. The Program recommended that cities be allowed to define their powers on the fairly broad basis that they not conflict with state law. While the courts would continue to mediate and interpret, as provided for by Dillon's rule, the state legislatures would stop functioning as an additional force limiting municipal powers. Leo S. Rowe wrote to explain this point:

The courts have always required [in the past] a specific grant from the Legislature to justify an exercise of local authority. In giving the municipality all powers not inconsistent with the general laws of the State, the endeavor has been made to reverse the policy of the past and to create the presumption in favor of the broadest exercise of municipal powers. The history of municipal government clearly shows that the constant appeals to the State Legislature for additional powers has been one of the most unfortunate influences in our public life. It has created the impression that the real seat of city government is in the State Legislature, rather than in the city authorities, and has developed the unfortunate habit of constant interference by the former body in local affairs.[22]

Second, by obtaining the agreement of groups from many states to the principle that "with slight local variations, the system [of improved municipal government] applicable in New York is applicable in Kentucky" and elsewhere, innovators at the national level assured themselves that their work would not meet with loud protestations that only locally contrived improvements were appropriate to the circumstances of a particular city or state.

Third and finally, by uniting activists, analysts and groups of all kinds behind a commitment to strong city self-government, the Program helped to justify the further development of a major field of municipal political science. The assurance that the effect of reform would be to make city governments more and more like "true" governments, and less and less like administrative branches of the state government, was crucial to the elaboration of a special branch of political science for the analysis of city politics and government.

With these three advances established, a new kind of urban political innovation could begin.

CHAPTER 4

The Census Bureau's Model of Good City Government

Once the formulation of a systematic approach to municipal innovation was well under way, the participants in the innovation process began to concentrate their attention upon a generalized model of improved city government structure and accompanying methods of administrative management. In the years from 1894 to the publication of the Municipal Program in 1899, the reorienting of basic legal and political principles had been most important. Individuals enamored of particular reform schemes, such as Dorman B. Eaton, who insisted that municipal civil service reform was an all-purpose solution to the city government problem, contributed little to the progress made in the late 1890s. The 1899 Program contained the rough outlines of a structural model and a system of administration, but no more. Giving substance to the model was the next task to accomplish.

The generalized model of strong city self-government that emerged between 1899 and 1913 consisted of a centralized administrative structure headed by a mayor and his immediate staff, and a set of function-oriented departments, each headed by an official appointed by, and directly responsible to, the mayor. I have called this the "Census Bureau's" model of good city government because after 1902 the urban statistics experts of the federal Bureau of the Census assumed chief responsibility for developing it. The bureau mounted a major program of comparative statistical reporting and research designed to advance the new approach to municipal administration, and to make structural and administrative innovations accessible to city governments. Later, around 1909, municipal political scientists combined the generalized model, the associated innovations in administrative methods, and the legal and political assumptions of the Municipal Program into a complete theoretical treatment of American municipal government. This was the final step in the establishment of a standard framework for municipal political science, and for training and research programs in municipal administration. By 1913, the new approach to urban political innovation had acquired the standardized, institutionalized, and professionalized form in which it continued to function for the next twenty years.

At all stages of its evolution, the prescriptive aspects of the generalized model developed in conjunction with the analytic methods employed to investigate the nature of cities and city government. Conceptions of good city government and the analysis of existing city government went hand-in-hand with each other. The first section of this chapter deals with early analytic conceptions and the beginnings of annual comparative statistics programs. When the Census Bureau established its urban statistics program, it began elaborating the generalized model in considerable detail. As the bureau's program advanced, annual comparative statistics became both the measure and the standard of good administrative practice. These developments make up the second section. Finally, municipal political scientists incorporated the new analytic approach into their prescriptive theory of city government by making the necessity for performing the essential functions of city government depend upon the unique physical, social, and economic conditions of city life. This is the subject of the third section. In one sense, the American innovators borrowed much of their generalized model from European theories of government. But in another sense, the strictly American work of developing a proper context for the model was more important than the selection and assembly of its component parts. The last section briefly discusses the inadequacy of the hypothesis that the large industrial corporation was the general model for strong, centralized, functionally departmentalized city government.

The Mutual Development of Analysis and Prescription

From the earliest origins of the new approach to urban political innovation, the question of what constituted good city government was associated with the question of why cities had their own governments at all. Cooley recognized in the original edition of *Constitutional Limitations* that city government required a special rationale. The belief that local affairs should be controlled by local authority, he argued, "impels" the states, "as if by common agreement . . . to incorporate cities, boroughs, and villages wherever a dense population renders different rules important from those which are needful for the rural districts."[1] Despite Cooley's example, John Dillon did not recognize the need for a special rationale until considerably later. The third edition of his *Municipal Corporations*, published in 1881, continued to explain the existence of municipal governments by saying that there was a policy of establishing cities and towns and giving their citizens powers of self-government. "The effect of this policy . . . ," Dillon remarked, "has, upon the whole, been most happy."[2] It was in another section of the 1881 edition that Dillon first introduced a density-based rationale similar to Cooley's. There he explained that *"the fundamental idea of a municipal corporation proper* is to invest the people of a thickly populated place or district with the power of regulating their own affairs, which are of a nature not common to the state at large, and which it is supposed they can regulate for themselves better than the legislature can regulate them by general enactments."[3] Dillon's fourth edition included a more elaborate statement:

large and compact aggregations of people necessarily give rise to conditions and create wants peculiar to such circumstances. . . . [These circumstances] are not common to rural populations and to the state at large. Special provisions are therefore necessary for the health, safety, convenience, and good government of populous communities crowded within a narrow space, . . . a large and dense collection of human beings occupying a limited area have needs peculiar to themselves, which create the necessity for municipal or local government and regulation.[4]

The city's character as a large dense aggregation of people eventually became the chief concern of municipal analysis and prescription. George Waring, author of the first major Census study of cities: the two-volume *Report on the Social Statistics of Cities* in the Census of 1880, built his analysis on the premise that cities were a product of the natural, economic, commercial, social, and political forces operating in the nation's natural geographic regions. Waring postulated that these forces caused clumpings of dense population to develop around nuclei of political cities and towns. In addition, the national growth of European countries had caused population to concentrate around the nucleus of the national capital, forming a national "Metropolis," which Waring described as the "natural outgrowth of the original nucleus." Similar forces operated in the United States to generate the "Metropolis of the United States," New York City and its environs. New York City, Brooklyn, Jersey City, Newark, Hoboken, and numerous smaller surrounding communities, Waring argued, constituted "one great metropolitan community" with a "national hinterland."[5]

The first analyst to impute a systematic relationship between the unique conditions of city life and the necessity for the performance of public functions not required by the noncity population was John S. Billings, M.D., special agent in charge of vital statistics for the Census of 1890. Billings examined the large cities ward by ward in the reports on vital statistics in hopes of demonstrating a direct relationship between the physical and social environment of a city neighborhood, and the health of its residents. Then, in the second decennial report on the social statistics of cities, Billings attempted to validate his theory that poor city government service in a ward neighborhood was the direct and patent cause of death and disease. He subdivided the wards of the large cities into "sanitary districts" for purposes of the census enumeration, each district containing a "particular class of the population or some special aggregation of people in tenement houses."[6] While the census work was in progress, Billings predicted that these reports would reveal "whether the municipal authorities are to be blamed for the circumstances producing . . . greater death rates." The *Social Statistics* report presented tables designed to reveal a correlation between high death and disease rates and low per capita spending on sewers, street cleaning, and public health. The statistics of city government expenditures were a major achievement, but the testing of the theory was a failure. Billings found that he could not make the city death rates match his notions of which cities were well governed. He blamed this failure in part on his inability to eliminate from the analysis the intervening effects of such factors as climate, city altitude, population density, and the age and wealth distributions of the population. He refused to abandon his belief that death and disease rates could be used in some manner as measures of municipal performance.[7]

The next major conceptual advance was the introduction of an analytic discussion of the process of urban aggregation. In 1899, Adna Ferrin Weber published a major study of urbanization during the course of the nineteenth century which focused upon industry and industrialization as the principal cause of the conditions found in late nineteenth-century American cities. "New needs and purposes manifest themselves when a community attains a certain size," Weber wrote; the dense concentration of a large number of people "alters even the material conditions of life." This argument was familiar. Weber added to the evolving analysis a marvelously detailed study of the industrial nature of nineteenth-century urbanization. He emphasized that steam railroads and steam power in industry had accelerated the concentration of national populations in cities, and showed that this industrial concentration had produced the congested conditions of life plaguing the cities of the 1890s. The book focused upon the United States but included comparable statistics on all the industrializing countries. Weber described current urban conditions and concluded with possible remedies for city congestion, giving prominence to the use of electric streetcar systems for dispersing workers' residences, and possibly industrial plants as well, to the suburbs.[8]

At the same time that Weber was composing his discussion of industrial urbanization, the final developments preliminary to the formulation of a generalized model of American city government were taking shape. As with the preceding steps, analysis and prescription went hand-in-hand. In a discussion in 1896 of improved methods of studying city government finances, Frederick W. Clow recommended an analytic scheme based on the functional theory of government associated with the prominent Prussian institutional economist Adolf Wagner. Wagner's theory defined five obligatory functions of city government and one category of enterprises in which cities should have the power to engage if they so desired. The obligatory functions were maintenance of government, care of defective classes, public safety, public convenience, and "higher objectives," and the optional enterprises were known as "quasi-private undertakings." The first step towards a science of municipal government in America, Clow argued, had to be the creation of a comparative system of statistical description based upon the scientific classification of municipal government functions. "In scientific work," he proclaimed, "classification is the step preparatory to generalization. Facts and figures are like soldiers—they must be organized before they can be used."[9]

In response to Clow's and others' proposals, the National Municipal League initiated a program to advocate uniformity and comparability in municipal accounting and financial reporting. Accumulated uniform and comparable information from many cities could later be used to develop improved methods of municipal administration. Clow speculated that annually published municipal statistics might be valuable enough to become a profitable enterprise, something like the statistics and information on railroads published in Henry Varnum Poor's *Manual of Railroads*.

Enthusiasm for comparative municipal statistics stimulated Congress to authorize the Commissioner of Labor, in July 1898, to "compile and publish annually an abstract of the main features of the official statistics of the cities of the United States having over 30,000 population." The Commissioner of Labor was not a leading advocate of this program, but his agency was the only one capable of undertaking it in 1898.[10]

The annual reports issued by the Department of Labor did not attempt to derive generalizations from the statistics about the appropriate functions and administrative methods of city government. The reports arranged financial statistics for all the cities in standardized categories, but not according to a system of obligatory and optional functions such as Wagner's. Labor Commissioner Carroll D. Wright told the 1899 convention of the National Association of Officials of Bureaus of Labor Statistics that the program might eventually have "the same beneficial effect" in promoting cooperation among cities about improved administrative methods "that the action of the Interstate Commerce Commission had in bringing the railroads to a common understanding." Officials in "nearly every city" had shown tremendous interest in obtaining annual statistics for other cities that were uniform and comparable with their own statistics and financial records. But the Department of Labor lacked the resources to provide the kind of program that these officials really wanted. The only way to obtain comparable numbers for all cities was to send agents of the department to the cities to perform the proper calculations. Since Congress made no increases in the department's appropriation when it authorized the program, this field work fell upon the existing staff and was very onerous. Commissioner Wright was enthusiastic about the program's possibilities, but was not anxious to become a leading advocate for a kind of federal statistical reporting and analysis that differed from the philosophy of statistics that he had developed over a long career. After three years of working with officials in the cities, the Department of Labor reported to the 1901 Good City Government Conference that it appeared unlikely that greater progress would be made in the future, "unless some stronger and more powerful influence can be brought to bear for the purpose of securing greater uniformity and clearness of method among city officials."[11]

The Census Bureau Specifies a General Model

The "stronger and more powerful influence" came in the form of the transfer of the statistics-of-cities program to the new permanent Bureau of the Census in July 1903, and its expansion into a major aspect of the bureau's work. The bureau's program fell short of Milo Maltbie's prediction that the federal government would establish a "Municipal Statistics Bureau" comparable to the Local Government Board of the national government in England, but it was a tremendous advance from the beginnings made by the Department of Labor. Simeon N. D. North, who became director of the Census Bureau soon after its establishment as a permanent federal agency in 1902, viewed the design, collection, publication, and use of statistics as one of the crucial functions of national government, on a par with collecting revenues or providing national defense. He assigned the statistics-of-cities program a prominent role in his somewhat grandiose plans for the agency that he hoped would soon become the "Central Statistical Office" of the federal government.[12]

Despite the fact that the work on the Census of 1900 was still under way, North rapidly turned the statistics of cities into a major enterprise. He consolidated the annual reports for 1902 and 1903 with the report on social statistics of cities planned for the 1900 Census in order to produce one large document that would provide an impressive beginning for the bureau's urban statistics program. Next he adopted the functional classification system employed by the National Municipal League as the framework for collecting and publishing the data, and coordinated the preparation of the combined report for 1902 and 1903 with the work of the league's Committee on Uniform Municipal Accounting. He put LeGrand Powers, who was then chief statistician for agriculture, and William C. Hunt, chief of population, in charge of the report. Then he organized a conference in November 1903, for city government accounting and financial officials, to initiate them into what he hoped would become a permanent cooperative effort. Census Bureau field agents replaced the agents of the Department of Labor in visiting the cities and collecting the data, and the work began. Reviewing the first year's progress, North reported:

It is probable that the annual Census reports upon Municipal Finance for cities of 30,000 population and over will prove the most influential factor in securing the adoption of uniform classification, thus materially lessening the cost of compiling Census statistics upon this subject, increasing the accuracy of returns, making comparison possible between the itemized expenditures of cities of the same population and encouraging reform in public service.[13]

In material terms the program was impressive. It was far more time-consuming and expensive than all the activities of the National Municipal League combined. In the first years, when most of the cities were using accounting methods of their own peculiar evolutionary design, each total figure for each category of expenditure, debt, revenue, and so forth, had to be compiled and calculated by the bureau's own field agents. Even in later years, when many cities had adopted some form of the league's uniform accounting system, the labor of compiling an annual report was immense. In 1914, after more than ten years' experience, the field work of collecting the data required seven to eight months of full-time effort by about thirty bureau agents.[14]

The Census Bureau's program put into practice the scheme for annual comparative statistics suggested by Clow in 1896. In adopting the classification system of the National Municipal League, the bureau was replacing the largely descriptive format employed by the Department of Labor with a modified form of the Wagnerian functional system.*

---

*Each capitalized entry is a separate category in the respective classification system. Department of Labor categories are from *Bulletin* 24, pp. 688–689.

Clow, based on Wagner	Census Bureau	Department of Labor
Maintenance of government	General administration	No distinct category
Care of defective classes	Public charities and corrections	Police courts, jails, workhouses, etc. Hospitals, asylums, charities
Public safety	Public safety	Police department Fire department Health department
Public convenience	Public highways and sanitation	Sewers Care of streets Street lighting Garbage removal
Higher objects	Public education Public recreation	Schools Libraries, galleries, museums Parks and gardens
Quasi-private undertakings	Commercial functions	Waterworks Electric light works Gas works Docks, wharves, ferries, bridges, markets, cemeteries

The bureau also began to confront the analytic problem most crucial to the prescriptive aspect of its program: defining what constituted the "municipal government" of a city. The definition employed in preparing the statistics had to be sufficiently narrow to conform to each individual city's working conception of its own government, but sufficiently broad and general to provide statistics for all cities that could be compared with each other in ways that would be meaningful and beneficial. Before the composition of the bureau's report for 1902 and 1903, no such definition had ever been formulated for American cities. The definition selected was forceful and straightforward:

The "municipal government" for which the Bureau of the Census seeks to present financial statistics is not limited to the "city government" . . . but includes all corporations, organizations, commissions, boards, and other local public authorities through which the people of the city exercise any privilege of local self-government, or through which they enjoy the exclusive benefits of any municipal function.

The bureau's definition of municipal government functions was also notable for dispelling vagueness about which activities and institutions of a city should be considered part of its "government." Governmental functions were:

those municipal activities which are performed for all citizens alike without compensation, the expense being met by revenue obtained principally from compulsory contributions levied without regard to the benefits which the contributors may individually derive from any or all municipal activities. . . . The term *governmental functions* . . . includes those municipal functions which are as a rule performed for all citizens alike without any attempt to measure the amount of benefit conferred or exact compensation therefor. Most of them are essential to the existence and development of government and to the performance of the governmental duty of protecting life and property and of maintaining a high standard of social efficiency.

This definition had the added advantage of differentiating Wagner's five obligatory functions from the sixth functional category, quasi-private or commercial undertakings, which the bureau defined as "those activities from which a revenue is derived that represents a partial or full compensation or return for the privileges granted, commodity or property sold, or specific service rendered."[15]

Here, in these two definitions, lay the foundation of the bureau's generalized model of American municipal government. Following Wagner, the definitions delineated municipal government in terms of the *functions* that constitute local self-government. Similarly, the bureau made the functions that municipal government was to perform the core of their generalized model. They assembled the administrative structure required to perform the obligatory municipal functions around this central reason for cities to possess strong powers of self-government. The functions of municipal government also formed the hinge connecting the analysis of current city practices with the bureau's prescriptive conception of how city government ought to be organized and administered. The reports carried the mutual development of analysis and prescription to the point where comparative statistics of the current performance of municipal functions by all large cities could provide a comprehensive guide to improved operating methods for centralized, functionally departmentalized city governments. As the second definition emphasized, one of the bureau's prescriptions was "the governmental duty . . . of maintaining a high standard of social efficiency."

The most prominent feature of the bureau's reports was the presentation of per capita statistics of annual operating expenditures on the five obligatory municipal functions for all cities of over 30,000 population. These figures made it possible for each individual city to see statistics of its own expenditure practices cast in the format of the generalized model. Cities that had adopted the uniform accounting system designed by the National Municipal League were already keeping accounts according to the classification scheme used by the bureau in compiling these figures. For these cities, the bureau's statistics were a source of directly comparable information about the functional expenditures of other cities. Most cities that had not reformed their accounting practices obtained from the bureau reports not simply information about other cities, but a completely new statistical picture of their own practices. Many cities lacked the kind of function-oriented data compiled by the bureau because different parts of the city government kept separate financial records based on special taxes and funds, sometimes with fiscal years that ended on different dates. Often such cities did not distinguish between capital and operating expenditures in a rigorous manner, and therefore had no clear conception of what the appropriate level of annual operating expenditure on any particular function might be. The fiscal and accounting practices of most cities in 1902 were extremely specific and complex. While the officials of these cities might understand the complexities, their residents were left in the dark about how fiscal administration was being conducted. Even cities that had converted to the National Municipal League system did not usually go to the further trouble of calculating expenditures on a per capita basis and publicizing them annually. The per capita expenditure figures emphasized, for the individual city resident reading the bureau's report, that some cities were not performing certain of the municipal functions at all. In some cities, one or more functions were performed by state government agencies or other institutions that were not properly a part of the city's "municipal government," according to the bureau's definition. The emphasis on comparison made officials and residents of cities of this kind aware that their behavior was aberrant. In the report on 1902 and 1903, Fort Wayne, Indiana enjoyed the unique distinction of appearing to have spent no public monies in the category of public charities and corrections. Mostly the reports emphasized the tremendous variation in what cities were spending on a particular functional activity. Average per capita expenditure on fire departments (under Public Safety), for all cities was $1.33. Yet Scranton, Pennsylvania, had been spending $0.63 per capita, while Wilmington, Delaware, spent $0.56, Harrisburg, Pennsylvania, $0.35, Bayonne, New Jersey, $0.42, and Kingston, New York, $0.32.[16]

The comparative per capita expenditure tables both encouraged and facilitated the translation of the abstract obligation for municipal governments to perform the five essential functions into practical estimates of appropriate dollars-and-cents amounts of city spending. What constituted good protection of the public safety? The census reports provided data suggesting various answers. One possible answer was that the average per capita expenditure for all one hundred and fifty cities of over 30,000 population (1904) might be an appropriate amount for any individual city to spend. Another possible answer was the average per capita expenditure among cities of approximately the same population as the city in question. A third answer was to follow the lead of a city with a reputation for good and efficient service. Cities contending with climate, altitude, topography, or other complicating conditions could modify their chosen standard as they saw fit, or seek guidance in the statistics from cities facing similar difficulties. As early as its first report, the bureau included discussion of the implications of the statistical tables for improving the performance of municipal functions. The report for 1902 and 1903 emphasized that it was not sufficient for larger cities to expend greater *total* amounts of money in providing a particular service than smaller cities spent. Providing high quality service also required that larger cities expend greater amounts per capita. The report arranged the cities in the tables by population size, from largest to smallest. This helped to illustrate the "fact"

that in all municipalities expenditures and the burden of taxation increase faster than population, the *per capita* figures being, in almost all cases, greater in the large cities than in those of smaller size. For most of the objects of payment . . . the *per capita* figures . . . form a more or less regular series from the cities containing less than 50,000 inhabitants up to the five largest cities.

The tables showed that a general relationship existed of a kind expressed by the formula:

$$\text{per capita expenditure} = f \text{ (population)}$$

The text of the report recommended that cities evaluate this relationship for their own purposes either by observing its values for cities that had a reputation for administrative efficiency, or by taking the mean value for the size class in which their city fell and using that as a guide. Thus a city of 75,000 could observe that a city of 100,000 which it considered efficiently governed expended $3.00 per capita on public safety and an efficient city of 50,000 expended $2.50, and conclude that an appropriate level of expenditure for a city of 75,000 would be $2.75.[17]

The bureau was not reticent about its desire to assist the reform activities of the National Municipal League, elite activist groups in cities, and progressive city officials. LeGrand Powers, by this time the chief statistician for statistics of cities, addressed the 1908

Conference on Good City Government on the bureau's role "as an agent of municipal reform." The bureau, Powers reported, was providing the cities with "analytical statistical accounts" analogous to accounting systems that had "proved of great administrative assistance to all the most successful private enterprises of the day." The comparative statistics formed "the basis for making the experience of one city the text and measure of the economy, wastefulness, or efficiency of the administration of our larger cities." More than half of the nation's large cities had adopted the National Municipal League uniform accounting system and were using the bureau's comparative statistics as a guide to the planning of revenues and expenditures, and to the preparation of budgets. "To change the character of the accounts and reports of the cities of a nation is a great undertaking," Powers told the league convention, "one which, in its magnitude, can only be likened to the reformation of the governments of the same city [sic], and the placing of all municipal life upon a higher level." The bureau's reports had been "of the most vital assistance" in "increasing the efficiency of the democracy of cities." Powers concluded by firmly linking the bureau's hopes for the further success of its program with the efforts of the league, the accounting profession, citizens' associations, students of municipal life, emerging bureaus of municipal research, and "reformers generally."[18]

Bureau Director North made similar claims in a presentation to the American Statistical Association in which he cited the bureau's involvement in municipal reform as a demonstration of the importance of statistical science to governmental progress. "The most prolific source of municipal graft," North told the statisticians, "its securest hidingplace, its most effective agency in seeking immunity, is the chaos existing in municipal bookkeeping and in the classification of municipal accounts."

To each of the 157 cities of the United States having a population of 30,000 and over, a representative of the census goes every year, and so classifies the receipts and expenditures for every purpose that each city now knows just what it costs, in comparison with the cost in other cities of its class, to maintain schools, police, fire department, streets, sewers,—every important item of municipal expense. This is magnificent work, furnishing a most effective weapon in the crusade for municipal reform and rehabilitation now sweeping over the United States.[19]

The final step in the development of the generalized model was finding a solution to the problem of measuring and improving the efficiency of municipal service performance. The reports on financial statistics gave no indication of how much service actually resulted from the expenditure of money on police, fire, or health activities. The financial statistics reports also failed to provide cities with a means of evaluating whether reforms and innovations in municipal structure and administrative practice were producing beneficial results. The early reports made analogies to the role of profits in private business and lamented that public business lacked such a straightforward measure of performance, and of the value of innovations. By 1910, when the report for 1907 appeared, the Bureau had resolved these problems by deciding that "unit cost accounting," a recent development in private business administration, could be used in a modified form to suit the needs of city governments:

In private business , . . . every factor of business administration is brought under accounting control by means of what the business world now knows as "cost accounting." It is by such methods that the leaders in modern private business have made accounts and accounting of supreme administrative assistance in avoiding bad and securing good financial results. Their accounts are the ideal ones of the business world, and demonstrate the great part that accounting records can play in securing success and avoiding failure. In like manner, a few governmental officials have introduced general and departmental accounts which accomplish for nations, states, and municipalities what the analytical and statistical accounts above described accomplish for private enterprise. Their accounts are so arranged as to provide adequate accounting control over revenue, to aid in preventing waste or loss thereof in collection, and to apply the principles of private cost accounting for purposes of testing the efficiency and economy of all branches of governmental service.[20]

Unit cost accounting for cities meant the correlation of unit cost with unit output. Assistant Director of the Census W. F. Willoughby explained to the 1910 Good City Government Conference that the only way to make true progress towards increasing the efficiency of municipal government was by making it possible to compare financial inputs with physical output in such a way as to establish the cost of units of service. Cities would have to know how much it was costing them under existing methods to maintain a mile of sewer pipe, pave a square mile of street surface, or provide policemen for units of 10,000 population. In order to promote comparability, the bureau would have to develop a series of statistical reports on the physical units of municipal functional service that could be correlated with the existing statistics on financial expenditures. Bureau officials had planned the first such report for statistics of units of service provided during the year 1909.[21]

Some cities had attempted to correlate their own physical and financial statistics, Willoughby reported, but such information was of little value without comparable data from other cities. He proposed that the National Municipal League recognize that its 1899 Municipal Program had accomplished many of its aims, and that the time had come to enter a new phase of municipal reform: "that of improving municipal administration as distinct from municipal organization." He suggested that the league was the appropriate national organization to coordinate the various efforts to improve municipal administration through the design of a set of administrative methods "that might as far as practicable be adopted generally by cities, and administrative practices and procedure thus be standardized." Willoughby was uncertain about how much could be accomplished in this direction, but he felt that a league program to promote the adoption of the bureau's physical statistics accounting system by all cities would be a good first step.[22]

The bureau had made a first attempt at calculating physical statistics for police service in the financial statistics report for

1907. The report on "general statistics of cities" for 1909, published in 1913, presented a system of physical unit accounting that could be correlated with the financial statistics for 1909 on the basis of "common units of service." The 1909 report covered sewer service, refuse collection, street cleaning, dust prevention, and highway service. The Wilson administration chose not to continue with the 1910 plan to cover all areas of service and to repeat the report on each area on a five-year cycle. The 1909 report was sufficient to present the general method of correlating physical and financial statistics for units of service, however. The bureau had completed its specification of a generalized model of effective municipal government and produced comparative statistics illustrating all the model's aspects. By the time the 1909 report on physical statistics appeared, in 1913, the municipal political scientists had completed the work of incorporating the model of city government structure and administrative practice into a prescriptive theory of American city government. Experts in the subspecialty of municipal administration carried on the development of municipal unit cost accounting from the beginnings made by the bureau.[23]

Political Scientists Construct a Theory of American Municipal Government

The last major task in developing the new mode of urban political innovation was to elaborate a political theory of strong city self-government. A theory was required to establish the legitimacy of the principles put forward in the 1899 Municipal Program, and of the model of structure and administration specified by the Census Bureau, within the context of American federal and state constitutionalism. The theory of constitutional limitations, by now completely institutionalized in the legal system, absolved legal theory of this responsibility. Dillon and other legal commentators had placed the responsibility in the province of political science and welcomed the initial steps taken in the Municipal Program. The work accomplished between 1899 and 1909 was largely a matter of eliminating potential contradictions with federal and state constitutional principles, but it was important work nevertheless. Until it was finished, municipal political science could not complete its evolution from a method of approaching city government problems to a comprehensive paradigm for municipal analysis and prescription.

The authors of a successful theory faced two major difficulties. The first was that the theory of municipal government could not be a "social contract" theory, the type of theory inherent in federal and state constitutionalism. City governments did not exist as a result of either a real or an abstract act of contracting together by their citizens. Regardless of the assertion of the principle of city self-government since 1894, city governments could never be what were sometimes referred to as "true" governments by political scientists working on the theory. They were stuck with their origins as chartered corporations created by their state governments. The second difficulty was one of justifying the differential applications of principles to two otherwise indistinguishable groups of citizens of a state. In other words, for what reason should state citizens living in "cities" have a right to a form of local government denied to state citizens living outside of "cities"? This difficulty took the additional form that unless there were some legitimate reason why only the state citizens living in "cities" should be allowed to make legislative policy relating to their own affairs, then there was no reason for the state legislature to allow city councils to share even a small part of its power and responsibility for making policy for the citizens of the state. In the absence of good and sufficient reasons, the only legal alternatives would be either to grant every local jurisdiction within the state the *same* powers of legislation and self-government, or not to delegate legislative power at all and make all policy for cities in the state legislature.

Like the urban statisticians at the Census Bureau, the authors of the theory obtained assistance from the European functional theory developed by Adolf Wagner and others. They borrowed from the European theory the concept of basing the legitimacy of city self-government upon the necessity for a particular group of a nation's citizens (and therefore of a state's citizens in the United States) to have a special form of local government. The necessity of this particular group, the residents of cities, arose, they argued, from the special character of life in cities. Frank Goodnow published a preliminary formulation of such a theory in 1904 in a book called *City Government in the United States.* Goodnow published the classic complete formulation of the new theory in 1909 in a book entitled *Municipal Government.* Several other writers published their own versions of the theory, in part to indicate the consensus among political scientists on the form of an appropriate theory, and in part to provide textbooks for teaching the theory in university political science courses. Horace Deming, who had served as chairman of the league's Committee on the Municipal Program, published *The Government of American Cities: A Program of Democracy,* in 1909; Charles Beard, at this stage in his career a professor of political science at Columbia University, and a close associate of Goodnow's, published his version of the theory, *American City Government: A Survey of Newer Tendencies,* in 1912; and William Bennett Munro, Professor of Municipal Government at Harvard University, published *The Government of American Cities,* in 1913.[24]

All formulations employed the same central argument: (1) The purpose of government is to satisfy the *needs* of the people. (2) Such needs of a population for government arise out of the nature of the *conditions* of their life together in society: the character of the population in question as a group, and the nature of their environment. (3) The *needs* arising from these *conditions* in which the population lives together are of several varieties, and for each variety of need there is a corresponding *function* of government, the proper performance of which will alleviate the corresponding need. (4) The purpose of municipal government is to perform the *functions* required to alleviate the *needs* of the population arising from the nature of the *conditions* of city life. Given the nature of the central argument, it is appropriate to call this the "theory of the functions of municipal government" or the "functional" theory for short. It could, of course, also be called the "function" theory of city government. The authors of the functional theory used this argument to resolve the difficulties confronting them in the following way. First, they overcame the problem of having different governments for different groups of the citizens of a state by arguing that the conditions of life in cities were different from the conditions of life in which the noncity citizens of a state resided. The conditions unique to the cities generated needs for public service unique to cities, necessitating special governments, that is, city governments, capable of performing the governmental functions required to alleviate the unique needs arising from the unique conditions in which city residents lived.

Goodnow presented this part of the theory in an ingenious form. He established the existence of unique conditions in cities through a discussion of the historical evolution of cities, and of the appropriate form of city government for each major evolutionary city type. The types included the ancient city-state, the medieval city, the free imperial city, the English borough, and so forth. During the nineteenth century, Goodnow argued, industrialization had produced another major transformation of city conditions, requiring the development of a new form of city government. It was the task of modern theory to determine the form of municipal government appropriate to the new urban conditions created by industrialization. Any discussion of modern municipal government, therefore, necessarily had to begin with "a consideration of the ways in which trade and industry influence both the establishment of cities and the character of the urban population which their pursuit attracts." He went on to argue that industrialization in the United States had created increasingly great differences between urban and rural conditions of life, that state governments had done little to adapt preindustrial city government to this change, and that the proper resolution was for state governments now (1909) to provide a "governmental system" for cities "suited to the conditions of life in the city."

If . . . the formal system of government [meaning state government in the United States] has due regard for the conditions existing in the city, the endeavor will have been made to obtain in the first place a clear understanding of urban conditions as urban conditions, and not merely a fractional part of general social conditions, and to provide a governmental organization suited to these conditions.

The conclusion to be drawn from the analysis of urban conditions was that the cities of the industrial age required strong powers of self-government.[25]

Charles Beard, in his *American City Government*, expounded this part of the theory by devoting a chapter to the horrors of city life among those who could depend only upon the city government for aid and relief: the overcrowding, disease and suffering of the industrial working classes. Horace Deming considerably shortened the discussion of conditions and treated the argument leading up to the necessity for cities to have strong powers of self-government as largely self-evident.

It is self-evident that when a considerable population is massed within a limited area, a community life is developed whose needs and circumstances are very different both in degree and kind from those of the isolated individual lives of dwellers in agricultural or grazing regions.

If the truth of this proposition were granted, as Deming insisted it had to be, then state governments would also have to concede that communities with special needs and circumstances ought to have a form of local government suited to their needs:

A city should have all the powers requisite to satisfy the local needs of the community within its corporate limits. . . . The satisfaction of these needs is the primary function of a city, the fundamental reason for its existence as a local government.

A city without such powers would be a "subject province" of its state government, a status Deming emphatically denounced. "A city is not a province to be administered by some outside authority," he wrote, a city is "a government." Beard handled this part of his treatment by simply quoting directly from Deming.[26]

The first difficulty, the difficulty that they could not provide a social contract theory of city government, the formulators of the functional theory could not overcome. The government created by the social contract was the state government. Giving powers of legislation and execution to a city government involved usurping powers granted solely to the state legislature and the governor by the social contract inherent in the state constitution. The difficulties arising from the lack of a social contract basis for city government theory persist even today. Wallace Sayre and Nelson Polsby, writing in 1965, expressed a prevailing attitude among modern political scientists when they described these writings of Goodnow and his associates as "doctrinal prescriptions for the governing of cities in the United States," rather than as a contribution to organic American political theory. By and large, the functionalists overcame the social contract difficulty by a fait accompli. Leo S. Rowe had told the first Good City Government Conference that "the doctrine that a municipal government is but a *subordinate branch of the general governmental power of the State*" was "as false in principle as it is detrimental to progress in its operation." The difficulty then, in 1894, was that the doctrine of subordinate municipal status had been "confirmed from the . . . Supreme Court downwards," and that little would be accomplished until there was "a change in the attitude of the State towards the municipality." By 1909, that change had come about, at least to the satisfaction of political scientists and legal commentators. The authors of the functional theory were able to assert the necessity for cities to have strong powers of self-government largely because a consensus had emerged that such a necessity existed. State legislators and others who wished to oppose the new attitude of the state towards its cities were free to do their worst. John Dillon, who had been waiting for the political scientists to complete a formal justification for strong city self-government since the 1890s, quickly incorporated the functional argument into the fifth edition of his treatise, published in 1911.[27]

Having established the necessity for cities to have strong powers of self-government for the purpose of performing the essential functions of municipal government, each author devoted the major portion of his treatment to specific discussion of the six municipal functions defined by Wagner, and employed in the Census Bureau's generalized model. Their titles varied from one author to another, and the sixth nonobligatory category, "quasi-private undertakings," sometimes did not appear. Goodnow's functions, each of which received a chapter-length treatment, were called finance, charities and corrections (care of defective classes), police, local improvements (public convenience), and education (the most important of Wagner's "higher objects"). Goodnow omitted quasi-private undertakings. Beard devoted whole chapters to the following subjects: "Raising and Spending the City's Money" (maintenance of government), "Guarding the City Against Crime and Vice," "Guarding the Health of the People," and "Tenement House Reform" (a three-part treatment of the two categories: care of defective classes and public safety), "The Streets of the City" (public convenience), two chapters on higher objects: "Education and Industrial Training" and "Municipal Recreation," and a two-part discussion of quasi-private undertakings: "Franchises and Public Utilities" and "Municipal Ownership." Beard also included a chapter on "City Planning" in the hopes that it would become accepted as a necessary function.[28]

The "Functional" Mode Versus the Model of the Business Corporation

The publication of Goodnow's *Municipal Government* and the other formulations of the functional theory completed the development of the new mode of innovation. The *uses* of the new mode: the state constitutional change, legislative reform, city structural reorganization and administrative improvement constituting the new process of urban political innovation, are fairly well understood. The next chapter presents a statistical description of the changes in city administrative practices between 1904 and 1930 that illustrates some major consequences of functional innovation. A few words must be said, however, before proceeding, about one current hypothesis concerning the origins of functional innovation. The customary treatment of the origins of what I have called the functional mode, by urban historians, has been to refer off-handedly to the centralized, functionally departmentalized industrial corporation as the model for reformed city government structure and administration. Samuel Hays gave the hypothesis its most elaborate expression in 1964 when he argued:

> The guide to alternative action lay in the model of the business enterprise. In describing new conditions which they wished to create, reformers drew on the analogy of the 'efficient business enterprise,' criticizing current practices with the argument that 'no business could conduct its affairs that way and remain in business,' and calling upon business practices as guides to improvement. . . . The centralization of decision-making which developed in the business corporation was now applied in municipal reform.

"The model of the efficient business enterprise," Hays postulated in a more impressionistic vein, "rather than the New England town meeting, provided the positive inspiration for the municipal reformer."[29]

The reason that the accuracy of this hypothesis has yet to be tested is that the question of the *origin* of the general model of good city government was not considered important as long as it was believed that it originated with innovations in the world of business. Historians have been prepared to believe, as Hays asks them to do, without demonstration, that innovations originating in the world of business were sufficiently accessible, and sufficiently influential, to legal commentators, elite city reformers, federal statisticians, municipal political scientists, and progressive city officials and politicians, to render the task of actually documenting how business innovations made their way into the municipal realm of minor importance.

This was a mistake. At approximately the same time that Hays's article appeared, Alfred Chandler published the first detailed history of structural and administrative innovation in late nineteenth and early twentieth century American business. Chandler showed very convincingly that as late as 1902, when Pierre duPont and his two cousins took control of their family's hundred-year-old chemical company, the centralized, functionally departmentalized structure was not regarded by American entrepreneurs as a fixed and coherent model of administrative organization. Joseph Litterer's investigations of the business magazine literature of the 1890s dealing with administrative structure provided important support for Chandler's argument about the timing of the appearance of centralized functional structure. Before the innovations made by the duPont cousins became widely known, after 1910, the centralized, functionally departmentalized structure was not easily available even to businessmen as a model for innovation, much less to municipal innovators.[30]

Hays may have meant to use the term "model" less exactly, for in other passages in his article he implied that city politics acquired from the world of business no more than the "centralized" system of decision making. Hays postulated a dichotomy between "centralized" decision-making processes, which are "inherent in science and technology" and in the realm of business, and "decentralized" decision-making processes, which are "inherent in representative government," and argued that municipal reform in the early twentieth century "involved a tendency" for centralized processes to "prevail" over decentralized ones. Why the realm of business should be the unique locus of "centralized" decision-making processes, Hays did not explain. The likelihood that the army was the source for the first model of complex business organization—the "line and staff" structure employed by railroads in the middle of the nineteenth century—suggests that it is dangerous to make any strong a priori claims about the origins of forms of complex organizational structure.[31]

Less sweeping arguments about business, such as assertions that specific methods of business administration proved useful to municipal governments, have more validity. The adaptation of cost accounting to municipal finance by the Census Bureau is one of the chief examples. The questions of the *direction* of innovational influence between business administration and public administration, and of the *degree* of influence, remain at issue, however. I have only argued that innovation in urban politics from the 1850s to the mid-1930s was a process in which business played little part. Business administration and public administration as professions in the twentieth century have remained amazingly separate and distinct from each other. This seems largely a function of the fact that public administration began as a branch of political science. There has been no strong drive for public administration to move to a new home in the schools of business administration. If a larger context is needed for the origins of innovations in municipal government at the turn of the century, it seems preferable to retreat not to vague formulations of the nature of decision making in business, but to Robert Wiebe's concept of "bureaucratic orientation" as a new facet of American culture, and to the social scientific formulations of Max Weber and of experts in the process of political modernization.

CHAPTER 5

Municipal Progress, 1904–1930

"It has been a common superstition that municipal government is a failure," Charles Zeublin wrote in the revised edition of his *American Municipal Progress*, published in 1916.

It is not yet what we could wish. But the external accomplishments of American cities have been varied and creditable. If we assemble the best examples of their municipal successes, we produce a picture of a composite city inspiring and compelling. Each city is fragmentary and unsatisfactory; the composite city is already realized and provides a practicable vision.

The composite city is not the ultimate city, but it is a convenient working ideal. . . . Why should any city lack what man has worthily made in any other city?[1]

In this chapter, we will use the Census Bureau's financial statistics of cities to discuss the progress made in municipal administration between 1904 and 1930. The statistics reveal some major changes. The meaning and significance of those changes must be evaluated by comparison with changes in state and federal government, and with city administration in the more recent past.

The great problem of municipal service provision before the implementation of the strong centralized model of administration was that cities were attacking a complex of intricately interrelated problems with a hodgepodge of uncoordinated departmental programs and work efforts. The best that a city of the 1880s could hope for in the way of efficient service provision was economical handling of its purchases of supplies and labor. The city that could buy its paving materials and building stone, or hire street sweepers and day laborers, without having to make payments to political middlemen was accomplishing a great deal. If a city day laborer could also be supervised in such a way that he did a day's work for his day's pay, it was a great boon to the city's residents. The only way for a city government to know whether an adequate level of performance was being achieved was to invest time and effort measuring the amount of work completed. When such efforts were invested, however, the only way to make up for the failures that they revealed was to spend even more money on repeating work, and on providing better supervision. Municipal work was not amenable to the factory discipline, or to the piece-rate system, that allowed manufacturers to obtain high levels of worker performance.

City financial records from the 1890s reflect the difficulty that cities had in achieving effective performance. The financial reports of San Francisco in the 1890s, for example, consist of no more than page after page of itemized payments made to individuals and companies for labor and materials. San Francisco's knowledge of its annual expenditures consisted of no more than a totalling of these itemized purchases. When Carroll Wright and his Department of Labor field agents set out to prepare their report on the "official" statistics of cities for 1898, they discovered that San Francisco was among the more advanced cities in that it compiled and publicized any statistics at all. As late as 1910, San Francisco was still not ready for a comprehensive revision of its accounting and administrative methods. In that year, the Merchants Association of San Francisco hired four prominent accounting firms to prepare a report entitled "The Necessity of a Revision of the Accounting System of the City Government of San Francisco." The report showed that the financial administration of the city was poor. The city's Board of Supervisors did nothing. In 1913, the independent, nonpartisan California State Tax Association organized to promote tax reform in state, city, and local government. The Tax Association announced in 1915, with much documentation from comparative Census Bureau statistics, that San Francisco was on the verge of a great tax crisis because of rising costs caused by waste and inefficiency. Its report asserted that California's other cities faced similar crises; San Francisco merely presented the best example of the problem.[2]

The warning of imminent crisis helped to clear the way for administrative restructuring, especially because it came from an elite, nonpartisan group with no special interest in San Francisco, and was based on statistics prepared by the Census Bureau. The San Francisco Real Estate Board seized the opportunity to commission the Bureau of Municipal Research of New York to study San Francisco's city government and recommend a program of reorganization. The board also organized the San Francisco Bureau of Governmental Research to assist the city in managing its administrative problems in the future. This time the Board of Supervisors responded and the administrative structure of the city was reorganized. Budget planning and uniform accounting methods advocated by the National Municipal League and the Census Bureau were adopted. The New York Bureau of Municipal Research recommended a form of centralized, functionally departmentalized structure based on the functional model and it was put into operation.[3]

Few cities undertook the restructuring of their governments in the radical manner of San Francisco, but most cities of over 30,000 population made reforms along the lines recommended by the Census Bureau and the National Municipal League. In 1902, only four cities used the league accounting system: Baltimore, Boston, Cambridge (Massachusetts), and Chicago. The system spread quickly between 1902 and 1907 as a result of the passage of uniform municipal accounting laws employing the league system in four states: Ohio, New York, Iowa, and Massachusetts. Nineteen other cities adopted the system on their own initiative by 1907, and the bureau's field agents found that the majority of all the remaining cities of over 30,000 population had made at least some modification in their accounting methods. By 1913, when the report for 1911 was published, the Census Bureau was reasonably satisfied with the general status of city government comprehension of the functional approach to municipal administration and with the uses that cities were making of its reports.[4]

The statistics of changing city administrative behavior in the period from 1904 to 1930 presented here are intended to be primarily descriptive. The form of much of the presentation derives from "determinant" analysis, a method developed by students of modern urban public finance. Determinant analysis attempts to account for differences in administrative behavior from city to city. We will look at five aspects of changing practices: (1) the relation of changes in city expenditures per capita to changes in per capita gross national product, federal government expenditures per capita, and state government expenditures per capita; (2) the functional components of changing city expenditures per capita; (3) the changing role of city population size as a possible source of differences in per capita expenditures from city to city; (4) the changing role of city residential population density as a possible source of differences in per capita expenditures from city to city; and (5) the changing inter-correlation of per capita expenditures on the various functional categories of expenditure.

Wherever it is relevant, I have compared the statistics for 1904–1930 with similar statistics for the early 1950s prepared by Harvey Brazer as part of the first major determinant analysis of city expenditure behavior. Using the Brazer study as a standard provides a means of evaluating the significance of many aspects of the 1904–1930 statistics that are difficult to interpret on their own merits. At the end, evaluations of municipal "progress" will be attempted.[5]

The Context of City Government Expenditure Practices, 1880–1930

City government was more important to city residents than state and federal government combined before World War I, and was still of roughly equal importance with the federal government at the beginning of the 1930s. Table 1 is an attempt to examine changes in per capita city government expenditures in the context of changing national productivity, and federal and state govern-

Table 1. Per capita gross national product, federal government expenditures, state government expenditures, and city government expenditures, for selected years, 1880–1932, in current and in 1904 dollars.

Year	Current $				1904 $			
	GNP	Fed. expen.	State expen.	City expen.	GNP	Fed. expen.	State expen.	City expen.
1880	205*	5.32		13.64†	197*	5.12		13.12†
1890	208	5.04		12.97‡	213	5.16		13.28‡
1902	273	6.13	2.35		278	6.25	2.40	
1904	279	7.10		12.06§	279	7.10		12.06§
1912	413	7.24		12.99§	348	6.10		10.94§
1913	407	7.45	3.50		345	6.31	2.96	
1922	673	30.64	9.95		343	15.60	5.06	
1923	760	29.43		27.68§	378	14.63		13.76§
1930	734	27.95		35.47§	379	14.45		18.34§
1932	465	37.32	16.36		295	23.66		10.37

* 1880 figure is an average for 1879–1888.

† 1880 figure is a mean for 310 cities of over 7,500 population.

‡ 1890 figure is a mean for 55 cities of over 50,000 population.

§ 1904, 1912, 1923, and 1930 figures are means for all cities of over 30,000 population.

Sources: For gross national product figures: Bureau of the Census, *Historical Statistics of the United States, Colonial Times to 1970* (Washington, D.C.: 1975), p. 224.

For federal expenditures: Bureau of the Census, *Historical Statistics of the United States, Colonial Times to 1957* (Washington, D.C.: 1960), p. 718.

For state government expenditures: *Historical Statistics, Colonial Times to 1957*, p. 728. Capital outlays have been excluded.

For city government expenditures: for 1880: Census Office, *Tenth Census of the United States, Report on Valuation, Taxation and Indebtedness* (Washington, D.C.: 1880), pp. 245–247; for 1890: Census Office, *Eleventh Census of the United States, Report on Wealth, Debt and Taxation* (Washington, D.C.: 1890), Part II, pp. 554–557; for 1902–1930: Bureau of the Census, *Bulletin 50, Statistics of Cities over 30,000: 1904* (Washington, D.C.: 1906); Bureau of the Census, *Financial Statistics of Cities over 30,000: 1912* (Washington, D.C.: 1914); Bureau of the Census, *Financial Statistics of Cities over 30,000: 1923* (Washington, D.C.: 1925); Bureau of the Census, *Financial Statistics of Cities over 30,000: 1930* (Washington, D.C.: 1932).

ment expansion. The results are somewhat unexpected. 1904, 1912, 1923, and 1930 have been chosen as the four sample years out of the Census Bureau series for 1902–1934. In later sections, we will concentrate on comparing two periods: changes during the period when the functional mode of innovation was coming into fashion, and changes during the period of its maturity. For the first period, 1904 is the earliest year in which the cities and the Census Bureau were sufficiently familiar with the methodology of the reporting system to assure minimal accuracy of the figures compiled. The year 1912 is a good example from the period 1911–1913 when the bureau concluded that cities had achieved a sophisticated familiarity with the new innovative mode. The period of maturity, when functional innovation was at the height of its popularity, runs from 1912 to 1930. The year 1923 is a good intermediate example falling neither during World War I, nor during the chaotic industrial inventory crisis of 1919–1921. 1930 is a desirable concluding year, since it is the last year before the Great Depression had a serious impact on city governments. Before 1902, aside from the Department of Labor reports for 1898–1901, the only sources of comparable figures for large numbers of cities are the Census reports on wealth, debt, and taxation for 1880 and 1890. The gross national product per capita figures and the federal and state government expenditures per capita have been chosen from the years closest to the sample years for city expenditure figures.

The unexpected revelation of this comparison is that the municipal services of 1880 were not simply ineffective, as we found in Chapter 1, they were also very expensive. City expenditures per city resident were more than twice as large as federal government expenditures per national resident. From 1880 to 1904, national production of goods and services per person rose dramatically, federal expenditures per capita rose less dramatically, and city expenditures per capita declined between 10 and 20 percent. Since the per capita figure for 1880 derives from all 310 cities of over 7,500 population, it is probably lower than would be a figure more directly comparable to that for the 150 cities of over 30,000 population in 1904. The 1890 figure derives from the 55 cities of over 50,000 population and is probably slightly higher than if it also included the cities between 30,000 and 50,000 population. Between 1904 and 1930, per capita current dollar gross national product more than doubled, current dollar federal expenditures per capita increased about fourfold, state government expenditures per person increased about sevenfold by 1932 over a very low base figures for 1902, and current dollar city government expenditures increased almost threefold. These trends are not as unexpected as those for the period 1880–1904.

The estimates of the various figures in constant 1904 dollars create a slightly different impression. The constant dollar figures reflect a deflationary trend extending from before the depression of 1873–1879 to a low point during the depression of 1893–1897, followed by an accelerating inflationary trend into the mid-1920s, and an accelerating deflationary trend beginning in 1930. The estimated real dollar increase in per capita gross national product and federal government expenditures from 1880 to 1904 is slightly greater than the current dollar increase, while the real decline in city expenditures per capita is smaller than the current dollar decline. The $12.97 per capita current dollar expenditure on city services in 1890 is actually larger, in real terms, than the $13.64 expenditure in 1880. The increases between 1904 and 1930 are smaller in real terms than in current dollars, and there is a significant decline in real city and federal expenditures per capita from 1904 to 1912.[6]

The high per capita city government expenditures in the 1880s and 1890s, and their decline in real terms, by from 10 to 20 percent by 1912, run counter to present generalizations about city services. Without seriously studying per capita expenditure figures of this kind, urban historians have tended to assume that the physical amount of city services per capita being provided increased steadily from the 1850s onward. It has also been assumed that services were produced quite inefficiently before 1900. The hypothesis of increasing services and persistent inefficiency up to 1900 suggests that per capita expenditures in 1880 should be significantly *lower* than in 1904. In fact, they were higher, in both current and real terms. Total expenditures by all cities increased greatly from 1880 to 1900, and historians have tended to assume that per capita expenditures were also rising in the 1880s and 1890s.[7]

The interpretation of the changes in per capita expenditures is difficult. The decline in per capita expenditure levels from 1880 to 1904 undoubtedly results from the circumstance that although cities were increasing their total expenditures fairly rapidly, and expanding the services that they provided, their populations were increasing even more rapidly. This would lead to declines in per capita expenditures. In the absence of major improvements in the efficiency of service production, lower per capita expenditure meant less benefit per resident from the activities of the city government. The failure of city government implied by this interpretation is further strengthened by the contrasting increase in the real per capita national production of goods and services from $197 per capita of national population in 1880 to $279 per capita in 1904 (both measured in 1904 dollars). It was the industrial production going on in cities that generated most of this increase. The situation suggested by these figures is that at the same time that industry and industrial workers in cities were generating a tremendous boom in national productivity, the governments of those cities were remarkably unsuccessful at diverting the growing per capita product towards the alleviation of city needs. In short, it seems appropriate to interpret declining per capita city expenditures in a context of rising per capita national product as an indication that impressionistic evaluations of the failure of city government in the 1890s have been insufficiently severe. Even in the period between 1904 and 1912, when per capita expenditures were increasing in current dollar terms, and the impressionistic evidence suggests that conditions were improving, the rapid inflation of the period meant that there was actually a decline in per capita expenditures in real terms. Table 1 suggests that it was not until the years between 1912 and 1930 that city residents obtained significant increases in per capita spending on municipal services, and, by extension, significant benefit from increased provision of services.

The Functional Composition of
Changing City Expenditures, 1904–1930

We will focus from now on upon the functional breakdown of "ordinary" or operating expenditures per capita by the group of cities of over 30,000 population during the emergence and maturity of the functional mode of innovation. Capital, or "extraordinary," expenditures are not included. The category of "total" expenditures refers to operating expenditures on the essential municipal functions, and interest expenses on city debt. The functions examined here relate to the Census Bureau's six-class designation of the essential municipal functions as follows: [8]

Census Bureau Functional Classes	*Title of Function Used in Present Analysis*
General administration	General administration
Public charities and corrections	Charities
Public safety	Police
	Fire
	Health
Public highways and sanitation	Highways
	Sanitation
Public education	Schools
Public recreation	not included

The analysis deals with the cities of over 30,000 *as a group*, and concentrates upon the behavior of the city governments, rather than upon the effects of expenditure practices experienced by city residents. The number of city governments in the group changes considerably, from 150 in 1904 to 310 in 1930. Due to the characteristics of the urbanization process, however, the rapid increase in the number of cities of over 30,000 population produced essentially no change in either the average population per city, or their average residential population density per acre, between 1904 and 1930. These varied minimally above and below the average figures of 150,000 population, and slightly less than 12 persons per acre. The hypothetically "typical" city whose expenditure behavior we will be examining remained surprisingly stable in size and density throughout the period. The numbers with which the analysis began were the per capita expenditure by each city on the designated function, and on all functions, for the indicated year. Per capita expenditure figures for each city were added together and divided by the number of cities to produce a mean, or average, per capita expenditure figure for the *group of cities*. Thus the numbers appearing in the tables are "unweighted" averages. Although weighted averages would give a better description of expenditure practices as seen from the perspective of a hypothetical city resident, the greater influence weighting gives to the decisions of cities of large population, and the diminished influence weighted averages reflect from the practices of cities of small population, are not appropriate to an analysis that is primarily concerned, as we are here, with how city governments behave.

The distribution of expenditures among the various municipal functions did not undergo any radical alteration between 1904 and 1930 (see Table 2). The only severely neglected function in 1904 was health services. The fourfold increase in school expenditures made up the lion's share of the almost threefold increase in total expenditures between 1904 and 1930. Health expenditures increased more than fourfold over a small base figure, but in general expenditures on particular functions increased between two- and threefold, in current dollar terms, from 1904 to 1930. Highway expenditures lagged somewhat.

Table 3 translates the figures in Table 2 into constant 1904 dollars, using a deflation factor based on annual earnings of government employees, rather than the 1958 gross national product deflator used in Table 1. Since labor costs are the largest component of functional operating expenditures, this estimate of the real changes in expenditures better approximates the amount of labor and material input obtained from dollar expenditures. Annual earnings of government employees rose much less sharply than consumer prices between 1904 and 1930. As a result, city governments did not suffer the ravages of inflation as severely as did workers and consumers. The current dollar increase in total

Table 2. Means of per capita expenditure, by type of expenditure, in current dollars, for all cities of over 30,000 population, 1904–1930

Type of expenditure	1904	1912	1923	1930
Total	12.06	12.99	27.68	35.47
General administration	.89	1.23	1.85	2.31
Police	1.21	1.31	2.41	3.06
Fire	1.34	1.51	2.75	3.23
Health	.17	.24	.63	.77
Sanitation	.70	1.03	1.83	2.22
Highways	1.74	1.70	2.62	3.02
Charities	.62	.60	1.19	1.83
Schools	3.50	4.47	12.01	15.60
Mean density per acre	11.2	11.4	12.4	11.5
Mean population per city	142,971	150,465	157,952	153,069
No. of cities	150	195	248	310

Note: The means of per capita expenditures are unweighted; that is, they are not adjusted in relation to the differing populations of the cities.

Sources: For 1904: Bureau of the Census, Bulletin 50, Statistics of Cities over 30,000: 1904 (Washington, D.C.: 1906). For 1912: Bureau of the Census, Financial Statistics of Cities over 30,000: 1912 (Washington, D.C.: 1914). For 1923: Bureau of the Census, Financial Statistics of Cities over 30,000: 1923 (Washington, D.C.: 1925). For 1930: Bureau of the Census, Financial Statistics of Cities over 30,000: 1930 (Washington, D.C.: 1932).

per capita expenditures between 1904 and 1912 does not turn into a real decrease, using this measure, as it did using the gross national product deflator in Table 1.[9]

The deflated figures provide a better basis for evaluating changes. Again, the major finding is that health is the only function severely neglected in 1904. In other words, there was only one essential municipal function of the centralized, functionally departmentalized model of strong city government that many cities were seriously neglecting at the time the new model began to be introduced. Also, the relative distribution of expenditures among functions, with the exception of health and schools, was not remarkably different at the outset, in 1904, from the relative distribution in 1930, when most cities had fully implemented the functional reforms that they intended to make.

The timing of the change in per capita expenditures between 1904 and 1930 has been roughly outlined already. Using the gov-

Table 3. Means of per capita expenditure, by the type of expenditure, for all cities of over 30,000 population, 1904-1930, deflated for increases in annual earnings of government employees

Type of expenditure	Deflated means				Percentage changes	
	1904	1912	1923	1930	1904-1912	1912-1930
Total	12.06	12.42	18.19	19.72	3%	59%
General admin.	.89	1.18	1.22	1.28	33%	8%
Police	1.21	1.25	1.58	1.70	3%	36%
Fire	1.34	1.44	1.81	1.80	8%	25%
Health	.17	.23	.41	.43	35%	87%
Sanitation	.70	.98	1.20	1.23	40%	26%
Highways	1.74	1.63	1.72	1.68	−6%	3%
Charities	.62	.57	.78	1.02	−8%	79%
Schools	3.50	4.27	7.89	8.67	22%	103%

ernment employees' annual earnings deflator produces a 3 percent real increase in average total per capita expenditures between 1904 and 1912, followed by a 59 percent increase from 1912 to 1930. It seems best to compromise on the suggestion that during the period when cities were acquiring familiarity with the functional innovative mode, before 1912, there was no significant change in their per capita expenditure practices. As Table 3 indicates, however, the functional breakdown of the differences between 1904 and 1912, and then between 1912 and 1930, reveals some interesting aspects. Average police, fire, highway, and charity expenditures per capita remained essentially constant from 1904 to 1912, while there were considerable percentage increases in general administration, health, sanitation, and school expenditures. General administration, health, and sanitation were three of the four lesser functions in terms of amounts of expenditure in 1904, and the large increases during the early period of functional innovation possibly reflect adjustments inspired by the influence of the new model. The large increase in average total per capita expenditure between 1912 and 1930 breaks down into very large increases for schools, charities, and health, but only an insignificant increase in general administration expenditures. The lack of increase in highway expenditures is largely an artifact resulting from the introduction of state and federal highway programs. A possible explanation for the divergent movement of general administration expenditures is that once cities had modernized their administrative practices, it was not necessary to continue increasing per capita expenditures on administration while increasing per capita expenditures on the other functions. The very large increases in health and school expenditures imply a continuing need to increase their relative standing vis-à-vis the other functions. Overall, however, the major difference between the 1904–1912 period and the 1912–1930 period, is the stability in the first and the large increases in the second. This supports the finding in the previous section that it was only after cities became thoroughly familiar with the functional mode of innovation, around 1912, that major increases in per capita levels of expenditure occurred.

City Population Size as a Factor in
Per Capita Expenditure Practices, 1904–1930

The relationship of the population size of a city to its per capita expenditures can be interpreted in several ways. The Census Bureau's reports argued that per capita expenditure levels should be higher in large cities than in small ones, and should be increased as the population of an individual city increased. They based this argument on the assumption that the "need" for municipal services increased with increasing city population size, not just for the city as a whole, but also for each individual resident.[10] In terms of modern determinant analysis, such an argument confuses the potential effects of several factors. One modern hypothesis about population size is that there are "diseconomies of scale" in the production of municipal services. Under this hypothesis, per capita expenditures would increase as a function of increasing city population size because units of service were more expensive to produce in larger cities than in smaller ones, all other factors being equal. A second modern hypothesis is that the "demand" for services by the city's population increases as a function of city population size. Modern analysis does not recognize the concept of "need" for service as employed in the Census Bureau's reports. In modern terms, "need" involves a combination of demand and production cost characteristics. The third modern position on population size is that its influence tends to dissipate in the company of other independent analytic variables, especially city residential density and measures of residents' income and wealth. Given these complexities, it is best to be cautious in interpreting correlations between per capita expenditures and population size.[11]

Table 4 presents simple product-moment correlations between per capita expenditures and city population size for all cities of over 30,000. The table covers total and individual functional expenditures in the four sample years, and roughly comparable correlations for 462 cities in 1951. The major trend revealed in the table is one of decline, from a relatively high level of corre-

Table 4. Product-moment correlations between per capita expenditures and city population size for all cities of over 30,000 population

Type of expenditure	1904	1912	1923	1930	1951*
Total	0.33	0.38	0.27	0.25	0.14
General admin.	0.37	0.48	0.44	0.42	0.10
Police	0.52	0.46	0.34	0.33	0.24
Fire	0.07	0.08	0.03	0.04	0.04
Health	0.18	0.24	0.13	0.20	
Sanitation	0.34	0.26	0.25	0.24	0.09
Highways	−0.03	0.13	0.07	0.14	−0.06
Charities	0.21	0.40	0.27	0.23	
Schools	0.20	0.15	0.09	0.05	
N	150	195	248	310	462
5% significance level	±0.16	0.14	0.12	0.11	0.09

* Harvey E. Brazer, *City Expenditures in the United States* (New York: National Bureau of Economic Research, 1959), Occasional Paper 66, p. 76.

lation between per capita expenditures and city population size in 1904, to a moderately lower level in 1930. Brazer's figures for 1951 reveal a further decline to the point where only total operating expenditures and police expenditures show dependably significant relationships to population size.

The relatively strong positive correlations for 1904 indicate that larger cities spent more per capita than smaller ones. The simplest explanation of the decline in correlation from 1904 to 1930 is that smaller cities increased their expenditures relative to larger ones in the belief that better administration demanded higher per capita expenditures. The early Census Bureau reports promoted this argument. An explanation relating to the issue of diseconomies of scale would be that production diseconomies were inherent in the characteristic administrative methods of 1904, and that changes in methods between 1904 and 1930 tended to reduce them. In 1904, larger cities spent significantly more per capita on police, sanitation, and general administrative services than smaller cities. The methods of 1930, on the other hand, possibly involved less excess production expense per capita for larger cities for police and sanitation. Brazer's figures can be interpreted to imply that such excess production costs declined even further by 1951. Brazer's figures suggest that the "scale" factor in production costs in 1951 is essentially constant. In other words, the cost of providing fire protection or general administrative service per resident in 1951 appears to be similar for cities of all sizes. Police costs seem to remain moderately higher for larger cities. Arguments based on higher demand for services on the part of the populations of larger cities are reasonable to propose, but difficult to substantiate. The lack of any significant relationship between fire protection expenditures and city population size in any year makes arguments employing the demand concept problematical.

Modern studies of scale economies in the production of municipal services have not been as helpful in resolving questions of this kind as they could be. Economists tend to predict that favorable production economies will be realized as population size increases. Lower per capita production costs are one of the greatest sources of expected benefit from metropolitan government.[12] But empirical studies have generated conflicting implications. Werner Hirsch reviewed a large number of studies of the relation between per capita costs and city population size and concluded that the per capita cost of producing municipal services probably *increases* as city population size increases above 100,000. The support for this conclusion was not particularly strong, however. Two studies of police protection, one done by Hirsch himself, showed that per capita costs remained constant as population size increased. Two studies of fire protection showed that costs declined with increasing population size, although one of these showed costs increasing as population size went above 110,000. One study of garbage collection and one study of sewage plants both showed constant per capita costs as population size increased. A study of 1967 data from cities in eight states aids Hirsch's conclusion by providing strong evidence of diseconomies above the level of 250,000 population.[13]

If we postulate that there was steady improvement in the efficiency of service production between 1904 and the 1950s, then it is fair to argue that the higher correlations of the early period represent diseconomies of scale for larger cities resulting from inefficient methods. However, in the absence of other information, the argument that Table 4 is reflecting excessively low per capita expenditures by smaller cities in the early years is equally valid. The decline in the correlation between school expenditures per capita and population size from a fairly significant 0.20 in 1904 to a not significant 0.05 in 1930 probably results from smaller cities increasing their spending to the level of the larger cities. Without support from other analyses, however, it is difficult to draw any firm conclusions from the relationship between per capita expenditures and population size.

City Residential Density as a Factor in
Per Capita Expenditure Practices, 1904–1930

The relationship between city residential density and per capita expenditures on city services suggests that cities made significant improvements in the effectiveness of their administrative practices between 1912 and 1930. Table 5 presents simple prod-

Table 5. Product-moment correlations between per capita expenditures and city residential population density for all cities of over 30,000 population

Type of expenditure	1904	1912	1923	1930	1951*
Total	−0.04	0.04	0.13	0.33	0.24
General admin.	0.02	0.04	0.20	0.28	0.12
Police	0.27	0.25	0.32	0.43	0.41
Fire	−0.17	−0.15	0.09	0.25	0.24
Health	0.05	0.12	0.10	0.23	
Sanitation	0.16	0.11	0.27	0.41	0.18
Highways	−0.19	−0.11	−0.10	−0.05	−0.26
Charities	−0.04	0.10	0.11	0.17	
Schools	−0.10	−0.02	0.01	0.22	
N	150	195	248	310	462
5% significance level	±0.16	0.14	0.12	0.11	0.09
Correlation between population size and density	0.18	0.21	0.20	0.24	0.27

* Harvey E. Brazer, *City Expenditures in the United States* (New York: National Bureau of Economic Research, 1959), Occasional Paper 66, p. 76.

uct-moment correlations between per capita operating expenditures on all functions, and on various individual functions, for the four sample years. Comparable correlations for 462 cities for 1951, prepared by Brazer, are also shown.

The sole dependably significant relationship between the variations in expenditure and the variations in residential density from city to city for the years 1904 and 1912, occurs in the case of police service. Yet by 1930, all categories of expenditures, except highways, show a significant relationship to residential density. Brazer's results for 1951 are similar to those for 1930, although some of the relationships are slightly weaker. Modern analysts tend to hypothesize that cities of higher density spend more per capita to provide a particular service because higher density increases the cost of providing a given quantity and quality of service to each resident. Services such as police, fire fighting, garbage collection, and health inspection are generally more costly to produce where density is high. By comparison, there is no hypothetical reason for general administrative costs per capita to be higher in cities of high density than they are in cities of low density. In theory, general administrative functions need not differ in production costs per capita simply because of differing conditions of residential density. The absence of a significant relationship between per capita expenditures and density in 1904 and 1912, and the emergence of a strong relationship by 1930, reflects an important change in city administrative practices.[14]

The relationships between costs of production and population density postulated by modern determinant analysis will appear in statistics on expenditures only when the money that cities expend is being effectively transformed into a corresponding amount of service. The lack of significant relationships between expenditures and density in 1904 and 1912 suggests that city expenditures on labor and materials in that period bore little relationship to the amount of service being provided for city residents. In a period when the relationship between the amount of money expended on fire services, for example, and the amount of fire fighting obtained, is unreliable, the higher cost of providing a given amount of fire service in more densely populated cities becomes obscured by variations in city-to-city costs caused by the differing effectiveness of their fire departments. Conversely, as effectiveness becomes more similar from city to city (effectiveness being the ability to convert expenditures on materials and labor to fight fires into the actual extinguishing of fires), the statistics will begin to reflect the higher costs of providing a given quantity and quality of fire service in cities of higher residential density. On the basis of this line of reasoning, it is appropriate to conclude that Table 5 reflects a significant improvement in the effectiveness of city service provision between 1912 and 1930.[15]

One aspect of the table suggests that cities achieved this improvement by following the recommendations about density in the functional literature on administration. General administration expenditures also show an emerging relationship to residential density between 1912 and 1930, despite the fact that the correlation for 1951 (0.12) reflects the modern presumption that higher residential densities do not necessitate higher administrative expenditures per capita. This anomaly suggests that cities may have originally implemented functional innovations by simply altering their expenditure practices to conform to the relationships prescribed in the Census Bureau reports and in the literature on administration. Cities with high residential density may have increased the per capita level of their expenditures between 1912 and 1930 not simply on the functions for which higher density produces higher costs, but on all functions, including general administration. Then, presumably, between 1930 and 1951, as administrative sophistication increased further, high density cities learned that administrative expenditures per capita could be reduced relative to total, police, fire, and sanitation expenditures per capita. The result would have been what appears in Table 5, the decline in the correlation between administrative expenditures and density from 0.20 in 1923 and 0.28 in 1930, to a barely significant 0.12 in 1951. The moderate relationship between school expenditures and density in 1930 may also reflect this kind of behavior. There is no strong reason for school costs to increase simply as a function of residential density.

The Interrelationship of Expenditures on the Various Municipal Functions, 1904–1930

Table 6 is an attempt to determine whether major changes occurred in the similiarity with which all cities of over 30,000 population distributed their expenditures among the various functions that they performed. Did all cities spend approximately the same proportions of total expenditures on police, fire, health, sanitation, and schools in 1904? Did the similarity of the distribution patterns from city to city increase between 1904 and 1930? Was the situation in 1930 significantly different from that in 1951?

Table 6 presents simple product-moment intercorrelation matrices for per capita operating expenditures on all functions, and on the various functional categories, for the four sample years, with a corresponding matrix for 462 cities in 1951. The table shows that for 1904, with the exception of fire and health expenditures, the relationship of the amounts spent by the cities on one function to the amounts spent on each other function, and on all functions together, is very high. The correlation between total per capita expenditures and per capita expenditures on general administration, for all the cities, is the closest (0.78). By the standard of 1951, when the same correlation for 462 cities was 0.49, this relationship is quite strong. These high correlations suggest that even in 1904 all cities over 30,000 population were practicing administration in similar ways.

The chief exceptions are the administration of fire and health services. The relationship between fire expenditures and police expenditures is particularly important to examine, since it tends to be the closest relationship between two functional categories in modern analyses such as Brazer's. For 1904, the correlation between fire and police expenditures, 0.42, is low relative to many other correlations in the matrix. In Brazer's matrix for

Table 6. Product-moment intercorrelation matrices for per capita expenditures

1904

	Total	Gen. admin.	Police	Fire	Health	San.	High.	Char.	Schools
Total									
General admin.	0.78								
Police	0.73	0.66							
Fire	0.51	0.37	0.42						
Health	0.34	0.29	0.37	0.16					
Sanitation	0.74	0.60	0.67	0.34	0.32				
Highways	0.72	0.45	0.38	0.30	0.20	0.52			
Charities	0.61	0.44	0.50	0.16	0.21	0.51	0.39		
Schools	0.68	0.48	0.33	0.29	0.14	0.33	0.55	0.29	

N = 150
5% level = ±0.16

1912

	Total	Gen. admin.	Police	Fire	Health	San.	High.	Char.	Schools
Total									
General admin.	0.79								
Police	0.77	0.63							
Fire	0.55	0.37	0.51						
Health	0.57	0.43	0.49	0.26					
Sanitation	0.66	0.51	0.62	0.34	0.47				
Highways	0.77	0.47	0.49	0.40	0.44	0.47			
Charities	0.63	0.52	0.65	0.30	0.48	0.42	0.47		
Schools	0.67	0.44	0.26	0.22	0.19	0.22	0.44	0.15	

N = 195
5% level = ±0.14

1923

	Total	Gen. admin.	Police	Fire	Health	San.	High.	Char.	Schools
Total									
General admin.	0.74								
Police	0.77	0.69							
Fire	0.71	0.40	0.63						
Health	0.56	0.46	0.52	0.35					
Sanitation	0.68	0.53	0.67	0.44	0.41				
Highways	0.67	0.44	0.44	0.39	0.45	0.41			
Charities	0.48	0.49	0.49	0.23	0.39	0.38	0.31		
Schools	0.75	0.40	0.32	0.48	0.19	0.31	0.33	0.04	

N = 248
5% level = ±0.12

Table 6 continued

	Total	Gen. admin.	Police	Fire	Health	San.	High.	Char.	Schools
				1930					
Total							N = 310		
General admin.	*0.74*						5% level = ±0.11		
Police	*0.79*	*0.68*							
Fire	*0.67*	0.38	*0.66*						
Health	*0.68*	*0.53*	*0.59*	0.44					
Sanitation	*0.76*	*0.55*	*0.67*	0.48	*0.55*				
Highways	*0.62*	*0.52*	0.45	0.31	0.43	0.42			
Charities	*0.60*	*0.51*	*0.50*	0.34	*0.61*	0.39	0.42		
Schools	*0.77*	0.44	0.42	0.42	0.33	0.46	0.31	0.16	

	Total	Gen. admin.	Police	Fire	San.	High.
				1951		
Total					N = 462	
Gen. admin.	0.49				5% level = ±0.09	
Police	*0.57*	*0.51*				
Fire	*0.68*	0.44	*0.67*			
Sanitation	0.43	0.30	0.45	0.33		
Highways	0.31	0.18	0.48	0.28	0.17	

Note: Figures of 0.50 and greater are given in italics.
Source: Harvey E. Brazer, *City Expenditures in the United States* (New York: National Bureau of Economic Research, 1959), Occasional Paper 66, p. 73.

1951, it is 0.67, by far the highest correlation between two individual functions, and higher than all but one of the correlations between total expenditures and individual functions. Between 1904 and 1930, the correlation between fire and police expenditures increased from 0.42 to 0.66, one of the stronger relationships in the 1930 matrix. The relatively low correlation in 1904, and the increase to 1930, imply that fire services were administered in much more diverse ways from city to city in 1904 than other services, including police services. By 1930, changes had occurred that brought fire administration into greater conformity with administrative practices for the other functions.

The correlations between health services and other functions are the lowest of those for any function in the 1904 matrix. This implies extreme diversity from city to city in health administration. Some of this diversity is a statistical artifact stemming from the small proportion of total expenditures spent on health. By 1930, however, correlations between health expenditures and other functions had increased tremendously. The correlation between health expenditures and total expenditures doubled, from 0.34 to 0.68. These changes in the correlations for fire and health services imply increasing conformity on the part of all cities of over 30,000 population to one pattern of relative distribution of expenditures among the various functional categories.

With a few exceptions, such as the correlation between charities and school expenditures (0.16), the matrix for 1930 suggests great similarity in the practice of municipal administration from city to city. Brazer used the standard 0.50 in evaluating his matrix for 1951, and found it significant that only two correlations between individual functions, police and general administration, and police and fire, were higher than 0.50. This led him to conclude that expenditure patterns among cities were "extremely diverse," and that individual functions were subject to wide variations from city to city as a result of "specific circumstances." (Correlations of 0.50 and greater have been italicized in all five matrices to facilitate comparisons based on Brazer's standard.) Applying the 0.50 standard to the matrix for 1930 reveals eleven inter-functional correlations of 0.50 or greater, ten between 0.42 and 0.48, and only seven lower than 0.42. This is a considerably stronger pattern of conformity than in the 1951 matrix and seems to justify a different conclusion from Brazer's.[16]

Drawing a general statement from these findings is difficult, however. Presumably the diversity of 1951 stems from administrative sophistication about specific conditions peculiar to individual cities, while the diversity for 1904 stems from ignorance and ineffective methods. The relatively high level of conformity in 1930 may represent the influence of the functional model of administration, brought to bear in similar ways on all cities pri-

marily through the influence of the professional public administration associations. The decline in conformity from 1930 to 1951
could be interpreted to reflect the decline of the functional approach, the relaxing of professional rigidity about administrative
methods, and an increasing influence of citizen demand for expenditure patterns tailored more closely to each city's individual
circumstances. The great increases in the conformity of health
expenditures to expenditure patterns for the other functions between 1904 and 1930 seem to reflect the revolution in public
health that transpired during the early twentieth century.

Conclusion

We cannot assemble statistical evidence that replicates the
subjective judgments most meaningful to individual city residents, such as: How much *benefit* does each resident obtain per
dollar of municipal expenditure? Such questions posit mechanis-
tic relationships between city problems, and municipal attempts
to alleviate them, that do not exist. Some additional work relating
dollar expenditures to amounts of physical units of service produced for the period between 1904 and 1930 should be done, and
the results would be of considerable interest. Constraints on time
and energy prevented me for carrying the analysis into that
area. Such statistics would give some indication of changing
productive effectiveness. They would not adequately evaluate
the "efficiency" of city performance, however, since efficiency
depends upon measurements of quality, and of benefit to the
city's residents, in addition to measurements of the number of
units of service produced. Urban public finance has yet to adequately master the measurement of service efficiency even for
present-day cities. The complexity of the processes involved
raises questions about whether efficiency as applied to manufacturing, or engines, or railroads, is an appropriate concept for
evaluating municipal administration.[17]

We can ask a less precise question, however. Do the various
approaches presented here appear to reflect "improvement" in
municipal government under the influence of functional innova-

tion? The evidence we have collected includes: (1) the development of an ability to channel increases in per capita national production of goods and services into significant increases in city government expenditures per capita; (2) significant increases in per capita expenditures on all the major functions of city government; (3) significant efforts to expend more per capita in cities of higher residential density; and (4) increasing consistency in the inter-functional distribution of expenditures among all cities. While subjective generalizations from the evidence must remain largely impressionistic, it seems fair to argue that city residents of the late 1920s were "better off" as a result of the expenditures and activities of their city governments than the city residents of 1904. Functional innovation appears to have aided in producing at least a modicum of municipal progress.

CHAPTER 6

Dilemmas of Municipal Democracy

Regardless of how effective it might be in improving the material conditions of people's lives, functional innovation confronted a serious dilemma if it produced improvement at the expense of the democratic character of city government. The authors of the National Municipal League's Municipal Program and the formulators of the functional theory were acutely aware of this danger and discussed it at considerable length. Where a prescriptive theory defined the tasks of city government, and a comprehensive scheme of administrative innovation elaborated the best methods of day-to-day city management, what role remained for the desires of the people of the city? Could a government that consisted much more of "administration" than of "policy" still claim to be expressing the will of its population in its decisions and actions?

The chief functionalist defense was the argument that no structural arrangement of a city's government could be effectively "democratic" if the city lacked strong powers of self-government. The most eminently democratic structural arrangement of mayor, council, and bureaucracy was no more than a facade if it lacked the power to make city policy and to administer that policy effectively. But *how* strong the city's powers of self-government should be, vis-à-vis the state government, was a controversial issue on which writers differed. The first section of this chapter describes that controversy.

The second pillar of the functionalist defense was the argument that only a large, representative city council could guarantee that city policy would be made in a democratic manner. The council would necessarily deal primarily with the best means of applying functional principles and methods to the administration of the city's affairs, but within that framework the public will would receive full expression. The alternatives to a strong, large city council were to allow policy to be made by the mayor, to allow policy to be made by some other administrative arrangement, or to allow it to be made by a small, unrepresentative council or commission. None of these alternatives would have been very "democratic," regardless of how popular they might be as practical reform schemes. The second section discusses these issues.

The question of whether the large, representative city council should be elected on an at-large basis, or by wards, did not concern the functionalists very seriously. A long history of corruption and ineffectiveness convinced them that ward-based councils in small cities were a practical disaster. For large cities, there were equally creditable arguments for either the ward or the at-large arrangement. Choosing between them was considered largely a pragmatic question. More important than the arguments on either side of the question was the principle established in the Municipal Program that cities of over 25,000 population should have the right and the power to write their own charters and make their own choices between ward and at-large representation. As long as the city council was large and representative, the system of choosing the representatives made no particular difference for the "democratic" character of the way the council would function. The third section elaborates this position.

The remainder of the chapter deals with functionalist treatments of lesser aspects of the democracy question: whether the city franchise should be restricted; whether functional theory should include such specific reform schemes as initiative, referendum and recall, or nonpartisan elections; and whether the massive introduction of university-trained professional administrators into city bureaucracies threatened the democracy of city government. Their defense of the large, representative city council put the functionalists considerably to the left of most of the popular reform movements in the cities, especially groups promoting the "commission-manager" system. The commission-manager movement adopted whole the functional approach to administration, but discarded the large, representative council, the one element of the functional model crucial to assuring democratic city decision making. While the unrepresentative character of commission and city manager policy-making processes made it impossible for orthodox functionalists to espouse these reforms wholeheartedly, their desire to improve the efficiency of city government prevented them from attacking the commission-manager system. This equivocation was pragmatic rather than fundamental, however, and must not be used as an excuse to lump the authors of the functional theory and the proponents of the commission-manager system together in one heap when considering the "democracy" of early twentieth-century municipal reform.

The Proper Strength of City Powers of Self-Government

All formulations of the functional theory proposed to assure the democracy of city government by providing the city with strong powers of self-government. Before any consideration was given to structure or procedure, municipal democracy demanded that the city have the power to shape its own policies. Differences within the functionalist camp about municipal democracy involved controversies about the appropriate strength of the city's powers of self-government, and about the amount of state government supervision and interference that should be tolerated.

The best measure of an individual functionalist writer's commitment to municipal democracy lay in the strength of the powers of city self-government he advocated. The distance between the extreme positions on this scale was considerable. At the conservative extreme was Frank Goodnow. After imitating the national system of checks and balances in the early part of the nineteenth century, Goodnow explained in *Municipal Home Rule*, city governments turned for aid in the Jacksonian era to the "unfailing and infallible panacea," democracy. Unfortunnately, this democracy was embodied in a governmental structure so "extremely loose and disconnected" that it became necessary to form "rings," that is, partisan machines, to make city government function at all. This was very damaging to the political faith of "naturally democratic" city communities.[1]

The transfer of power to the state in the latter part of the nineteenth century, in order to stifle the growth of rings and the power of their bosses, had been too extreme in the opposite direction, however, and when the Municipal Program Committee resolved to advocate strong home rule powers, Goodnow concurred. But he did not alter his own beliefs. "Urban life does not favor the development of democratic government," he wrote in *Municipal Government* in 1909; in fact, the character of his contemporary fellow residents of the great cities led him to doubt seriously their ability, in the context of broad suffrage, to "efficiently" accomplish the necessary functions demanded by the conditions of their urban environment. "Urban populations," he warned, "have in the past too easily and too generally fallen under the control of oligarchies and despots or bosses, to permit us to entertain the hope that under modern conditions their fate, if left to themselves, will be much different from what it has been in the past."[2]

Goodnow's remedy for this problem was not less electoral participation, nor elimination of representative city councils, but state government supervision of the city's use of its powers of self-government. The state government, he insisted, had a responsibility to protect the "interests of the city population" as a whole, by preventing the rise of oligarchical control. The state could not allow the "weaker classes" to be "despoiled by those of greater strength"; it must curtail the powers of the city in such cases and assume certain functions itself. The tendency to oligarchic dominance was a consequence of the great heterogeneity of city populations, while conversely, the "relatively greater homogeneity" of the entire state population made the state government much more likely to "exercise justly governmental power." Goodnow maintained that this was an unfortunate but inescapable conclusion, given the functional theory's assumptions about the character of urban populations and the effects of urban conditions. The tendency of the "wealthy few" in the cities to exploit the masses was inevitable according to Goodnow, and he insisted that functional theory had to provide some means for the democratic processes of the state government to resolve this tragic flaw in municipal self-government.[3]

Horace Deming, the chairman of the League's Municipal Program Committee, stood at the opposite extreme, insisting that as a "community" a city must have strong powers of self-government, and that a city without strong powers was no more than a "subject province" of its state government.[4] The Municipal Program came closer to Deming's position than to Goodnow's, especially in advocating that state legislatures should allow cities of over 25,000 to draft their own charters. The Program Committee rejected Goodnow's pet scheme for state administrative supervision.

Between the extremes advocated by Goodnow and Deming, writers used pragmatic means to determine the amount of autonomous power to be granted to self-governing cities. On page thirty-six of *American City Government*, Charles Beard quoted Deming's demands for strong home rule powers verbatim, and on page forty he quoted Goodnow's denunciation of "unlimited" municipal home rule as "a shibboleth of days that are past" that had "no just foundation in either history or theory," except in "a very limited sense" in modern urban circumstances. Then he concluded on his own behalf that no general principle could draw a boundary between the powers of the state government over the people of a city and the powers rightfully belonging exclusively to the city government. Considering the "great abuses" the cities had suffered under special acts of the state legislatures, however, the need to place "some check . . . upon the power of the legislature to control municipal affairs" was "also clear." This carefully moderated assertion rendered Beard something of a conservative on the issue of the strength of municipal self-government.[5]

The message of the Municipal Program was that the success of municipal democracy depended upon acquiring for cities the requisite powers of self-governing political communities. "The proposed Municipal Program has taken democracy for granted," Delos Wilcox wrote to explain why democracy was not discussed in detail in the Program's specific provisions, "and has attempted to organize municipal government in relation to this great fact." The belief that an excess of democracy was the source of municipal failure in America was ill-founded. Horace Deming reminded the Program's readers that the best governed European cities were "far more democratic," both in "conception" and "in actual practice," than their national governments. After comparison with the relative success of city government in Europe, Deming concluded, "The failure of municipal government in our own country can hardly be attributed to the democratic character of our institutions." America's "municipal problem" was the improper dominance of state legislatures, not the excesses of democratic self-government.[6]

Defending the City Council

An indispensable corollary of the demand for strong powers of self-government was the Municipal Program's designation of the city council as the central institution of municipal democracy. The Program separated "executive and administrative functions" from "legislative or policy-determining powers," and sharply focussed the city's representative and democratic processes upon the city council. The movement for home rule in the 1890s had favored the strong mayor structure as a means of guaranteeing direct official accountability. As strong mayor reforms were instituted in more and more cities, however, they threatened to destroy the city council. The League attempted to reverse the trend by means of a strong defense of the representative element against the encroachments of the executive and the bureaucracy.[7]

The role of the council remained uncertain after 1900. The crucial question was: Should the council retain, or where necessary be restored to, dominant responsibility for determining city policy? The strong distaste for city councils among reform activists was a consequence of their use by ward-based partisan machines to exchange benefits, jobs, and favors among neighborhoods and groups at the expense of the interests of the city as a whole. The strong mayor system resolved this problem by severely reducing the powers and responsibilities of the city council, by giving the mayor a very strong veto power, and by eliminating the council's role in choosing administrative department heads. But the League's Program Committee insisted that throttling the council meant eliminating the "representative" principle, the essence of the democratic process. The council had to be saved. They decided that the best way to proceed would be to forcefully advocate city councils with all members elected "at large," that is, on a city-wide basis. For large cities that preferred ward or district representation, Leo Rowe emphasized that this recommendation was superceded by the principle that cities of over 25,000 population should have the power to design their own structures according to their own best judgment. But for small cities, the decision of the Program Committee was very firm, and Rowe expressed their feelings in brusque terms: "For the smaller cities there is no valid reason for district or local representation. Our experience with such representation has been of a kind to discourage its continuance whenever and wherever possible."[8]

The Program's emphasis on the separation of policy from administration was part of this effort to promote the primacy of the city council. Not only had the distinction between determining and executing policy been made since time immemorial, Goodnow pointed out, it was also the true basis of "that fundamental principle of American constitutional law usually referred to as the principle of the separation of powers." While it was true that city government consisted largely of the administration of policies, it was also patently apparent that if there were no need for those policies to be determined locally, by a council representative of the city's residents, then there would be no reason why city policy could not be made by the state legislature. Under that circumstance, city government would be reduced to the status of an administrative agent of the state executive. In those cases where policy determination was vested in the mayor and his bureaucracy, Goodnow added, the result was to politicize the administrative branch and thereby destroy its efficiency. Hence the necessity for city councils.[9]

Ward Versus At-Large Council Representation

The character of city council representation was of distinctly less importance. The functionalists were unanimous in their distaste for ward representation in the councils of small cities, and indifferent to the competition between ward and at-large representation in the councils of large cities. Those who expressed a preference usually favored at-large representation because it supposedly denied ward bosses the opportunity to trade favors. Goodnow, in characteristically iconoclastic fashion, argued that because city populations consisted of numerous distinct classes of people having widely differing interests, it was very difficult for members of different classes to unite behind the same candidate in an at-large election. As a result, at-large systems tended to increase the ability of well-organized minorities to get their favorites elected. Discovery of this phenomenon had stimulated a preference in European cities, especially those of England and Germany, for ward representation. Despite the fact that most American city councils in 1909 were still elected by wards, Goodnow recognized that a revulsion against ward systems had developed in this country and that ward representation no longer "appeals to American opinion." Nevertheless, Goodnow argued, "theory, experience and present practice" were all on the side of ward-based councils.[10]

Ward councils were especially desirable to Goodnow because they made each council member personally responsible for whatever actions the council might take. In at-large councils, individual members could take refuge behind the barricades of factions and parties. Responsibility was divided among all of them, allowing each to avoid direct personal accountability. But a ward councilman always had to account to his ward constituents. If "supreme municipal authority" were vested in the mayor, Goodnow postulated, he could be kept under proper public control because he was a single individual. When central responsibility resided with a group of council members, as it necessarily had to in a democratic self-governing city, district representation was the only way to keep each of them under effective popular control.[11]

The principal argument in favor of city-wide council representation: viz., that only council members elected at-large can place the interest of the city as a whole above the interests of neighborhoods and groups, was only feebly voiced by the functionalists. The Municipal Program Committee members were perfectly willing to have ward councils in larger cities. In the chapter entitled "The Organization of Municipal Government" in his 1910 textbook *American Government and Politics*, Beard conceded that popular enthusiasm for city councils continued to decline, despite various kinds of reforms. The "inefficiency and dishonesty" of the councils in many cities had brought on what Beard described as their "complete abolition" and replacement by a "small board of directors elected at large" who held both legislative and administrative power. This was his way of describing the "commission" form of city government. Beard concluded his discussion with an apparently approving reference to claims that "a deliberative representative assembly is indispensible" for bringing various opinions into consideration, and for keeping party politics out of the administrative branch of the city government. He did not specify that any particular form of council representation had notable advantages or disadvantages. His only clear endorsement of city-wide councils was a brief aside in *American City Government* indicating that the idea of having ward-based councils write city budgets, on the theory that the larger public interest could be determined by aggregating the local interests of each ward, did not work in practice.

If the people of a city were asked directly whether they would favor appropriating $100,000 for ice and milk stations in the summer, or the same amount for paid jobs for party workers, they would not hesitate long in making their decision in favor of the former. But when a civic association demands such an important appropriation from a council built on ward politics, it generally finds that the necessity of meeting the local demands overrules the councilors' good will.

Apparently Beard felt strongly about the issue, but agreed that it was not of major significance compared with the issues of the strength of city powers of self-government, and council responsibility for city policy making.[12]

Functionalist Confidence in the Electorate

The functionalists displayed a remarkable confidence in the people of the cities, despite their apparently comfortable sharing of the racist and anti-immigrant attitudes of most native Americans of their era. The tone of the functionalist attitude towards popular participation, like the general tone of the functional theory itself, was set by Bryce. Although he considered the uneducated foreign-born a potentially dangerous element in municipal politics, Bryce admired the American faith in universal suffrage and did his best to direct reform efforts away from criticism of the characteristics of the electorate. His generalizations that "poison germs" dangerous to democracy breed vigorously in all cities of over 200,000 population, and that danger arises "when the population begins to exceed 100,000 and includes a large proportion of recent immigrants," have been quoted repeatedly without proper acknowledgement of his far more important recognition that native Americans did not strenuously object to the swelling of the partisan machine ranks by means of illegal enfranchisement of immigrants in violation of residency requirements. Despite the illegality of what the party bosses were doing, the native born tolerated their newly-immigrated fellow voters because of a profound faith in "democratic theory." Such excessive democratic optimism was somewhat foolhardy, Bryce admitted, for it naively "underrated the inherent difficulties of politics and failings of human nature." "Such a sacrifice of common sense to abstract principles has seldom been made by any country," he commented. But the optimism and the faith in democratic principles were important elements in the success of the American system. The manipulability of immigrant voters was not a major source of municipal misgovernment according to Bryce's larger argument, and fighting to reform abuses of the enfranchising power would have been a waste of the energies that Bryce hoped to direct towards more fruitful pursuits.[13]

Bryce even moderated condemnations of the moral character of the bosses by his American colleagues. In the chapter on the Tweed Ring that he contributed to the first edition of *American Commonwealth*, Goodnow had praised the new charter Tweed obtained from the state legislature in 1869 because it increased the city's control over its local affairs and concentrated responsibility in a "very few hands." Under such a charter, New Yorkers only had to fear for their municipal democracy if those hands happened to be "unclean and grasping," as in the case of Tweed and his henchmen. Goodnow found the Tweed machine guilty of criminal fraud, accusing them of running "the gamut of public dishonesty from abuse of official position for the advancement of private ends to transactions which can with difficulty be distinguished from actual theft." But Bryce, as part of his initiation of the theoretical concern with overall social conditions rather than with characteristics of individuals, contended that bosses and their retinue were men corrupted by their situation. Bryce accused the public-at-large for the evils of machine corruption, on the grounds that they had failed to make the obligations and duties of their officials clear and compelling. "It must not be supposed that the members of Rings, or the great Boss himself, are wicked men," Bryce wrote. "They are the offspring of a system. Their morality is that of their surroundings."[14]

Bryce's optimism prevailed, and Goodnow became one of his most enthusiastic converts. In the Tweed era there had been considerable enthusiasm for limiting the city franchise to property-owning taxpayers as a means of assuring "responsible" voting behavior. Francis Lieber had proposed that one chamber of the city legislature be elected by property holders only, and such ideas reappeared often in lists of reform proposals of the 1870s and 1880s. Bryce, however, showed no interest in limiting the franchise, and by the 1890s property restrictions were rarely suggested. More typical of the approach fostered by Bryce, and by the rise of functional innovation, was Goodnow's suggestion in *Municipal Government* that more responsible voting behavior could be obtained not by restricting the franchise to property owners, but by altering the tax system so that as many voters as possible felt its incidence directly. While cities continued to depend on real property taxes for the bulk of their revenue, Goodnow pointed out, property owners would always be inclined to oppose large expenditures, even if they were vital to the performance of "necessary functions," while renters of housing would tend to "hurry the city into undertakings which, however useful they may be, are in excess of the city's economic resources," because they failed to recognize the indirect impact of tax increases upon them in the form of higher rents.[15]

The one conspicuous bar to an optimistic faith in individual human nature was Philadelphia. Bryce felt compelled to agree with his chief informant on the City of Brotherly Love, Henry C. Lea, that there was no satisfactory explanation for Philadelphia's corruption. On the contrary, Philadelphia seemed to Lea "almost an ideal community in which to work out practical results from democratic theories." Its general social conditions were admirably suitable; "nowhere" was Lea able to find "a more general diffusion of property or a higher average standard of comfort and intelligence—nowhere so large a proportion of landowners bearing the burden of direct taxation, and personally interested in the wise and honest expenditure of public revenue." In fact, as Bryce quoted from Lea's conclusions: "In existing conditions, it would be difficult to conceive of a large community of which it would appear more safe to predicate judicious self-government than ours." Both Lea and Bryce expected the citizens of Philadelphia to learn from their mistakes, but seventeen years later Lincoln Steffens's still found Philadelphia the "worst-governed city in the country" and Goodnow concluded, after reviewing Steffen's writings, that Philadelphia appeared to be the prominent exception to the rule that bad city government resulted from undesirable social and economic conditions rather than from failings of human nature. "The experiences of particular cities such as Philadelphia" demonstrated that in one case, at the least, there was "something in the moral character" of the people "which militates against good city government." What was particularly strange was that these flawed moral characters belonged primarily to native Americans, Philadelphia having a proportionately smaller foreign-born population than most other large cities.[16]

Their commitment to the importance of social conditions rather than individual character also led the functionalists to reject claims that the successes of democracy in America were a function of character. Thus Woodrow Wilson's review of *American Commonwealth* for the recently founded *Political Science Quarterly*, although expressing a standard belief of the period, revealed a grave misunderstanding of the intentions of Bryce's approach to American politics. Democracy, Wilson pontificated, was "conduct," and the "only stable foundation" of conduct was "character." Americans had succeeded with democratic institutions because they were of the English race. Their success was the result neither of "accident merely" nor of "good fortune, manifestly," but of the fact that only the English "race" and the "race" of "quiet, closeted Switzerland," were capable "amidst the fierce contests of national rivalries," of "establishing and maintaining the most liberal forms of government." Given their racial character, the success of their political institutions was "a perfectly natural outcome of organic development." Although Bryce and his American colleagues probably agreed, to some extent, with such bombastic racial nonsense, they carefully avoided it for fear of undermining the operative principles of their theory of municipal improvement. If successful municipal democracy depended on having a city population of native Americans, Englishmen, and "quiet, closeted" Swiss, there was little hope for American cities.[17]

Functionalist Positions on Reform Schemes

Despite the controversy over the strength of self-government that cities should be granted, the functionalists unanimously agreed that municipal improvement depended upon developing in the city's population a strong interest in their own city government. The way to do this was to make the politics of city affairs totally independent of state and national politics, and to give each city independent control over its own electoral processes. The Municipal Program recommended that beyond guaranteeing to each city a "democratic-republican form of government," the states should allow their cities "complete freedom to control the methods of the exercise of municipal suffrage in purely municipal elections." This would provide the cities with an opportunity to determine the worth of various electoral systems through trial and error.

The functional theorists did not encourage the numerous schemes for electoral reform current around 1900, with the exception of those intended to make city politics independent of state and national party politics, such as banning state and national parties from city elections, and holding municipal elections on separate dates from all other elections. The functionalists were not opposed to city political parties, provided they confined themselves strictly to city politics; nor did they object to the partisanship of city residents in state and national politics. But the functionalists were not conspicuous advocates of primaries, preferential voting, short ballots, proportional representation, or other instant schemes to purify municipal democracy. Even initiative, referendum and recall were not considered unmixed goods because of a strong suspicion that they would have a detrimental effect on the workings of state legislatures and representative city councils. In the introduction to a collection of materials on state-wide initiative, referendum and recall, Beard pointed out that *in theory* the ideal way to conduct popular government was through a representative assembly of delegates apportioned according to districts. Because the "practice" of representative government tended to be so far inferior to the theoretical ideal, however, it was both necessary and desirable to resort to supplementary methods of direct popular legislative action. Beard did not go beyond the discussion of state government to recommend initiative and referendum to the cities.[18]

Since the functionalists were doing their best to strengthen the city council, they were not inclined to advocate improvement schemes whose desirability stemmed from the practical failures of representative councils. They preferred the mayor-council system of functional policy making and administration, and with one exception they supported reforms compatible with that system. The one prominent omission from their list of desirable schemes was women's suffrage. The functionalists showed almost no interest in women's suffrage, despite the obvious part it could play in increasing popular participation and interest in city affairs. Women were rarely discussed in any context in their writings, and women's suffrage was practically never mentioned, much less encouraged. In reviewing reform developments for the first issue of the National Municipal League's magazine, the *National Municipal Review*, in 1912, Woodruff remarked on the possible benefits of greater activism on the part of women that "the largest contribution of women has been in the direction of improving municipal housekeeping," and he commented that "the entrance of women into the housekeeping of cities is one of the cheering developments of the decade."[19]

The Dangers of Efficiency

There was a strong self-interest in the success of functional innovation in the functionalists' discussions of municipal democracy. Their resolution of the controversy over the relative roles of mayors and city councils, for example, ultimately depended upon accomplishing two goals: providing cities with the power to perform the essential municipal functions adequately and efficiently, and securing a high level of public concern about the quality of city government. In the interest of the practical success of their ideas, the functionalists tended to emphasize the two goals, and to minimize the problem that the functional approach to managing urban conditions imposed fairly severe constraints on the role of popular participation in city policy making. Thus Leo S. Rowe could write that: "The essence of popular government is such popular control as will enforce certain definite standards of efficiency in the administration of public affairs," without concern that he was eliminating all controversy over the proper tasks of city government from his conception of municipal democracy. What mattered, Rowe insisted, was the strength of public concern rather than the democratic orthodoxy of the governmental machinery.[20]

The "search for a self-acting governmental machine" had not only been "fruitless," Rowe argued. It had led to the mistaken belief that electoral surveillance by itself could assure honest, efficient administration. What was really required was ever-constant watchfulness, of which Rowe gave an example. The new charter of New York City had made the power of the mayor "so great that the community feels the necessity of watching his policy at every step." The mayor's power had made him dangerous, and fear of the danger compelled the public to properly scrutinize his behavior. Only militant public opinion could really bring about good city government. Only organized public opinion could permanently protect the cities from state legislative interference, Rowe argued in another example, for recalcitrant legislatures could not be depended upon to abide by the terms of constitutional amendments and general incorporation laws unless they were watched carefully and constantly. "Instead of expecting a mechanism of government to maintain a high standard of public service," by which Rowe meant expecting the electoral process alone to assure honesty and efficiency, "these standards will be furnished by the public opinion of the community." "The democracy toward which we are approaching will be a democracy of pleasures and enjoyments rather than a democracy of the suffrage." Rowe allowed himself to be carried away by his own rhetoric in this unfortunate passage, but his message was the standard Brycian assertion that good city government was the best interest of every municipal citizen.[21]

Even the leaders of the municipal research bureau movement, who are often mistakenly considered mere technocrats of administrative machinery, derived their conception of "efficient" municipal democracy directly from the tradition founded by Bryce. William H. Allen, joint founder of the New York Municipal Research Bureau, wrote in 1907 in a book called *Efficient Democracy*:

Democracy's greatest problem is this, how can we utilise without excessive waste the tremendous potential force of the small percentage [of municipal citizens] who, feeling keenly the injustice, the discrepancies and inefficiencies of government, are willing to make sacrifices, if thus they can help remove discrepancy, inefficiency and injustice. Today there is enormous waste of civic interest and of potentially efficient citizenship.

Efficient democracy meant mobilizing "facts" and conclusions based on facts, to "enlighten and convince public opinion." The means that Allen advocated called for specialization and division of labor, but his conception of the municipal political process, and of the role of potential leaders, derived directly from the prescriptions of the *American Commonwealth*.[22]

The practical desire for efficiency and improvement was so strong that it overcame whatever distaste the functionalists harbored for the numerous socialist victories in municipal elections in 1911 and 1912. Woodruff, in describing these victories in the *National Municipal Review*, wrote of the platform of the San Francisco Socialist party that "but for the introduction of the word 'class' in the first line," the "average municipal progressive could give conscientious adhesion" to most of the planks. The socialists' constant harping on working-class struggle against capitalism was "divisive," and might eventually prove dangerous "if allowed to go unchecked," but if they would emphasize the best features of their platforms, and agree to work willingly with the other people interested in the "advancement of high ideals of city life," without regard for party, they would "contribute an earnestness and an aggressiveness" that could be "of great value."[23]

Much of the suspicion that might justly be directed against the proponents of municipal efficiency is dispelled by the vigorous participation of Charles Beard in the municipal research bureau movement. At the same time that Beard was earning a notorious reputation as a radical democratic critic of the Founding Fathers and the federal Constitution, he was also busy writing his formulation of functional theory, sitting on National Municipal League committees, and working with the New York Municipal Research Bureau. Beard's positions on the specific issues of municipal democracy were tremendously pragmatic. He characterized the trend of reforms implemented by the cities as of 1912 as a "revolt" against bicameral and large ward-based councils that constituted "a revolution in municipal government." He gave the impression of a personal distaste for the most popular form of this revolt, the "commission" system of government, because it "destroys the deliberative and representative element in municipal government, and may readily tend to reduce its administration to a mere routine business, based largely upon principles of economy, to the exclusion of civic ideals." However, during the very same year, 1912, Beard sat on the league's committee to evaluate commission government, and concurred in its conclusions, including such statements as:

Commission government is a relative success [emphasis theirs].
This relative success . . . *results primarily because it is more democratic* (i.e., sensitive to public opinion), than the old form.
Commission government is in general to be recommended *for cities of 100,000 population* and under, and *possibly* for cities of much larger size in preference to any other plan now in operation in any American city.[24]

Beard's treatment of municipal socialism was similarly contradictory. In the chapter of *American City Government* corresponding to the chapter in other formulations of functional theory in which "urban conditions" were described, Beard made numerous references to such things as the separation of workers from ownership of the "instruments of production" leading to "the creation of two rather sharply marked classes in society," the "capitalist class" and the "working class"; to the "landless, homeless and propertyless" character of the resulting "proletariate [sic]," which constituted the great majority of the population of the large industrial cities; to the tendency of the "modern system" to discourage these workers from accumulating property; and to the "collectivist" demands of trade union and socialist movements arising from the development of working class "solidarity." The rest of Beard's formulation of functional theory differed not at all from that of other writers, however. His belief that class struggle was an important aspect of social conditions in great cities did not lead him to propose a different conception of the functions that municipal government ought to perform in order to ameliorate those conditions from the conception of more conservative functionalists such as Goodnow.[25]

Beard's attitude toward the socialists was as purely pragmatic as Woodruff's. In a later issue of the *National Municipal Review*, of which he was an associate editor, Beard presented an updated list of municipal socialist officeholders to supplement Woodruff's original compilation. He appended to the list a quotation from

Robert F. Hoxie of the University of Chicago, which read in part:

> Investigation shows that these Socialist successes represent on the whole a liberal and progressive type of socialism—not ultra theoretical or revolutionary—which stands for honesty and efficiency of administration and a broad and practical program of social reform. As such they are, in the opinion of the writer, one phase of the progressive democratic movement which is sweeping the country.

The statement itself evinced a modest sympathy for the socialists, but Beard's publication of someone else's opinions, rather than taking direct responsibility by writing his own statement, represented a curious equivocation about his personal commitments.[26]

On the assumption that Beard's activities are the best guide to his true beliefs, he emerges as a leading proponent of efficient functional administration headed by highly trained experts. Despite his popularity as a teacher of political science at Columbia University, Beard occupied more and more of his time after 1909 with municipal affairs. The New York Bureau of Municipal Research founded the first graduate school of public administration, the Training School for Public Service, in 1911, and soon negotiated full affiliation for the school with Columbia. In 1915, Beard became director of the school, and in 1918, following his resignation from his professorship in political science at Columbia, he became director of the entire bureau, serving until 1921.[27]

Beard was vigorously committed to expert administrative leadership as the key to municipal improvement. However, he was sufficiently sensitive to the antipathy between democracy and expert administrative efficiency to compose a major statement in 1916 defending the Training School approach to municipal improvement. Again, as with his fellow functionalists, Beard's commitment to the success of functional innovation led him to distort somewhat the meaning of municipal democracy. "Modern social and industrial conditions," Beard wrote, had "imposed" upon government "great tasks." Could a thoroughly democratic government perform these tasks efficiently?[28]

He attacked the problem by postulating that the attempt to reconcile efficiency and democracy had never been made. American democracy meant "public officers . . . elected for short terms by popular vote and compelled to keep their attention fixed upon pleasing the public at every turn." Efficiency meant "experts," nonpartisan administrative bureaucracy headed by trained and talented specialists. The essence of the conflict between democracy and efficiency was that "democracy distrusts the expert." Beard conceded that such fears were justified. Reconciliation could be achieved by keeping administration separate from policy and politics, and training the experts to be modest, humble, and responsive.

The only kind of an expert that democracy will and ought to tolerate is the expert who admits his fallibility, retains an open mind and is prepared to serve. There are many things in this world worse than very dirty streets, a very high death rate and a large percentage of crime. Anyone who is so overcome by passion for efficiency and expertness that he is willing to sacrifice everything else for the sake of securing any kind of mere mechanical excellence has no message for democracy in America.[29]

The remainder of the article was an advertisement for the kinds of university programs originated by the bureau's Training School for Public Service. The tasks of government should be undertaken by experts in the "new science of administration" who were responsive to the public will. Then, if "public opinion" could be "properly educated to appreciate" the abilities of experts, the just fears of democracy would be put to rest.[30]

Conclusion

Beard's rhetoric can be read in an antidemocratic tone of voice, but in practice the functionalists were considerably to the left of the mainstream of practical municipal reform activism during the first two decades of the century. The functionalists placed a very strong emphasis on city self-government. Their hopes of seeing cities of over 25,000 obtain the power to write their own charters were only marginally fulfilled. Amidst the rage for strong mayors, and then for commission government, their struggle to preserve and strengthen truly representative city councils was a courageous defense of democratic principles. The most fascinating aspect of the functionalists' position was their confidence in the ability of community self-government to master a complex of urban problems that they themselves had defined as technological and industrial in origin.

Despite the impossibility of transferring ultimate responsibility for governing the city from the state governments to the cities themselves, the functional theorists did do whatever they could to transform the municipal corporation into a true government. Their assumption that every citizen of the city had an equal and identical interest in "good government," regardless of class, wealth, or condition, cut through the very real difficulties of reconciling administrative efficiency with democratic processes, and made possible simplistic solutions such as Beard's. But by championing the representative city council, they constituted themselves the vanguard of a movement to preserve a democratic process of formulating municipal policy for the administrative experts to implement. The functionalists defended broad municipal suffrage in an age of fierce racial and ethnic prejudice and steadfastly attributed corruption to the failings of the citizenry as a whole rather than to the evil designs of scheming politicos.

Within the context of their larger program of converting the cities to functional administration, the functionalists built up and defended an admirable position on the central questions of municipal democracy. In the end, they found themselves demanding more than the state legislatures would willingly grant, and more than the city reform groups were able to achieve, in terms of strong municipal self-government, independent municipal politics, and democratic city council policy making. The functionalists were not municipal social democrats, not even of the mild Fabian variety flourishing in Great Britain at the time. However, promotion of "gas and water" socialism was never the test of democratic commitment in American cities. Luther Gulick, one of the first graduates of the Training School for Public Service, wrote in his foreword to Jane Dahlberg's 1966 history of the New York Bureau of Municipal Research that the functionalists were men "driven by a profound devotion to democracy."[31] He meant by this, democracy of a practical kind, commensurate with the American variety of twentieth-century pragmatic liberalism. While democracy of that kind has its shortcomings, we can hardly afford to disparage Gulick's assertion on the basis of any radical advances in municipal democracy in the sixty-odd years since the functionalists devised their defense of the democratic virtues of strong, centralized, functionally departmentalized city self-government.

CHAPTER 7

Metropolitan Problems and the Decline of Functional Innovation

By the time that functional innovation began enjoying its greatest usefulness, between 1910 and 1930, the social and economic characteristics of urban development that functionalism was designed to ameliorate were already being supplanted by new forces of urban growth. National industrialization in the second half of the nineteenth century had been accompanied by urbanization with tremendous centripetal force. Up to the 1890s, urbanization not only shifted the domestic and immigrating population into the urban sector, it also concentrated the urban population towards the centers of cities, producing dangerous levels of residential density. In the absence of mitigating technology, conditions in slums at the centers of large cities became unspeakable by the standards of American culture. The density of New York City's Tenth Ward, on the Lower East Side, reached 900 persons per acre (ca. 500,000 per square mile), possibly the highest residential density achieved anywhere in the world in recent times.[1] Social reformers had one all-encompassing term for the problems of the cities in the 1890s: congestion.

Between 1890 and 1900, however, the prevailing forces of urban development began to reverse direction. By 1900, concentration had begun to give way to deconcentration, and centripetal to centrifugal forces. Residential density in the central areas of cities continued to increase, and population density during working hours in central business districts increased even more rapidly, but the *relative* distribution of residential population throughout the city, and what were coming to be known as its "suburbs," began to shift towards the perimeter. While the centers of urban areas were still the fastest growing portion in 1900, the districts between five and ten miles from the central foci of the cities had become the fastest growing area by 1920.[2] Technology was the immediate cause. The elevator and structural steel for buildings allowed business uses to price residential uses out of the market for space at the center of the city. The electric streetcar accelerated a trend already begun by the horsecar and the steam-powered cable car, making it feasible for people to live in larger quarters at lower rents more than two miles from the city center and also afford to pay to commute. The electric streetcar was probably the most rapidly implemented invention in American history. Frank Sprague got the first electric streetcar system working effectively in Richmond, Virginia in 1888, and by 1895, 850 trolley systems had been built and put into operation. The systems of 1895 included approximately 10,000 miles of track. By comparison, it took more than twenty-five years from the time that Alexander Graham Bell demonstrated the first working telephone, in 1876, for cities to install extensive telephone systems. In 1900, the total number of telephones in use nationally was 800,000, only slightly more than one for every hundred people. Around 1900 came the internal combustion automobile, followed shortly by the truck. Also of importance was the role that high voltage alternating current electricity, suitable for long distance transmission by wire, played in allowing industry to move towards the outskirts of cities.[3]

The Census Bureau was very quick to perceive and publicize the dominance of deconcentrating forces. As early as 1905, the bureau was working on the "industrial district" concept, a general conception of an urban area that captured the major aspects of the new centrifugal trend. In 1911, bureau officials developed the concept of the "metropolitan district," the forerunner of the modern "metropolitan area." The metropolitan district conception of an urban area ignored political boundaries almost entirely. The bureau did its best to devise definitions that would correspond appropriately to the functionalist analysis of urban conditions. After experimenting with delineation rules based on industrial ties to the core of the urban area, they settled upon a fixed minimum level of residential density for census enumeration districts at the periphery of the urban area as the basis for deciding where a metropolitan district had its boundary with the countryside. The use of density as the crucial quality of urban conditions coordinated excellently with the discovery of the importance of density as a factor underlying the need for urban services, and as a crucial variable in the cost of producing services.

The presentation of statistics for metropolitan districts cast the relationship of the large cities to their urbanized areas and suburbs in a new light. The statistics revealed that what seemed to be a very ambitious annexation and "Greater City" expansion movement on the part of most very large cities between 1890 and 1910, had in fact not kept pace with the centrifugal expansion of their residential population. In the race between suburban growth and central city consolidation, the suburbs, rather than the cities, suddenly appeared to be winning. By 1930, annexation had declined substantially and suburban growth had mushroomed. The era of the metropolis was beginning.

The functionalist municipal political scientists perceived metropolitan deconcentration as a crisis. The "community" constituted by the social and economic metropolis was politically fragmented, and the consequences were potentially dangerous. The functionalist response to the emerging fragmentation crisis was consolidation of the metropolitan area and the promotion of centralized, functionally departmentalized metropolitan government. The mode of innovation that had mastered the crisis of the industrial city would presumably also resolve the problems of the metropolitan district.

Ultimately, proponents of centralized metropolitan government expected political fragmentation to result in real crises within metropolitan areas, crises such as water shortages, or sewage overflows, resulting from the inability of fragmented governments to cooperate in planning and building capital improvements that had to be of metropolitan scale. By the late 1920s, however, it became clear that such crises were not about to occur, not even in one or two districts. The anticipated indigenous movements for metropolitan consolidation also failed to arise. Metropolitan areas became increasingly fragmented, politically, but consolidation and metropolitan government came to seem less and less relevant as responses to the political disorganization of metropolitan areas.

Finally, between 1930 and 1933, functionalism was abandoned. Two prominent studies of the metropolitan area, one undertaken by the National Municipal League, and the other by President Herbert Hoover's Research Committee on Social Trends, examined the probable future course of metropolitan development and concluded that the functional approach could not be appropriately transferred from the realm of city political innovation to that of the metropolis. While neither study attempted to speculate on what a new approach to innovation in urban political development should consist of, the authors of the studies, and many of their readers, came away recognizing that the time to replace functional innovation with a new mode of analysis and prescription had arrived.

The "Metropolitan District" Concept

George Waring made use of the concept of a "metropolis" in his special report on cities for the Census of 1880, but not in a manner related to the modern concept of a metropolitan area. In 1880, "metropolis" still meant the capital city of an empire or nation. Waring was using the term in this sense when he suggested that the United States had a metropolis similar to those of great European countries. The "Metropolis of the United States": New York City, Brooklyn, Jersey City, Newark, Hoboken, and the numerous smaller surrounding municipalities, constituted "one great metropolitan community" with a "national hinterland," Waring argued, and played a role in national life similar to that of London, Paris, or Berlin in their respective countries.[4]

The Census Bureau's later use of the concept of a "metropolis," in developing a means of describing the effects of deconcentrating forces on very large cities, owed nothing to Waring's "Metropolis" of 1880, however. The first analytic conception of a city under the influence of centrifugal economic and social forces was the "single urban center," a concept introduced by E. Dana Durand in a report on street and electric railways in 1902 that was part of the bureau's census of electrical industries. Durand coined the term "single urban center" to describe situations in which horsecar and trolley lines connected a city to surrounding industrial and residential areas with a combined city-hinterland population of greater than 100,000. Durand argued that the railways unified conditions in such areas, and made them indistinguishable from incorporated cities of 100,000 and over.[5]

In 1905, the bureau's Chief Geographer, Charles S. Sloane, carried Durand's conceptualization of industry, dense population, and intraurban railways one step further by suggesting the preparation of a special report on "population and industrial districts" as part of the census of manufactures of 1905.[6] Where Durand had considered transportation lines the crucial factor in unifying an urban center, Sloane proposed that the entire fringe of industrial development extending around a large city should be considered part of that city's urban area. The final report, published in 1909, explained:

The development of the telephone, electric railway, and other means of transportation and intercommunication has to a great extent done away with the necessity of close physical association in industrial enterprises; therefore the increase in our urban population and industries is in many instances due to the development of the suburbs of the cities rather than to growth within corporate limits. Under these conditions the publication of the statistics for population and industries included within the corporate limits of the city often conveys an erroneous idea of the importance of the district in which the city is located.[7]

The report presented statistics for thirteen districts, the smallest being that of Providence, Rhode Island, with a total population of slightly less than 350,000. The industrial district was in part an attempt to convert the analytic concern with industrial causes of urban density into a workable device for organizing comparative statistics of urban conditions. But Geographer Sloane's imagination had also been jogged by a controversy between Bureau Director North and the Boston *Herald* in August of 1905. The *Herald* had suggested that the bureau compare city sizes in terms of "the natural basis of centres of population." City growth was a "natural" process, the *Herald* editors argued, and the full extent of a city's natural growth, not simply its corporate area and population, ought to be the measure of its size in relation to other cities. North had replied that the bureau did take into account the area surrounding large cities, but that it could not go beyond corporate boundaries in compiling statistics for a city unless the conditions in the surrounding area were "in a marked degree dependent upon the existence" of their "great centre." Such dependence had to involve not only population but also manufacturing.[8]

The *Herald* responded that Boston "suffers more than any other great city by the disparity between its corporate limits and its true population." If the bureau would present Boston's "true population," the population of the "metropolitan district," as the city's official population, it would reveal that in truth Boston was "the tenth great city in the world."[9] The *Industrial Districts* report provided some official recognition of the size and population of Boston as an urban conglomeration, but delineated according to industrial interrelationships rather than concepts of a city's "true population."

Industrial interrelatedness did a great deal to resolve the bureau's conceptual problems, but it did not provide an exact mechanism for drawing boundaries around an urban conglomeration. The bureau had to be prepared to defend its districts against complaints that one partially industrialized suburban municipality had been included in an urban district, while a contiguous municipality that was only slightly less industrialized had been excluded. Sloane was aware of a proposal by the New York *Sun* in September 1905 that New York's true population should be calculated by taking the population of an area equal in size to that of metropolitan London. He ignored this suggestion at the time, but may have been making some use of it in January 1911 when he began assembling data from the 1890 and 1900 censuses for New Orleans and San Francisco and their surrounding areas into "industrial metropolitan districts." During the course of 1911, Sloane, Durand, who was now director of the bureau, and others on the staff experimented with various defining principles on data for specific large cities, trying to devise a good working method of drawing boundaries. Among the methods considered was a form of the idea suggested by the New York *Sun* in 1905. The San Francisco Merchants' Association made essentially the same conceptual suggestion in the February 1911 issue of their *Review*, by proposing that centers of population be compared with each other on the basis of the "Greater London" area. "Political lines of all sorts" they wrote, were "wholly artificial" where the "essential unity, both geographic and industrial" of a great urban community was concerned, and should be ignored. Instead, great cities should be compared in terms of their metropolitan character, using Greater London as the model of a "metropolis." An area of seven hundred square miles, the approximate area of Greater London, should be mapped out, with the city at its center, and data should be aggregated for that entire area. Such a method would properly standardize comparisons. In particular, the *Review* emphasized, the Greater London area method would produce a valid comparison among the three great cities of the western states, and prove conclusively San Francisco's "proud position as the Pacific Coast metropolis."[10]

Sloane made some use of this method in March 1911, when his office began studying the population density of the area within a ten-mile radius of the center of each corporate city of over 100,000 population. From these studies, the Geographer's

Office prepared urban area delineations of two kinds. For cities of over 200,000 population, the areas delineated included all cities, towns, and minor civil divisions of municipalities lying within a ten-mile radius of the center city that had a population density of greater than 150 persons per square mile. For cities of 100,000 to 200,000, the areas included *all* cities, towns, and minor civil divisions within a ten-mile radius, regardless of density. These prototypes incorporated some aspects of the Greater London concept, although Sloane apparently considered a circle with a ten-mile radius a more appropriate area than one of the size of metropolitan London. The prototypes also made use of a fixed minimum level of residential density, the standard that eventually became the crucial factor in the bureau's method of delineation.[11]

In October 1911, Durand put out a press release to test the popularity of the concept of a "metropolitan district." The release was entitled "New York Leads London" and was framed as a counter to the statistics on the Greater London metropolitan area in the recently released British census of 1911. The British census gave statistics for London city, the "Administrative County of London," and "Greater London." Durand explained that since "Greater London" lacked significant political organization, and since New York City had a larger population than London County, New York was now officially the "largest organized municipality in the world." In addition, Durand presented statistics for "what is taken by the Census Bureau to form the Metropolitan District of New York." Using diagrams to extrapolate the rates of population growth for this New York Metropolitan District and also for the Greater London metropolitan area as defined in the British census, Durand showed that if growth continued in both cases at the average rate prevailing from 1861 to 1911, then around the year 1915 the New York District would surpass Greater London in population.[12]

The press release used the term "metropolitan district," but the statistics it presented for New York were compiled for the same area as that of the industrial district of New York in the

1905 report. A strong adverse reaction emanated from John R. Rathom, the managing editor of the Providence, Rhode Island, *Journal* and *Evening Bulletin*, who called the release "utterly absurd," "unfair," "inconsistent," "untruthful," and tending to make the bureau appear "ridiculous." Rathom objected on the grounds that Greater London was the administrative area for police, fire, and water districts, while New York Metropolitan District was "a series of entirely separate communities not connected in any official way with one another." Using the kind of logic employed by the San Francisco Merchants' Association, Durand responded that he saw no reason why the New York District, with an area of 702 square miles, could not properly be compared with Greater London's 693. More important, Greater London was not politically a city, and on other grounds it differed little from the New York District.

Jersey City, Newark, and other adjacent towns in New Jersey are as much a part of the industrial and social life of New York metropolis as Brooklyn is. Moreover, Jersey City, for example, is hardly more independent politically from New York than the towns in the outer ring of London outside London county are independent of the political organization of London. . . . I did not put out these statistics with regard to New York and London for the sake of pleasing the pride of New York, although doubtless it will have that effect. Personally I think it is a great disadvantage to have cities of such enormous size.

Rathom protested that taking the industrial district concept and implying that industrial ties, in the absence of political consolidation of any kind, were sufficient to unify a metropolis, was unacceptable reasoning. But the Secretary of Commerce and Labor sided with Durand in the three-sided correspondence that transpired, and Durand proceeded with plans for a full report on metropolitan districts in the 1910 census publications.[13]

In December 1911, Sloane and Durand reviewed the draft report in preparation for its inclusion in the 1910 *Census Abstract*. The draft argued that the urban environment of a great city extended outward from the center throughout the contiguous area in which the residential population density was greater than 150 persons per square mile.[14] For cities of 100,000 to 200,000, the environment could be considered to extend to a radius of ten miles, even though density in some parts might be below 150 persons. "Metropolitan districts" defined in this manner represented the true and complete communities of the great cities.

All of our great urban communities . . . extend far beyond the confines of the official city limits, and have suburban districts with a comparatively dense population adjacent to the boundary and so closely connected with the business center of the city by numerous electric and steam car lines as to be practically a part of the city. The wage earners residing in these suburbs are employed in the city, but through the restrictions of the city boundary are not counted by the Census as a part of its population.[15]

The final text published in the *Abstract* explained that the dense suburbs of great cities were "in a certain sense . . . as truly a part" of the city as the districts inside the city's political boundary. The purpose of the "metropolitan district" concept was to annex, descriptively, to the great cities, "adjoining communities which may be considered as intimately associated with the urban center," in order to "show the magnitude of each of the principal population centers taken as a whole."[16]

The Discovery of Metropolitan Deconcentration

The subdued form in which the metropolitan district concept appeared in the ponderous volumes of the census of 1910 belied its importance to the bureau's overall analysis of urban conditions. The metropolitan district concept successfully translated the abstractions of the functional analysis of industrialization, population concentration, and urban conditions into a workable method for presenting statistics of the social environment of a large city. Industrialization was the major force producing urban agglomeration, but population density was the factor producing the urban conditions that required the services of functional municipal government. By relying primarily on an absolute value of minimal urban density to mark off the boundaries of the urban environment of a large city, Durand and Sloane were not necessarily accommodating everyone's conception of a "community," but they were providing a statistical picture of urban conditions that conformed to the precepts of functional theory.[17]

The 1910 metropolitan district report attempted to demonstrate that all cities of over 100,000 were "metropolitan" in character. As concentrations of dense population, they were all divided into a large central political city and a surrounding urbanized area. Of slightly more than twenty-seven million people living in these metropolitan districts, 25 percent resided in the fringe areas. This revelation posed serious practical problems for the functional approach.

One reason that the functionalists had not concerned themselves with annexation, consolidation, or the various turn-of-the-century "Greater City" movements, was that these activities seemed to be resolving both practical and theoretical questions about the size and shape of the political city without the assistance of functionalist analysis and prescription. Before the Census Bureau presented its "metropolitan" descriptions of the extent of urban conditions in large cities, large city unification was regarded as reasonably successful, with the exception of such special cases as San Francisco and Boston. The central cities described in the metropolitan district report for 1910 had increased their political area by 45 percent between 1870 and 1890, and between 1890 and 1910 Greater City movements had helped to spur their territorial expansion to an even higher rate of 59 percent (see Table 7). Before the publication of the metropolitan district report, it was reasonable to assume that the large cities had been doing a first-rate job of incorporating within their political boundaries the fringe areas where urban conditions were constantly developing as national urbanization proceeded.

The 1910 metropolitan district statistics cast the annexation activity of 1890–1910 in a different light. The statistics showed that despite extremely vigorous annexation and consolidation, the

Table 7. Central city area, increases in area by annexation, percentage increase due to annexation, and proportion central city population is of total urban area population for the forty-seven central cities of the forty-four metropolitan districts of 1910 for the period 1870–1940

Year	Area of central cities of 1910 (sq. miles)	Increase in area by annexation (sq. miles)	% increase due to annexation*	Proportion of metropolitan area population in central cities†
1870	985			
1890	1,432	447	45%	
1910	2,273	841	59%	75%
1930	3,088	815	36%	65%
1940	3,119	31	1%	64%

* The area of the 47 cities in the beginning of the decade is the basis for the percentages: i.e., increase 1870–1890 ÷ 1870 total area.

† See Table 9.

Sources: Area: for 1870 and 1880: Roderick D. McKenzie et al, *The Metropolitan Community* (New York: 1933; reprinted by Russell and Russell, New York, 1967), Appendix Table IX; for 1890: Census Office, *Report on the Social Statistics of the Cities in the United States at the Eleventh Census* (Washington, D.C.: 1895), prepared by John Shaw Billings, M.D.; for 1900: Bureau of the Census, *Financial Statistics of Cities over 30,000: 1910* (Washington, D.C.: 1913); for 1910: Bureau of the Census, *1910 Census, Population* (Washington, D.C.: 1913), I, 74–76, "Cities and Their Suburbs"; for 1920, 1930 and 1940: Warren S. Thompson, *Population, The Growth of Metropolitan Districts in the United States: 1900–1940* (Washington D.C.: Bureau of the Census, 1947), General Table 2.

central cities of the nation's forty-four largest urban areas had managed to bring within their boundaries only 75 percent of the total population of those areas. A proportional distribution of 75 percent to 25 percent between central cities and their urbanized fringes tended to suggest that the centrifugal forces of deconcentrating urban growth had entirely neutralized the consolidating efforts of the annexation movement. The kinds of urban growth facilitated by the electric streetcar, the automobile, the truck, and other recent technological advances, were not simply making large cities bigger than ever, they were also rapidly transforming them into urban areas of a very different kind from the large industrial city of 1890.

The 1910 statistics were the functionalists' first introduction to the full implications of the phenomenon of deconcentrating metropolitan expansion. Tables 8 and 9 show the further effects of deconcentration between 1910 and 1940, when annexation activity was far less vigorous. Since urban areas tend to grow at the same rate as the rate of growth of the nation's total urban population, any given group of metropolitan districts will tend to contain the same proportion of the national urban population over long periods of time. Table 8 illustrates this constant proportionality phenomenon for the forty-four districts of 1910, which contained 62 percent of the nation's urban population in 1910, 61 percent in 1920, 66 percent in 1930, and 65 percent in 1940. It shows the same constant proportionality for the fifty-eight metropolitan districts identified by the census of 1920, which included 66 percent of the national urban population, and 71 percent in 1930 and 1940, and for the ninety-seven districts of 1930, which contained 79 percent of the national urban population in both 1930 and 1940. The combined effects of more rapid population growth in the fringe areas of metropolitan districts than in the central cities, and of the reduction in annexation activity after 1910, however, led to a severe decline in the proportion of the total district population of the forty-four 1910 districts encompassed within the central cities. This deconcentration process within metropolitan districts is illustrated in Table

Table 8. Urban population and its metropolitan district components, 1870–1940, illustrating the constant proportionality of metropolitan district to total urban population

Year	U.S. urban population	Population of metropolitan districts			Proportion of urban population in district area		
		1910 dists.	1920 dists.	1930 dists.	1910 dists.	1920 dists.	1930 dists.
1870	9,902,361						
1890	22,106,265						
1910	41,998,932	26,039,836			62%		
1920	54,157,973	32,970,096	35,992,323		61%	66%	
1930	68,954,823	45,186,403	49,013,484	54,753,645	66%	71%	79%
1940	74,423,702	48,424,642	52,740,537	59,118,592	65%	71%	79%

Sources: For U.S. urban population: Bureau of the Census, *Historical Statistics of the United States, Colonial Times to 1957* (Washington, D.C.: 1960), Series A 195–209; 1940 definitions of urban population apply for all years. For population of metropolitan districts: Warren S. Thompson, *Population, The Growth of Metropolitan Districts in the United States: 1900–1940* (Washington, D.C.: Bureau of the Census, 1947), Table 1, p. 3; 1930 definitions of metropolitan districts have been used.

Table 9. Deconcentration in the metropolitan districts of 1910, 1910–1940

Year	population U.S. urban	Population of metropolitan districts	Proportion of urban population in district area	Population of central cities	Proportion of district area population in central cities
1910	41,998,932	26,039,836	62%	19,538,782	75%
1920	54,157,973	32,970,096	61%	24,262,276	74%
1930	68,954,823	45,186,403	66%	29,575,958	65%
1940	74,423,702	48,424,642	65%	30,929,246	64%

Sources: For U.S. urban population and district population figures, see Table 8. For population of central cities: for 1910: Bureau of the Census, *1910 Census, Population* (Washington, D.C.: 1913), Volume I, pp. 74–76, "Cities and Their Suburbs," Tables 50 and 51; for 1920 and 1930: Bureau of the Census, *Fifteenth Census of the U.S.: 1930; Metropolitan Districts, Population and Area* (Washington, D.C.: 1932), prepared under Clarence E. Batschelet, Geographer, Table 4; for 1940: Thompson, *Population*, Table 2.

9. In 1910, the proportion of the total population of the metropolitan districts of 1910 living within their forty-seven central cities was 75 percent. This proportion fell to 74 percent in 1920, to 65 percent in 1930, and to 64 percent by 1940. The 1910 metropolitan districts maintained their proportional relationship to the overall urban sector of the nation, but the deconcentrating character of their growth significantly altered the relationship of the central cities to their districts.[18]

There was little that even the kind of annexation practiced between 1890 and 1910 could have done to overcome the centrifugal force of deconcentrating metropolitan growth between 1910 and 1940. Largely as a product of the use of the automobile and the motor truck, population in the fringe areas of metropolitan districts did not grow, between 1910 and 1940, merely by means of peripheral expansion. Fringe areas also grew by means of tremendous increases in their own average density, especially after 1920. The metropolitan fringe areas became increasingly "urban," despite their retention of the designation "suburban." We can see what this meant by observing Los Angeles as an example (Table 10). Between 1910 and 1920, the fringe population of Los Angeles Metropolitan District increased almost threefold, from 119,028 to 302,335, with an accompanying areal increase of even more than threefold, from 295.8 square miles to 933.7. Average fringe density probably increased slightly, but annexation of 266 square miles of fringe to the central city removed the densest areas.[19] Between 1920 and 1940, fringe population increases were also very great, from 302,335 to 1,400,319, but they consisted almost entirely of the filling up of vacant suburban land within the existing fringe area, and the growth of subcenters within the fringe. The fringe grew in area from 933.7 square miles in 1920, to 1,175.1 square miles by 1940, but lost 82.6 square miles of its densest territory to central city annexation. Despite this loss, population density in the fringe increased from 323.8 to 1,281.8 persons per square mile, making the suburban fringe almost as densely populated in 1940 as the central city itself had been in 1920. Yet only 241.4 square miles of terri-

Table 10. Metropolitan deconcentration in Los Angeles metropolitan district, 1910–1940

District component by year	Population		Area		Density (persons per square mile)
	Number of persons	% of district population in central city	Number of square miles	% of district area in central city	
Total district					
1910	438,226		395.0		1,109.4
1920	870,008		1,299.4		676.5
1930	2,318,526		1,474.3		1,572.6
1940	2,904,596		1,540.8		1,885.1
Central city					
1910	319,198	73%	99.2	25%	3,217.7
1920	576,673	66%	365.7	28%	1,576.9
1930	1,238,048	53%	440.3	30%	2,811.7
1940	1,504,277	52%	448.3	29%	3,355.5
Fringe					
1910	119,028		295.8		402.4
1920	302,335		933.7		323.8
1930	1,080,478		1,034.0		1,044.9
1940	1,400,319		1,092.5		1,281.8

Source: Warren S. Thompson, *Population, The Growth of Metropolitan Districts in the United States: 1900–1940* (Washington, D.C.: Bureau of the Census, 1947), Table 2, p. 29. The 1910–1930 figures are based on 1930 definition rules; the 1940 figures are based on 1940 rules.

tory on the outer edge of the 1920 metropolitan district increased in population density above 150 persons per square mile between 1920 and 1940.

This kind of deconcentrating urban growth had a very demoralizing effect on the annexation and consolidation drives of the great cities. In this instance, Los Angeles is the best example, because of its tremendous efforts to maintain a high rate of central city expansion. Between 1910 and 1920, the central city annexed 266.5 square miles, approximately one-half of all the territory annexed by the forty-seven metropolitan central cities during that decade. But although this incredible expansion increased the proportion of the metropolitan district *area* incorporated in Los Angeles central city by 3 percent, it did not prevent a 7 percent decline in the proportion of the metropolitan district *population* incorporated in central city Los Angeles.

Los Angeles central city expansion was a hopeless enterprise in the face of deconcentrating forces. The only way for a city to hold its own against its outlying fringe was by a cessation of deconcentration, such as the one occurring during the Depression. Residential density within central city Los Angeles increased by 19 percent during the 1930s, only slightly less than the 23 percent increase in the density of the fringe, allowing the central city to hold its own without significant annexations. An incredible lust for trucks, automobiles, and highways, and the low density conditions that they made possible, led Los Angeles to suffer more severely than other central cities from the impact of deconcentration. But the Census Bureau's 1920 and 1930 metropolitan statistics revealed that deconcentration was producing similar effects in most of the nation's metropolitan districts.

The Functionalist Response to Metropolitan Deconcentration

Municipal political scientists did their best to force the effects of deconcentration into the functional mold. While they recognized metropolitan areas as new phenomena, they tried to interpret them as large cities transformed to a gargantuan scale, but otherwise unchanged. A belief that the political forces associated with urban conditions in a metropolitan district, like those of a large industrial city, would necessarily be centripetal ones, led some political writers to suggest that state government involvement with metropolitan areas was an undesirable hindrance to metropolitan good government that should be curtailed. Robert C. Brooks of Swarthmore College, a fellow Cornell graduate student of Durand and A. F. Weber, and a close follower of Bryce, argued in 1915 that great "metropolitan communities" such as New York, Philadelphia, Boston, and Chicago, whose annual budgets were becoming larger than those of their state governments, should be allowed to sever their state ties and become "free city commonwealths" under the federal system, like the free cities of Hamburg, Lübeck, and Bremen in Germany. In orthodox functionalist fashion, Brooks insisted that "the unique character of metropolitan conditions" demanded subway and highway systems, metropolitan area-wide sanitation, city planning, and other unique metropolitan services. Brooks suggested that metropolitan self-government, free of state interference, was the appropriate means to deal with such unique conditions and necessities. As for the metropolitan suburbs, Brooks predicted that once they were part of an independent metropolitan government, they would give up their "reactionary" jealousy and contribute their "intelligent, clean-living, high-spirited citizenship" to achieving good metropolitan government.[20]

The evidence that the centrifugal and multinucleating forces in metropolitan areas were stronger than the unifying centralizing ones was impossible to ignore, however. Deconcentration led to the growth of subcenters: small cities and towns in the metropolitan district fringe with strong preferences for their own municipal governments and independence of central city control. Where a metropolitan district contained a second central city of reasonable size, strong forces arose that threatened to split the district in two. When San Francisco initiated a "Greater City" movement in the hopes of consolidating Oakland within its corporate limits, for example, Oakland mounted a Greater Oakland movement to defend its independence.[21]

By 1922, the leading functionalist analysis of metropolitan areas was that they were suffering from "political disintegration." Chester C. Maxey of Western Reserve University, in a prominent article in the *National Municipal Review*, called for a national metropolitan unification movement to be led by activists from all the nation's metropolitan district central cities. These great cities were truly "metropolitan communities," according to Maxey, but they needed outside assistance in unifying their population and territory. He drew an analogy with the consolidating large cities of the turn of the century and before, none of which had been able to unify themselves without the aid of state legislation, constitutional change, and, in some cases, legislative "fiat." Gradual consolidation by means of numerous small annexations had yet to produce full unification of any metropolitan community, Maxey reminded his readers. For those metropolitan communities that had been successfully unified, it had sometimes been necessary for the state legislature to override the strong opposition of suburbs and satellite cities. A national unification movement would help to overcome the difficulties hindering central cities in their pursuit of greater metropolitan political unity.[22]

The National Municipal League, the obvious group to catalyze such a movement, discussed the question at its 1924 convention and formed a committee on metropolitan government to conduct thorough research of the issues.[23] Paul Studenski undertook direction of the project with the apparent expectation that metropolitan communities would eventually develop centralized, functional administrative government analogous to functional city government, but appropriately transformed to metropolitan scale. The league seemed to expect that while the project was under way, the larger metropolitan cities would begin to initiate campaigns for metropolitan government. In 1927, this confidence was still sufficiently strong for Harvard Professor of Municipal Government W. B. Munro to predict in his textbook on municipal government that a unification movement for "broad treatment of metropolitan problems by a centralized authority," was "sure to arise, in due course." Where social and economic unity pertained, there should be political unity also, and Munro anticipated that political scientists would soon be confronted with metropolitan governments in need of good theoretical and practical models for their internal structure and operation.[24]

The Speedy Demise of Functional Metropolitanism

The metropolitan government movement failed to materialize. Studenski's research proved so disappointing that he did not feel he could recommend centralized government as a solution to the metropolitan government question. "Recent experience appears to demonstrate," he concluded, "that for the time being at least complete consolidation is not a practicable solution for any [metropolitan] region as a whole. Under these circumstances federation offers itself as an attractive, although by no means the only, alternative."[25] Judging from experience since 1930, Studenski's predictions of how various approaches to metropolitan government would fail, including county consolidation, annexation, city-county consolidation, and functional special districts, were remarkably accurate.[26]

While praising Studenski's report as "one of the most important contributions to municipal government in recent years," Charles Merriam of the University of Chicago also identified its principal shortcoming when he evaluated the results of the project as "a little inconclusive."[27] The National Municipal League responded to Studenski's report by abandoning its interest in metropolitan government. In 1933, Roderick McKenzie's famous volume for President Hoover's Research Committee on Social Trends, *The Metropolitan Community*, administered the final blow to functional metropolitanism by demonstrating not only that there was no pressing necessity for centralization, but that metropolitan areas were not suffering ill effects from the existing fragmented arrangement of independent municipalities.

Thomas H. Reed, who had been intimately involved in the Studenski project, wrote an eight-page chapter for McKenzie's book in which he summarily reiterated the functional view of the necessity for metropolitan government: "Every great city now has around it a metropolitan area, one with it economically and socially but without political unity. The consequences in many instances have been little short of disastrous." But this position had become hopelessly obsolete. Over the eleven years since Maxey's article appeared, the inevitable disasters kept failing to occur, and Reed had no examples to offer in support of his claims.[28] McKenzie himself, in another chapter, not only emphasized the unlikelihood of central cities converting themselves into metropolitan governments, but also pointed out that residents of small suburban municipalities enjoyed some unique benefits from metropolitan fragmentation. "At least part of the stimulus" behind the tendency for metropolitan fringes to become increasingly "multinucleated," was "the desire to move to communities where life may be organized on a smaller scale and where individual participation can be more effective."[29] McKenzie's tone implied that he did not agree with Reed's conclusion that sooner or later metropolitan problems would become so intense as to make centralizing reorganization unavoidable.[30]

The problem, as McKenzie clearly underlined in his overall conclusions to *The Metropolitan Community*, was that unified, centralized government was not appropriate to the centrifugal character of metropolitan development. "The spread of population under the influence of motor transport," he wrote, "is far too rapid and too extensive to be dealt with adequately by annexation, even if annexation were not vigorously resisted by most of the suburban communities." Since the dangers inherent in such fragmented political circumstances (according to the precepts of the functional theory) had not materialized, the problem must lie with functional analysis itself, rather than with the metropolitan "problem" to which functionalists were applying it. McKenzie suggested that a new model of "governmental functions" would have to be devised "before the political unity of the real functional metropolitan community can be achieved."[31] This reinforced Studenski's conclusion that the metropolitan government problem was beyond the capacities of the functional mode of innovation. Another three uneventful years had passed since the appearance of Studenski's report, however, and McKenzie did not repeat Studenski's call for national leadership of a metropolitan government movement that would include research, "new speculations" by "scholars of distinction," application of European metropolitan forms to American cases, and a large infusion of "American political ingenuity."[32]

CHAPTER 8

Urban Political Innovation and National Development

Compared with the long period of pragmatic experimentation that preceded the emergence of functional innovation, the transition away from functionalism to a new mode of urban political innovation was extremely rapid. In June 1937, only four years after the appearance of McKenzie's *The Metropolitan Community*, the Urbanism Committee of President Franklin Roosevelt's National Resources Committee published *Our Cities, Their Role in the National Economy*, the federal government's first formal statement on national urban policy. *Our Cities* proposed the framework for a new approach to urban political innovation, while a supplementary Urbanism Committee report on urban government offered a conclusion and retrospective appreciation for three decades of functional innovation. Not everyone immediately abandoned the functional approach to metropolitan development; there were those who continued to hope, as late as the mid-1950s, that some form of centralized, functionally departmentalized metropolitan government might be achieved. But most of the political scientists, elite reform activists, city officials, and other participants in the innovation process were prepared to become involved in the approach introduced by the Urbanism Committee's report.[1]

In this concluding chapter, I want to use the findings from the investigation of innovation in the period from the 1850s to the 1930s as the basis for discussing several general problems of devising forms and methods of urban government capable of mitigating the impact of national development upon urban life. One reason that it was possible to make a very rapid transition from functional innovation to a new approach was that the functionalist experience provided the innovators of the 1930s with an understanding of these general problems that had not been available to their predecessors in the 1890s. The problems include (1) the relationship of urban innovation to national development, (2) the importance of the joint pursuit of analysis and prescription, and (3) the need to provide practical models of improved governmental structure and administrative practice. I have also included brief descriptions of how the current approach to urban political innovation has dealt with these general problems. My purposes here are to provide a basis for comparative evaluation of functional innovation and to use what we have learned about functional innovation as a guide to understanding how modern political science participates in improving urban government.

Modes of Innovation and Periods of National Development

Because they are the means by which urban governmental responses to the forces of national development are devised, we can expect modes of urban political innovation to emerge, flourish, and decline in conjunction with distinct periods of national development. As the means for fashioning responses to the impact of industrialization, urbanization, and modernization, functional innovation was an effective mode for the period of national development in which that three-faceted transformation occurred, the years between the 1850s and the 1930s. During the 1930s a new period of national development began, the functional mode of innovation was abandoned, and participants in the innovation process turned their efforts to fashioning a new mode of innovation that would be appropriate to the new characteristics of national development.

American participation in World War I forced social scientists to recognize that a highly industrialized and urbanized United States would be different from a nation in the midst of an industrial-urban transformation. The war effort demonstrated the significance of American leadership of world industrial production. The industrial inventory crisis of 1919–1921 provided a first taste of the behavior of a mature industrial economy. The census of 1920 revealed that the nation's population had become more than 50 percent "urban" during the preceding decade. Social scientists began to perceive that the nation was approaching its industrial and urban maturity.

In Chapter 7, we dealt with the application of the functionalist approach to metropolitan areas, and with the general decline of functionalism precipitated by the failure of that effort. The activities that led to the introduction of a new approach in 1937 grew out of the recognition that it was changes in the character of national development that were making functional innovation inappropriate, not internal faults in the functionalist approach to metropolitan government. Efforts to fashion a new approach began with assumptions about the new character of national development, and proceeded by proposing approaches to innovation appropriate to the new characteristics.

Two of these efforts received significant attention. The first, the study directed by Roderick McKenzie that appeared as *The Metropolitan Community*, was part of the first major attempt to define the new character of national development, the *Recent Social Trends* project. In 1929, the Social Science Research Council, a committee of representatives from the various social science professional societies founded in 1923 to encourage philanthropic support for a coordinated program of national social research, undertook to form a "President's Research Committee on Social Trends" for President Herbert Hoover. This committee spent three years preparing a report that would "supply a basis for the formulation of large national policies looking to the next phase in the nation's development." The result, which reached Hoover's desk less than a month before the election of 1932, was a hodgepodge of empirical generalizations about where America's social institutions were taking her, institutions ranging from the family, to the arts, to religion, to the legal system, to the fundamental "vitality of the American people." At the very end of the report, Charles Merriam, professor of political science at the University of Chicago and a key figure in the project, argued that it was crucial to consider "the movement of American political theories and attitudes," if one hoped to understand "the trend of American government."[2]

The *Recent Social Trends* project recognized that new trends of development were emerging, but had no comprehensive framework for describing the changes. The chief findings of the *Metropolitan Community* study, as we saw in Chapter 7, were that the economic and social characteristics of metropolitan development did not require the kind of political unification and strong centralized government that functional innovation had prescribed for the industrial city of the 1890s. The study suggested that the complex social and economic interdependencies of the metropolitan community would probably allow separate central city, subcenter city, and suburban town governments to coordinate with each other without the overarching authority and power of a metropolitan government. As the dominant trends of national development became more clear, the appropriate political response to the social and economic character of the metropolitan community could also be more clearly specified.

The second new approach to innovation was part of the work of the Local Community Research Committee of the University of Chicago. This project began in 1923 as an "experiment in social science research" designed to develop a multidisciplinary analysis of the Chicago community. Charles Merriam, who was very active in this enterprise as well, soon shifted its emphasis from analysis to prescription. The shift led, by 1933, to the publication of *The Government of the Metropolitan Region of Chicago*, which strongly advocated centralized metropolitan government. Merriam and his associates argued that metropolitan development was itself one of the major new characteristics of national development. Using an early form of the analytic method based on the concept of a social system, they defined the political aspect of the Chicago metropolitan region as a metropolitan political "system," and then asserted that the metropolitan political system ought to "work." "Does the system work effectively?" was the all-important question Merriam and his associates asked about how the Chicago metropolis should be governed. "Does it [the metropolitan political system] function in practice? Does the great Region obtain the governmental services adapted to its needs as a community?" Above all, was there "popular control" over the functions of the 1,642 different governments the study found operating within the regional area?

By introducing the assumption that metropolitan areas were going to be playing an important role in shaping national development in coming decades, the Chicago study presented an analysis of national development for which strong, centralized metropolitan government was the appropriate approach to urban political innovation. The study used this approach to attack metropolitan governmental fragmentation head-on.

The governmental confusion in the Chicago Area begins at the center and extends to the circumference. The city corporate of Chicago, the County of Cook, and the whole region illustrate progressively the stages in the decentralization and disintegration of government in this great community.

From such a perspective, there was no question that 1,642 governments did not operate in the way one strong centralized metropolitan administration would. From the perspective of popular control over government's behavior, the study found that the "system" of metropolitan Chicago was "the very definition of political irresponsibility, a situation inherently adapted to misgovernment and waste, a situation fundamentally incompatible either with democratic government or with any form of central control." How do 350 police departments cooperate with each other, the study asked, or 343 health agencies, or 1,000 school systems?[3]

Either the approach suggested in *The Metropolitan Community*, or that taken in *The Government of the Metropolitan Region of Chicago*, might have served as the introduction to a new mode of urban political innovation. But by 1935 it was clear that the new characteristics of national development were going to include one very important factor that neither of these studies had looked forward to: forceful planning of, and participation in, national development by the federal government. The organizers of the *Recent Social Trends* project responded eagerly to this prospect. They pushed President Franklin Roosevelt to establish the National Resources Committee, a cabinet-level agency that would use social science analysis to devise an appropriate strategy for the new federal role in development. Charles Merriam abandoned the approach put forward by the Chicago project and concentrated his energies in the work of the new committee. In 1935, the committee published *Regional Factors in National Planning and Development*, its conception of the new character of national development and its initial strategy for federal participation in development.[4]

The National Resources Committee established a subcommittee on "urbanism" to develop an approach to urban development and urban government appropriate to its larger conception of national development. *Our Cities, Their Role in the National Economy*, published in June of 1937, was the result. *Our Cities* presented a conception of national development in which the plans, policies, and programs of the federal government were the most important single factor. The report looked forward to federal development policy that would take account of the needs of city residents and to a mode of urban political innovation in which city governments would work in concert with the federal government.

The *Our Cities* report resolved the first problem in the construction of a replacement for the functional mode of urban political innovation. It specified the major characteristics of the period of national development that opened during the 1930s, and it anticipated the ways in which national development in the new period would affect urban life. Working from the basic principle that the federal government would be guiding and stimulating national development, *Our Cities* argued that greatly increased consideration needed to be given to the cities in the formulation of federal goals and programs. The report also emphasized that what the cities required in the new period of development was the guidance, coordination, and long-range perspective that only a federal urban policy could provide. In the foreword to the report, the National Resources Committee declared:

It may be questioned . . . whether the National Government has given sufficient attention to some of the specific and common problems of urban dwellers as it has for farmers through the Department of Agriculture, and it is the purpose of this inquiry to indicate some of the emerging city problems in which the Nation as whole has an interest and in which the National Government may be helpful. It is not the business of the United States Government to assume responsibility for the solution of purely local problems any more than it is the business of local governments to assume responsibility for the settlement of national problems. Yet, the United States Government cannot properly remain indifferent to the common life of American citizens simply because they happen to be found in what we call "cities." The sanitation, the education, the housing, the working and living conditions, the economic security—in brief, the general welfare of all its citizens—are American concerns, insofar as they are within the range of Federal power and responsibility under the Constitution.[5]

The National Resources Committee's charge to its Urbanism Committee had been to investigate "the facts, the processes, the problems, and the prospects of urban America as they are related to national life and policies." The Urbanism Committee concluded, after analyzing the results of its investigation, that radical changes were needed for the cities to receive the kind of consideration in the formulation of "public policy" appropriate to their significance in national life. "In their most fundamental aspects . . . ," the Urbanism Committee reported, "the relations between cities and the Federal Government still remain in an amorphous and anachronistic state. Although a substantial majority of our population is urban, we continue to live politically in a rural society." The city had come to occupy "a preponderant role in our national existence," and it had therefore become "imperative that it acquire a central position in the formulation of national policy."[6]

The Urbanism Committee also prepared a report that wrote a conclusion to the functional approach to urban political innovation, described the significance of its accomplishments, and reiterated the need for the new approach to innovation introduced in the *Our Cities* report. Albert Lepawsky, one of Merriam's associates on the Chicago metropolitan region study, wrote in this report, *Urban Government*, concerning the accomplishments of functional innovation: "Structurally and technically, urban government has witnessed a development comparable to, though less heralded than, the growth of the nation's private corporate system and industrial machine." Lepawsky described the restructuring of city government along functional lines as "one of the most extensive transformations in our urban and national life." In the future, however, "because of the intimate relationships between local government and the entire national economy," a different kind of urban innovation would be necessary. There would have to be a "national program" of urban innovation that was part of a "well-devised national plan of government" interrelating city, state, and federal government in a single conception.[7]

The Joint Pursuit of Analysis and Prescription

Once the prevailing characteristics of national development have been defined, the construction of a mode of innovation for devising responses to the impact of national development depends upon the joint formulation of an analytic method and a prescriptive format that coordinate with each other. The governmental responses promoted by the prescriptive aspect of the mode of innovation must effectively confront the social and economic forces detected by its analytic method. In the development of the functional mode of innovation, this coordination of analysis and prescription went through several stages. First the experts in municipal law developed a crude argument that the special conditions produced by dense population settlement (analysis) required that cities and towns have local self-government (prescription). Then the Census Bureau developed a comparative statistics program that used a functional model to both analyze present city government efforts to confront the conditions of urban life, and prescribe a pattern of municipal expenditures and service provision that would increase the effectiveness of such efforts. And finally, functionalist political scientists constructed a theory of municipal government that analyzed urban conditions as consequences of industrialization and urbanization forces in national development, and prescribed the functional model of city government as the means of ameliorating those conditions. Progress towards an effective mode of innovation consisted of the *joint* improvement of a *coordinated* approach to analysis and prescription by moving from stage to stage.

Progress towards an effective mode of innovation in the current period was more rapid. The framework introduced by the *Our Cities* report looked forward to mechanisms on two levels: a federal means of planning and guiding national development, and means for urban governments to coordinate development in urban areas and take advantage of opportunities for improvement. The best example of the report's joint approach to analysis and prescription is its major recommendation. The Urbanism Committee argued that the worst problems of the cities in 1937 were primarily a function of the national economic crisis:

Because many of the most acute and persistent problems of the city cannot be solved until the fundamental issue of adequate and secure income is met, the Committee urges that efforts already made by Government, industry, and labor toward raising the level of family income and increasing economic security be continued and intensified.

Proposed mechanisms for the urban level of the two-level approach called for incorporation of urban governments into a national planning system that would include a federal urban research bureau, creation of a "clearing house of urban information" in the Census Bureau, incorporation of city planning agencies into national "public works planning," and the requirement that federal aid for housing construction and slum removal be "conditioned on the existence of a comprehensive city plan and a housing program meeting satisfactory standards."[8]

Development of the modern mode of innovation next jumped directly to the use of sophisticated theories of analysis and prescription on both the national and urban levels. On the national level, *Our Cities* looked forward to the emergence of a theoretical formulation of national development on which federal strategy and participation could be based. It proved possible to borrow such a formulation from the work of the English economic theorist John Maynard Keynes, whose *General Theory of Employment, Interest and Money* in advanced capitalist economic systems was first published in the United States in 1936. By 1946, analysis and prescription at the national level had taken the form of the Keynesian theory of national economic planning and development.[9]

Keynes postulated that national prosperity depended upon attaining "full" employment of all willing workers in the economy, that attaining full employment depended upon "effective demand" for the goods and services those workers would produce, and that attaining a "full-employment" level of effective demand required a certain determinable amount of aggregate spending throughout the economy within a given period. That is:

Spending $\longrightarrow$ Effective Demand $\longrightarrow$ Employment

and full employment would mean income to support an adequate style of living for the nation's individuals and families. Such a formulation made spending the crux of the problem of attaining national prosperity. Keynes divided spending into three major components: private consumption spending, private investment spending, and government spending. Together, the three components generated effective demand. In any short-run period, private spenders and government made plans to spend a certain amount, and this created a corresponding amount of effective demand. Keynes argued that if this resulting level of effective demand were too low, some workers would not be needed, would therefore not be employed, and would not receive income. Since the level of spending in the next period depended on the level of income in the preceding period, current unemployment would tend to lead to lower private spending in the next period, leading to lower effective demand, leading to still lower levels of employment. After several cycles of this process, a prosperous economy would move into Depression. Spending would also fall off if savers made plans to save (not spend) more money than investors planned to invest. In the next period, this would also lead to a decline in effective demand.

Given such conditions of economic interaction, how could an economy pursue and maintain prosperity? The answer, Keynes demonstrated, lay with government. Government could promote full employment and prosperity by (1) estimating the level of effective demand necessary to elicit full employment during a coming short-run period, (2) estimating expected private consumption and private investment in the coming period, and (3) setting government spending at a level equal to the difference between a full-employment level of effective demand and the expected level of private consumption and investment. For American followers of Keynes, the experience of the 1930–1945 period provided an ideal demonstration of the validity of this approach. The New Deal failed to pull the economy out of the Depression because it never generated sufficient government spending to attain a full-employment level of effective demand. Conversely, during World War II, government spending was so high that total effective demand was greater than the full-employment level, resulting not just in full employment and prosperity, but also in inflation. Lawrence Klein's abstraction of the 1930–1945 experience in his 1947 book *The Keynesian Revolution* typified its use in explaining the power and significance of the *General Theory* to the intelligent American layman:

> In the years before the war, the type of policy needed was one to combat deflation. The depression conditions of the 1930s were never successfully eradicated by government action. Looking back, at this

time [1947], on our policy we can easily see why the United States remained in a depressed state for a decade. The size of the deflationary gap was never properly estimated, and the government activity needed to restore full employment was actually much greater than that which was instituted. The impact of the war on our economy showed clearly that if the government expenditure is sufficiently high, full employment follows automatically. The war activities of the government were, of course, larger than the necessary full-employment activities of a peacetime situation. That is why we experienced an inflationary pressure. But an intelligent politico-economic policy need not necessarily be either too great, or too small. It could be just right.

The pervasive fear that the boom of the mid-1940s would be followed by another, perhaps more catastrophic, depression helped the Keynesians win adherents to their theory of national economic planning and management.[10]

The other half of the modern mode of urban political innovation, the mechanism of analysis and prescription at the urban level, emerged from the application of the kind of systemic approach pioneered by Charles Merriam and his associates in the 1920s and 1930s to the cities and metropolitan areas of a national economy managed on Keynesian principles. Methods of analyzing "behavior" within political systems were also employed. Characteristics of urban political systems generated by Keynesian national economic management included a surrounding environment of national economic growth, relatively high levels of employment in urban areas, assurance of minimally decent economic security for urban families and individuals, and considerable federal government "investment" in urban renewal, housing, transportation, and other aspects of urban development as an aspect of federal spending to generate full employment.[11]

Research and theorizing in the 1950s led directly to the formulation of a sophisticated mode of analysis and prescription for cities and metropolitan areas, the approach usually referred to as "urban pluralism." The originators of urban pluralism focused on the "processes" of politics and government in urban systems, and produced an approach in which the analytic side defined the various processes and explained how they functioned, while the prescriptive aspects emphasized that improvement would come through increased participation by individuals and groups in the processes described by the analytic findings, and through structural changes that encouraged and facilitated greater participation. The term "pluralism," meaning "rule by the many" and intended to serve as an antonym for "oligarchy," meaning "rule by the few" or rule by an elite, signified both the analytic finding that the processes of urban politics and government in the context of a Keynesian climate of national development were, in fact, open, accessible, and not dominated by powerful elites or individuals, and the prescriptive argument that efforts should be made to facilitate even greater access and participation.

Three major studies were particularly important to the formulation of urban pluralism: Robert Dahl's *Who Governs?*, a study of the political system of New Haven, Connecticut in the mid-1950s, *Governing New York City, Politics in the Metropolis*, a study of New York City supervised by Wallace Sayre and Herbert Kaufman, and *1400 Governments*, an analysis of the metropolitan political system of the New York metropolitan region by Robert C. Wood. Each of the three books was both a report on a major case study and a formulation of urban pluralism as an analytic and prescriptive approach.[12]

Dahl cast his book as an answer to the question: "In a political system where nearly every adult may vote but where knowledge, wealth, social position, access to officials, and other resources are unequally distributed, who actually governs?" He proposed to discover whether the existing governmental structure and political processes of a typical city, functioning within a national society pursuing prosperity and economic growth according to Keynesian principles, produced results that could be characterized as "democratic." The two contemplated alternatives were that city politics might be dominated by a cohesive and powerful "elite," or that city politics might not "work" at all, producing frustration, alienation, and destructive conflict. Sayre and Kaufman took a less pointed approach, presenting their study as a description of *how* city politics worked. Both studies demonstrated, at least to the satisfaction of their authors, that the political system of the American city functioned in a satisfactorily democratic manner. Sayre and Kaufman concluded that New York was admirably democratic and probably better governed than other American cities:

The most lasting impressions created by a systematic analysis of New York City's political and governmental system as a whole are its democratic virtues: its qualities of openness, its commitments to bargaining and accommodation among participants, its receptivity to new participants, its opportunities for the exercise of leadership by an unmatched variety and number of the city's residents new and old. Defects accompany these virtues, and in some situations overshadow them, but the City of New York can confidently ask: What other large American city is as democratically and as well governed?

Dahl found that the political system of New Haven was also responsive to the interests of diverse groups, but more because the city's political leaders anticipated adverse reactions than as a result of the application of pressure and influence upon them. Dahl stressed that *"most citizens use their political resources scarcely at all"*, between 40 and 50 percent not even bothering to vote in city elections.[13]

In contrast, Wood found that the New York metropolitan region's political system really was not working. Wood argued that there were actually *two* political systems in the region: the system of local governments, of which there were more than 1,400, and the system of "Regional enterprises," such as the region-wide transportation and water supply agencies. Rather than producing meaningful decisions and forceful action, Wood found that the combined effect of "the attitudes of the participants, the nature of the political processes, and the rules of the political game" was only to strengthen the region's prevailing "economic trends." The two systems of politics, he wrote, "leave most of the important decisions for Regional development to the private marketplace. They work in ways which by and large encourage firms and households to continue 'doing what comes naturally.' "

Thus, little opportunity exists for the development of Regionwide public policy. Each government is preoccupied with its own problems, and collectively the governments are not prepared to formulate general policies for guiding economic development, or to make generalized responses to the financial pressures generated by urbanization. They are neither in a position to establish and enforce public criteria for appropriate conditions of growth nor to provide public services which the private sector requires on a Regionwide basis. By their organization, financing, and philosophy, they foreswear the opportunity for the exercise of these large powers.

Wood's prescriptive position on these findings was similar to Dahl's conclusion about New Haven. Enthusiastic activism could probably increase the "usefulness of the Region's human and material resources," but in fact, most metropolitan residents had no strong expectations about the effectiveness of local or metropolitan politics.[14]

Practical Models of Better Urban Government

For a mode of innovation to be useful in improving the conditions of urban life, its approach to analysis and prescription must be translated into practical models of improved forms of urban governmental structure and administration. The functional innovators were extremely interested in practical results and concentrated great energy on the specification and promotion of models for structural and administrative reform. The Census Bureau's chief objective for its urban statistics program was to provide assistance to city officials and activists working to convert their city governments to functional structure and administration. The functionalist municipal political scientists also concentrated on detailed specifications of structure and practice, and on training professional municipal administrators in the functional approach. Charles Beard served as a consultant to city governments and devoted much energy and time to the New York Municipal Research Bureau and the Training School for Public Administration. Most other functionalists were also intimately involved in the work of municipal research bureaus and in administrative training programs. By about 1912, implementation of the functional model had become the chief activity of participants in functional innovation. The network of individuals, organizations, university programs, research bureaus, and private consulting firms involved in implementing the functional approach to urban government and administration was much larger and more influential than the currently available urban history literature on the early twentieth century suggests. A full study of this network is very much needed, especially for the corrective it would provide for the excessive significance presently attributed to the struggle for political power among groups *within* cities in explaining how functional structure and administration became the prevailing form of American urban government by the late 1920s.[15]

Participants in what can best be labelled the "Keynesian-pluralist" mode of urban political innovation have certainly not been any less interested in practical results than their functionalist predecessors. The preparation of computerized models of the national economy that can be used to formulate and implement Keynesian management and development policy has grown into a multimillion dollar industry. There are also Keynesian models that individual cities and metropolitan areas can use to forecast their economic condition over the short and the long run. Federal urban renewal and urban development programs have stimulated almost all cities, towns, and metropolitan areas to use such Keynesian approaches to their own economic condition and future prospects as the basis for physical, social, and economic planning. These and other programs have also involved much federal spending on urban physical, economic, and social improvement.

It is the "pluralist" aspect of the current mode of innovation, however, that deals directly with the improvement of urban government. Here, at the city and metropolitan level, there has been much interest in using the products of analytic research to construct practical models of the "processes" of politics in city and metropolitan systems. An approach known as "federalism" has even developed, which deals with the interaction *between* federal pursuit of Keynesian objectives for the national economy and city and metropolitan political processes. Sayre and Kaufman's *Governing New York City* has become not just an important case study of a complex political system, but a guide to the workings of New York City's government that officials and politicians who are part of the system find indispensible. The War on Poverty, with its emphasis on "maximum feasible participation," is a prominent example of a pluralist approach to improving the conditions of life in large cities. The various "client advocacy" approaches to professional practice in city government departments and agencies, such as social service departments and city planning agencies, are also practical models of pluralist innovation. Other examples of pluralist innovation include the tremendous growth in the use of citizen advisory boards, the increased use of public hearings for the airing of discontent, and, on the side of the discontented, the greatly increased use and effectiveness of organized protest demonstrations in influencing decision-making and administrative policies and practices.[16]

The practical aspects of urban pluralism have also included a distaste for structural reform, especially at the metropolitan level. Pluralist analysis of metropolitan political systems has emphasized, above all else, the complexity of metropolitan political processes, leading almost inevitably to prescriptive arguments that structural changes will do no more than rearrange the character of the complexity. Most later discussion has tended to agree with Wood's suggestion in *1400 Governments* that major metropolitan structural reforms are only likely to come about under drastically critical circumstances. This is exactly the opposite of the prescriptive argument of the 1933 study of the Chicago metropolitan political system by Charles Merriam and his associates. The difference between the two approaches derives from their differing premises about the role of metropolitan areas in national development. Merriam worked from the assumption that metropolitan areas would be crucially active units in driving national development forward and determining its direction. Modern metropolitan pluralism, employing the Keynesian approach to national development, assumes that metropolitan areas play a passive role and therefore sees no necessity for strong local governmental means of organizing and managing metropolitan economic and social development. The one type of structural reform that pluralists *have* favored is administrative decentralization. The rationale for this has come not from a concern for structure, however, but as an extension of the prescriptive approach to processes. Pluralism favors decentralization because it distributes authority in numerous hands, and increases the access of individuals and groups to decision making and implementation. Pluralist innovators have been willing to bear a certain amount of increased expense in running decentralized school systems, for example, in order to obtain the benefits of increased citizen participation in school decision making and management.[17]

Urban Political Innovation in the 1970s

After the present era of national development has given way to a new era, characterized by new forces of change and new kinds of urban conditions, it will be the task of historians to give meaning and coherence to the events, policies and changes of the period that began in the 1930s. For the moment, no one has suggested that this present era has come to an end. It has become customary to use the term "post-industrial" when referring to our present circumstances, for lack of a better phrase. "Post-industrial" doesn't even mean what it appears to mean, however, since American society continues to be highly industrialized. Instead, it is an improper term for indicating the era following the conclusion of the industrialization process, a term that tells us no more than that we are presently living in the period *after* the era of industrialization, urbanization, and modernization, the era with which we have been concerned in this book.

Since modes of urban political innovation depend for their effectiveness on how acutely they confront the forces of national development, the onset of an urban crisis, such as the one American cities have been experiencing since the mid-1960s, should suggest not just that the Keynesian-pluralist approach to innovation may require adjustment, but also that the character of national development may be undergoing major changes. When we turn our attention to the past, and examine urban political development in an era for which we can clearly specify a beginning, an end, and a set of major characteristics of national development, it is appropriate to argue that the era's prevailing mode of urban innovation, functionalism, was abandoned in the late 1920s and early 1930s as a response to changes in the character of national development. Making decisions about how to pursue urban analysis and political innovation in 1977, and in the next five years, or ten years, requires that we make similarly strong judgments about the present urban crisis. If we conclude that the present crisis is only a more dramatic manifestation of the kinds of change we have been experiencing throughout the period since the 1930s, then it will be appropriate to retain our confidence in the Keynesian-pluralist approach to innovation. There are, however, two major alternatives to consider.

One alternative is that the years from the 1930s to the 1970s form a very short period of national development that has already come to a close. This may have been a brief era in which a mature industrial-urban national social system enjoyed constant growth and increasing prosperity, a minimum of internal social conflict, and the leadership of a rapidly developing international economic system. The loss of American influence in southeast Asia, the crisis of the structure of the international production and distribution of petroleum, and the world-wide economic crisis of the non-Communist nations in the mid-1970s, may all be aspects of a major transition to new characteristics of American development. If we are entering a completely new era of our history, however, the "urban" aspects of the transition should soon become less important than the larger changes in the national economic and social system. Social science concern with crisis in the cities should give way to efforts to formulate new conceptions of national economic and social change, and to controversy over new approaches to national economic and social policy. While there has been considerable talk about the obsolescence of Keynesianism as an approach to national economic policy over the past three years, it remains to be seen whether a real transition is under way or not.[18]

The other alternative is that Keynesian-pluralist innovation is not the approach to urban governmental improvement best suited to the character of national development in the present era. Our discussion of Keynesian-pluralist innovation has been far too sketchy to support an examination of this question here. I only want to reiterate our findings about the failures of indigenous pragmatic efforts at innovation by cities in the 1860s, '70s, and '80s, and about the importance of the decision in the 1890s to make a complete transition to a new approach to innovation. The 1890s were a decade of crisis in the course of industrialization, urbanization, and modernization but they were not years of transition from one period of national development to another. The municipal innovation problem of the 1890s, as we have delineated it in this study, stemmed from the lack of an adequate conception of the character of national development and the nature of its impact on urban life. There is considerable reason to suggest that the difficulties urban political science is having in dealing with the present urban crisis are of a similar nature.

An entirely separate fourth possibility is that political scientists and urban activists will abandon their conviction that innovation can make city government better. I have tried to demonstrate that the functionalist innovators at the turn of the century made an important contribution to the development of effective city government. I feel it is fair to insist that without the National

Municipal League, without the Census Bureau and its urban statistics program, without the university municipal political scientists, and without a well-conceived model of strong centralized, functionally departmentalized city government, it would have been extremely difficult for the cities to develop effective means of alleviating the miserable conditions produced by industrial urbanization. Today, political science is highly professionalized and has powerful internal norms concerning the kinds of work individual political scientists should do. Wallace Sayre and Nelson Polsby, in their 1965 history of American urban political science, explain that the modern urban political scientist has two major roles to play. One is the role that *all* urban political scientists played in the functionalist era, in which one addresses the question "What are the political prerequisites for making our cities more livable?" The other is the new role of "clinical observer and analyst" in which political scientists "view urban communities as political systems capable of yielding answers to some of the enduring problems of political science as a discipline." While both roles are important, they present the individual with the temptation to retreat entirely into the role of detached observer when the question of how to improve urban government becomes excessively difficult. It is unlikely that we will make our way out of the present urban crisis just as well, and as quickly, if most urban political scientists are concentrating on the "enduring problems" as we will if more effort is invested in innovation and reform.[19]

Notes

Introduction

1. As yet, there is no treatment of American development in the period from the 1850s to the 1930s that makes full use of recent advances in the analysis of industrialization, urbanization, and modernization. Development has been differentiated into these three elements for the purpose of studying currently developing nations, but the three processes have yet to be reintegrated into a type of analysis appropriate to countries such as the United States, where all three transformations occurred through one process of development. For an introduction to the problems of constructing an analysis of this kind, see Eric R. Lampard, "The Evolving System of Cities in the United States: Urbanization and Economic Development," in Harvey S. Perloff and Lowdon Wingo, Jr., eds., *Issues in Urban Economics* (Baltimore: Johns Hopkins University Press, 1968), pp. 81–139. Of the three components, industrialization is the oldest and most familiar. For an introduction to the analysis of urbanization see Philip M. Hauser and Leo F. Schnore, eds., *The Study of Urbanization* (New York: John Wiley and Sons, 1965); and for modernization: David Apter, *The Politics of Modernization* (Chicago: University of Chicago Press, 1965), which suggests means of differentiating between modernization and industrialization.

2. For a complete discussion of assumptions about the relationship between cities and national urban development in recent urban history research, see my paper: "Urban History and Urban Community, The National Development of Urban Government in the Industrial Age: 1870–1930" Urban Institute Working Paper No. 705–82, Washington, D.C., 1971. For a pathbreaking re-examination of traditional arguments about city growth, including a case study of the rise of San Diego from village to city in the late nineteenth century, see Eugene Smolensky and Donald Ratajczak, "The Conception of Cities," *Explorations in Entrepreneurial History*, second series, II (Winter, 1965), pp. 90–131.

1. The Municipal Problem of the Late Nineteenth-Century City

1. James Bryce, *The American Commonwealth* (1st ed., 2 vols.; London: Macmillan, 1889), I, 618.

2. For a concise survey of changing historical themes, see Charles N. Glaab, "The Historian and the American City: A Bibliographic Survey," in Philip M. Hauser and Leo F. Schnore, eds., *The Study of Urbanization* (New York: John Wiley and Sons, 1965), pp. 53–80.

3. For a discussion of the importance of perspective, or point of view, in writing urban history, see Kenneth Fox, "Urban History and Urban Community, The National Development of Urban Government in the Industrial Age: 1870–1930," Urban Institute Working Paper no. 705–82, Washington, D.C., 1971.

4. David R. Johnson, "Crime Patterns in Philadelphia, 1840–1870," and Bruce Laurie, "Fire Companies and Gangs in Southwark: The 1840s," in Allen F. Davis and Mark H. Haller, eds., *The Peoples of Philadelphia: A History of Ethnic Groups and Lower-Class Life, 1790–1940* (Philadelphia: Temple University Press, 1973), pp. 89–110 and 71–87, are two excellent studies of the antecedents of the ward machine, and of city political and social processes before the 1850s.

5. Gustavus Myers, *The History of Tammany Hall* (New York: 1901, 2nd ed., 1917, reprinted by Burt Franklin, 1968), and Jerome Mushkat, *Tammany: The Evolution of a Political Machine 1789–1865* (Syracuse: Syracuse University Press, 1971).

6. This description is pieced together from information in Myers, *Tammany Hall*; Alexander B. Callow, Jr., *The Tweed Ring* (New York: Oxford University Press, 1965), esp. pp. 115–131; and Matthew P. Breen, *Thirty Years of New York Politics Up-To-Date* (New York: pub. by the author, 1899).

7. Edward C. Banfield and James Q. Wilson, *City Politics* (Cambridge: Joint Center for Urban Studies–Harvard-MIT, 1963), pp. 115–118.

8. Breen, *New York Politics*, pp. 147–153; William L. Riordon, *Plunkitt of Tammany Hall* (New York: Alfred A. Knopf, 1948), pp. 121–132. For general discussions of the functioning of the ward machine, see Robert Merton, "The Latent Functions of the Machine," and Eric R. McKitrick, "The Study of Corruption," both first published in 1957 and conveniently reprinted in Bruce M. Stave, ed., *Urban Bosses, Machines, and Progressive Reformers* (Lexington: D. C. Heath, 1972), pp. 27–45; and Harold F. Gosnell, *Machine Politics: Chicago Model* (Chicago: University of Chicago Press, 1937).

9. Joel A. Tarr, *A Study in Boss Politics: William Lorimer of Chicago* (Urbana: University of Illinois Press, 1971), esp. pp. 3–47.

10. Robert H. Wiebe, *The Search For Order, 1877–1920* (New York: Hill and Wang, 1967), pp. 44–75; Harold Zink, *City Bosses in The United States* (Durham: Duke University Press, 1930), pp. 69–84; and Moorfield Storey, "Municipal Government in Boston," *Proceedings of the National Conference for Good City Government . . . , January . . . 1894* (Philadelphia: The Municipal League, 1894), p. 66.

11. James F. Richardson, *The New York Police: Colonial Times to 1901* (New York: Oxford University Press, 1970), pp. 86–108.

12. Roger Lane, *Policing the City: Boston, 1822–1885* (Cambridge, Mass.: Harvard University Press, 1967), esp. pp. 85–86, 118–156.

13. Charles E. Rosenberg, *The Cholera Years: The United States in 1832, 1849, and 1866* (Chicago: University of Chicago Press, 1962), pp. 192–212. Readers of Rosenberg's discussion of the Metropolitan Board must be careful about his real arguments about its achievements. In the text, he states that the board "had, by its efforts, turned away a cholera epidemic" (p. 210). In introducing the chapter on 1866, however, he concedes that "it is, of course, doubtful that the mildness of New York's cholera epidemic was due entirely, or perhaps even partially, to the efforts of the Metropolitan Board." Rosenberg excuses the misconception perpetrated in his text by protesting that historians are compelled to "deal with the felt reality of the time," which was that the board had saved the city.

14. For the only analysis of the Tweed machine that recognizes its decentralized nature, and that Tweed did not make the structure function by using "power," see Seymour J. Mandelbaum's *Boss Tweed's New York* (New York: John Wiley and Sons, 1965).

15. Sources for the details generalized here are Callow, *The Tweed Ring*; Myers, *Tammany Hall*; Breen, *New York Politics*; and Zink, *City Bosses*.

16. Mandelbaum, *Boss Tweed's New York*, pp. 77–78; Callow, *The Tweed Ring*, pp. 163–165. Tweed borrowed his financing methods from the railroad barons; see Matthew Josephson, *The Robber Barons* (New York: Harcourt, Brace and Co., 1934), esp. pp. 121–141; and, on the Union Pacific-Credit Mobilier scheme: Wallace Farnham, " 'The Weakened Spring of Government': A Study in Nineteenth Century History," *American Historical Review*, LXVIII, no. 3 (Apr. 1963): 662–680.

17. American securities totaling $110 million were marketed in London in the year 1871, for example, much of it New York City bonds. In the depression of 1873–1879, Europeans lost approximately $600 million invested in American stocks and bonds. See Thomas C. Cochran and William Miller, *The Age of Enterprise: A Social History of Industrial America* (New York: Macmillan, 1942; rev. ed., New York: Harper and Row, 1961), pp. 135–140. On New York City debt in the 1890s see: Edward Dana Durand, *The Finances of New York City* (New York: Macmillan, 1898), p. 295.

18. Mandelbaum, *Boss Tweed's New York*, pp. 131–140.

19. For the Gas Ring, see Bryce, *American Commonwealth*, II, 354–371; Zink, *City Bosses*, pp. 194–229; Charles N. Glaab and A. Theodore Brown, *A History of Urban America* (New York: Macmillan, 1967), pp. 206–208. On Boss Shepard, see Glaab and Brown, *Urban America*, pp. 209–211; and Monte A. Calvert, "The Manifest Functions of the Machine," in Stave, *Urban Bosses*, pp. 45–55.

20. Claudius O. Johnson, *Carter Henry Harrison I: Political Leader* (Chicago: University of Chicago Press, 1928). The quotation from Merriam is from his introduction to Johnson's book, pp. vii–ix. See also Bessie

Louise Pierce, *A History of Chicago* (3 vols.; New York: Alfred A. Knopf, 1957), III, 340–380.

21. For a discussion of the "pietistic-ritualistic" dichotomy in nineteenth-century midwestern politics, see Tarr, *Lorimer of Chicago*, pp. 3–23. See also Johnson, *Carter Harrison*, pp. 180–205; and Pierce, *History of Chicago*, III, 304–307, 351–363, 375–380.

22. Lloyd Wendt and Herman Kogan, *Bosses in Lusty Chicago: The Story of Bathhouse John and Hinky Dink* (Bloomington: Indiana University Press, 1967; originally published by Bobbs-Merrill, 1943, under the title *Lords of the Levee*), see esp. the introduction by Paul Douglas, late Senator from Illinois.

23. Henry David, *The History of the Haymarket Affair* (New York: Farrar and Rinehart, 1936), pp. 198–220.

24. Pierce, *History of Chicago*, III, 320–321.

25. Harold Syrett, *The City of Brooklyn, 1865–1898* (New York: Columbia University Press, 1944), pp. 87–137, 159–179; Gerald Kurland, *Seth Low, The Reformer in an Urban and Industrial Age* (New York: Twayne Publishers, 1971), pp. 25–49; Seth Low, *The Problem of Municipal Government in the United States, An Address . . . , Cornell University, March 16, 1887* (Ithaca: Andrus and Church, 1887).

26. Wiebe, *The Search for Order*, pp. 145–149.

2. *Municipal Law and Municipal Political Science*

1. Francis Lieber, "Reflections on the Changes Which May Seem Necessary in the Present Constitution of the State of New York," published by the New York Union League Club, May, 1867; reprinted in Francis Lieber, *Contributions to Political Science* (2 vols.; Philadelphia: J. P. Lippincott, 1881), II, 214–215.

2. Ibid., II, 214–217.

3. Thomas M. Cooley, *A Treatise on the Constitutional Limitations Which Rest Upon the Legislative Power of the States of the American Union* (Boston: Little, Brown, 1868).

4. For an introduction to Cooley's importance, see Sidney Fine, *Laissez-Faire and the General Welfare State: A Study of Conflict in American Thought, 1865–1901* (Ann Arbor: University of Michigan Press, 1956; paperback, 1964), p. 128 and following. The influence of Richard Hofstadter and his school of "conservative" liberal historiography on the analysis of legal and social ideas in the late nineteenth century has produced a very unfortunate misrepresentation of Cooley's intentions and significance. Hence works dealing with Cooley that have been influenced by Hofstadter, such as Clyde E. Jacobs's *Law Writers and the Courts; The Influence of Thomas M. Cooley, Christopher G. Tiedeman, and John F. Dillon upon American Constitutional Law* (Berkeley: University of California Press, 1954), and Robert G. McCloskey's *American Conservatism in the Age of Enterprise, 1865–1910* (Cambridge, Mass.: Harvard University Press, 1951; Harper Torchbook, 1965), do more to obfuscate Cooley's importance than to explain it. For the beginnings of a most necessary reinterpretation, see

Alan Jones, "Thomas M. Cooley and 'Laissez-Faire Constitutionalism': A Reconsideration," *Journal of American History*, LIII, no. 4 (Mar. 1967): 751–771. Hofstadter first presented his conservative interpretation of late nineteenth-century liberalism in *Social Darwinism in American Thought, 1860–1915* (Philadelphia: University of Pennsylvania Press, 1944). For an introduction to the approach to the legal and constitutional history of the 1860s and 1870s that is superceding the conservative-liberal interpretation, see Harold Hyman's excellent recent study *A More Perfect Union; The Impact of the Civil War and Reconstruction on the Constitution* (New York: Alfred A. Knopf, 1973). The last revised edition of Cooley's treatise, number eight, appeared in 1927. Cooley died in 1898.

5. Jones, "Cooley and Laissez-faire Constitutionalism," pp. 758–759. Cooley's treatise distilled out of a mass of state constitutions, laws, cases, precedents, and traditions a body of knowledge in which law students could be educated. *Constitutional Limitations* "had a broader circulation, greater sale, and was more frequently cited," according to Jones, "than any other book on American law published in the last half of the nineteenth century."

6. Cooley, *Constitutional Limitations*, 1st ed. (1868), p. 189.

7. Ibid., pp. 189–191.

8. Ibid., pp. 191–193.

9. Ibid., p. 200.

10. Ibid., p. 211.

11. Ibid., pp. 200–201.

12. Ibid., p. 203. The principle of reasonableness was central to Cooley's entire approach, not just to municipal corporations. It is the principle that conservative interpreters have used to prove that Cooley intended to found a philosophy of law that would shield industrial capitalism from social and economic regulation. Such interpretations rest largely on the reference to Cooley's rule of reasonableness in the case of *In Re* Jacobs (New York Court of Appeals, 1885) which struck down a law prohibiting cigar-making in tenement houses on the ground that it was pursuing the preservation of the public's health in an unreasonable way, and thereby interfering with the property rights of tenement house residents. See Fine, *Laissez-Faire and the General Welfare State*, pp. 156–157, and Jacobs, *Law Writers and the Courts*, pp. 50–55. Alan Jones has begun to show very convincingly that Cooley developed this and other rules from the traditions of the common law, and that he cannot be made to bear responsibility for the attachment of his name to perversions of the rule by lawyers and judges with capitalist sympathies that he never intended to support. See Jones, "Cooley and Laissez-Faire Constitutionalism," esp. pp. 751–752 and 764–766.

13. Cooley, *Constitutional Limitations*, 1st ed., pp. 211–212.

14. John F. Dillon, *Treatise on the Law of Municipal Corporations* (Chicago: J. Cockroft and Co., 1872).

15. See James Willard Hurst, *The Legitimacy of the Business Corporation in the Law of the United States, 1780–1970* (Charlottesville: University Press of Virginia, 1970), esp. ch. 2. This is an unjustifiably neglected book.

16. Ibid., p. 70.

17. Dillon, *Commentaries on The Law of Municipal Corporations* (Boston: Little, Brown, 1881), I, 115–116. On the *ultra vires* doctrine, see Lawrence M. Friedman, *A History of American Law* (New York: Simon and Schuster, 1973), pp. 462–463.

18. Anna Haddow, *Political Science in American Colleges and Universities, 1636–1900* (New York: D. Appleton-Century, 1939; reprinted by Octagon Books, 1969), pp. 122–123 on Lieber, and 180–181 on Burgess. See also Albert Somit and Joseph Tanenhaus, *The Development of Political Science: From Burgess to Behavioralism* (Boston: Allyn and Bacon, 1967), pp. 16–21.

19. Haddow, *Political Science in American Colleges*, pp. 178–182, 239–240, 194–196. Herbert Baxter Adams, *The Germanic Origins of New England Towns* (Baltimore: Johns Hopkins Studies in Historical and Political Science, 1882), 1st ser., vol. II. Studies by Adams students who later became prominent in municipal political science include: Albert Shaw, *Local Government in Illinois* (Baltimore: Johns Hopkins Studies, 1883), vol. III; and Edward Bemis, *Local Government in Michigan and the Northwest* (Baltimore: Johns Hopkins Studies, 1883), vol. V.

20. Haddow, *Political Science in American Colleges*, pp. 248–250. Haddow reports that in its early years *American Commonwealth* had no rivals as the textbook for political science courses.

21. James Bryce, *The American Commonwealth* (1st ed., 2 vols.; London: Macmillan, 1889), II, 212–215.

22. Ibid., II, 212–214. Bryce had little confidence in the value of education, because it was the propertied classes that received the education in most cases, and its chief effect on them was to overstimulate their faith in the value of existing institutional arrangements.

23. Ibid., II, 214–215, 296, 466.

24. Ibid., II, 281–296, 450–460.

25. Ibid., I, 609–613; II, 67, 87, 141. Wallace Sayre and Nelson Polsby properly recognize Bryce's importance in the initiation of a special field of municipal political science, but make the mistake of assuming that Bryce agreed with the Tilden Commission about the failings of city politics and about the appropriate remedies. They fail to recognize that Bryce placed his hopes for political improvement on his theory of public opinion leadership, and on the municipal reform movement he hoped it would help initiate. See Sayre and Polsby, "American Political Science and the Study of Urbanization," in Philip Hauser and Leo Schnore, eds., *The Study of Urbanization* (New York: John Wiley & Sons, 1965), pp. 115–120.

26. Bryce, *American Commonwealth*, 1st ed., II, 295–296, 460.

27. Also in this seminar were John Dewey and John Franklin Jameson. Bryce's most prominent American friends were Oliver Wendell Holmes, and Charles W. Eliot, the president of Harvard, whom he met on his first visit in 1870. See Edmund S. Ions, *James Bryce and American Democracy, 1870–1922*. (London: Macmillan, 1968). Bryce also formed a close association with Thomas Cooley, who contributed considerable insight, information and criticism to *The American Commonwealth*. See Everett S. Brown,

"The Contributions of Thomas M. Cooley to Bryce's *American Common-wealth*," *Michigan Law Review*, XXXI (1933): 346–355.
28. Frank J. Goodnow, *Municipal Home Rule: A Study in Administration* (New York: Macmillan, 1895), pp. 45–55, 225, 233, 260.
29. Ibid., pp. 258, 267–272.

3. City Self-Government Becomes an Objective of National Political Reform

1. Ari Hoogenboom, *Outlawing the Spoils: A History of the Civil Service Reform Movement, 1865–1883* (Urbana: University of Illinois Press, 1961). Again, as in the case of legal and social theory, historians of late nineteenth-century political reform are in the process of revising a conservative interpretation originally propounded by Richard Hofstadter. Hofstadter argued in *The Age of Reform* (New York: Random House, 1955) that the younger generation of reformers coming of age in the 1880s feared the social and economic transformation going on around them and responded to it with reform movements whose ultimate objective was to reassert the treasured values of an earlier agrarian and commercial society. The leading revisionist formulation is Robert Wiebe's *The Search for Order, 1877–1920* (New York: Hill and Wang, 1967), which argues that elite reform groups and an emerging middle class took an active role in imposing a progressive institutional framework upon the evolving industrial and urban society. The best interpretation of federal civil service reform comes from neither of these traditions, however. It can be found in Matthew Josephson's brilliant popular Marxist interpretation of late nineteenth-century politics: *The Politicos* (New York: Harcourt, Brace and World, 1938), esp. pp. 276–340. There is also an excellent treatment of federal civil service reform by Leonard D. White, one of the founders of the political science field of public administration; see *The Republican Era: A Study in Administrative History, 1869–1901* (New York: Free Press, 1958), esp. pp. 278–345.
2. The investigation proved too expensive for the Reform Club to complete and had to be transferred in 1892 to Dr. Charles Parkhurst's Society for the Prevention of Crime. See Robert Muccigrosso, "The City Reform Club: A Study in Late Nineteenth-Century Reform," *New York Historical Society Quarterly*, LII (July 1968): 235–254.
3. James B. Crooks, *Politics and Progress: The Rise of Urban Progressivism in Baltimore, 1895–1911* (Baton Rouge: Louisiana State University Press, 1968), pp. 13–15 and app.
4. On the New York Committee of Seventy of 1871, see Seymour J. Mandelbaum, *Boss Tweed's New York* (New York: John Wiley & Sons, 1965), pp. 80–86. On the Chicago Committee of Seventy of 1872–1873, see Bessie Louise Pierce, *A History of Chicago* (3 vols.; New York: Alfred A. Knopf, 1957), III, 341. See also William Tolman, *Municipal Reform Movements in the United States* (New York: Fleming H. Revell Co., 1895), pp.

58–59 on the Citizens' Club of Cincinnati and pp. 64–65 on the Citizens' Municipal Association.

5. Crooks, *Politics and Progress*, pp. 15–24 (on the Baltimore Reform League); Tolman, *Municipal Reform Movements*, pp. 124–128 (on the Reform League), pp. 103–104 (on the Massachusetts Society). "Man-milliner" was a catchall term for anything from "unmanliness" to homosexuality.

6. Without the 1,000 votes of defecting Republicans, Cleveland would have lost New York State's 218 electoral votes, and the election. The fact that this crucial role of the Mugwumps was largely a matter of coincidence does not detract from their importance to Cleveland's victory. For the popular vote for each state, see U.S. Bureau of the Census, *Historical Statistics From Colonial Times to 1957* (Washington, D.C.: 1960), pp. 683–689.

7. For an excellent study of the Mugwumps as a group, both in 1884 and after, see Gerald McFarland, *Mugwumps, Morals and Politics, 1884–1920* (Amherst: University of Massachusetts Press, 1975), esp. pp. 35–80. For Deming's explanation, see *Proceedings of the Louisville Conference for Good City Government . . . , 1897* (Philadelphia: National Municipal League, 1897), p. 282.

8. James C. Carter, "President's Annual Address," *Proceedings of the Third* [sic] *National Conference for Good City Government . . . , 1896* (Philadelphia: National Municipal League, 1896), p. 44. This was actually the fourth conference. For what he calls "municipal mugwumpery," the involvement of prominent Mugwumps in municipal reform between 1884 and 1920, see McFarland, *Mugwumps*, pp. 81–106.

9. Frank Mann Stewart, *A Half Century of Municipal Reform: The History of the National Municipal League* (Berkeley: University of California Press, 1950), pp. 11–15; Tolman, *Municipal Reform Movements*, pp. 70–71, 91–96; *Proceedings of the National Conference for Good City Government . . . , January . . . 1894* (Philadelphia: The Municipal League, 1894), pp. 315–318, 324–326; McFarland, *Mugwumps*, pp. 92–95. The City Club expressly barred women from membership. "Severing municipal from national politics" meant detaching city politics from the control of the state and national political parties. See below, Chapter 6.

10. *Proceedings of the Conference for Good City Government . . . , January . . . 1894*, pp. 332–334.

11. David P. Thelen, *The New Citizenship: Origins of Progressivism in Wisconsin, 1885–1900* (Columbia: University of Missouri Press, 1972), pp. 156–175. Thelen's analysis of the relationship between "Mugwumpery" in the mid-1880s and municipal reform in the 1890s is similar to the one presented here.

12. *Proceedings of the National Conference for Good City Government . . . , January . . . 1894*, pp. 46–48.

13. John A. Butler, "A Plea for High Ground in Municipal Reform," in ibid., pp. 230, 232.

14. Ibid., passim; Stewart, *Half Century of Reform*, pp. 15–22. The *Proceedings* reported that the conference had "brought the subject of needed reforms forcibly before the minds of those who realize that municipal

government is the one conspicuous failure in the political system of the United States," a paraphrase of Bryce's famous conclusion; see p. iv.

15. Woodruff was the moving spirit behind the entire league enterprise. Carter and Deming had been prominent New York Mugwumps in 1884 and leaders of the "bar association" movement to improve the legal profession. See Stewart, *Half Century of Reform*, pp. 176–177 on Woodruff and p. 174 on Carter, and McFarland, *Mugwumps*, p. 94 on Carter and pp. 89–90 on Deming. For Deming's speech, see *Proceedings . . . , January . . . 1894*, pp. 259–260.

16. *Proceedings . . . Second National Conference . . . December . . . 1894 . . . and . . . Third National Conference . . . May . . . 1895* (Philadelphia: National Municipal League, 1895), pp. 160–161, 146.

17. *Proceedings of the Louisville Conference for Good City Government . . . May . . . 1897* (Philadelphia: National Municipal League, 1897), pp. iii, 6–10.

18. Stewart, *Half Century of Reform*, pp. 28–29. For reasons I have not been able to determine, Dillon did not become involved in the committee's work.

19. Horace Deming, "The Municipal Problem in the United States," in National Municipal League, *A Municipal Program: Report of a Committee of the National Municipal League, Adopted by the League, November 17, 1899, Together with Explanatory and Other Papers* (New York: published for the League by Macmillan, 1900), pp. 36–58.

20. Leo S. Rowe, "A Summary of the Program," *A Municipal Program*, pp. 157–173; followed by the amendments and the municipal corporations act, pp. 174–224. Delos F. Wilcox's "An Examination of the Proposed Municipal Program," pp. 225–239, is a very useful guide to the elements of the amendments and the act. One reason the Municipal Program is now thought of as a "model city charter" is that the League's Second Municipal Program, issued in 1919 after more than six years of controversy, did take the form of a model charter. The fact that the first Program consisted of constitutional amendments and a state legislative act, rather than a model city charter, was very significant strategically.

21. Rowe, "Summary," pp. 172–173.

22. Ibid., p. 160.

4. The Census Bureau's Model of Good City Government

1. Thomas M. Cooley, *Constitutional Limitations* (1st ed.; Boston: Little, Brown, 1868), p. 189.

2. John F. Dillon, *Commentaries on the Law of Municipal Corporations* (3rd ed.; Boston: Little, Brown, 1881), I, 16–17.

3. Ibid., I, 33–34.

4. Dillon, *Municipal Corporations*, 4th ed., 1890, I, 5–7.

5. Census Office, *Tenth Census: 1880, Report on the Social Statistics of Cities*, George E. Waring, Jr., Expert and Special Agent (Washington, D.C.: 1886), pp. 531–532 and passim.

6. Census Office, *Report on the Vital and Social Statistics in the United States at the Eleventh Census: 1890, Part II, Vital Statistics of Cities of*

100,000 Population and Upward (Washington, D.C.: 1896); John S. Billings, M.D., *Report on the Social Statistics of the Cities in the United States at the Eleventh Census: 1890* (Washington, D.C.: 1895). For Billings's theory of the relationship between city public health and city government effectiveness, see: John S. Billings, M.D., *Public Health and Municipal Government*, Supplement to the *Annals of the American Academy of Political and Social Science*, Feb. 1891.

7. Billings, *Public Health and Municipal Government*; Billings, *Social Statistics of Cities: 1890*.

8. Adna Ferrin Weber, *The Growth of Cities in the Nineteenth Century* (New York: originally published as Volume Eleven, Columbia University Studies in History, Economics and Public Law, 1899; reprinted by Cornell University Press, 1963). The book was the published form of a doctoral dissertation written primarily under the direction of Walter F. Willcox when he was Assistant Professor of Social Science and Statistics and Political Economy at Cornell. Weber actually received his degree from Columbia. See Cornell reprint, pp. ix–xi, and 467–475.

9. Frederick R. Clow, "Suggestions for the Study of Municipal Finance," *Quarterly Journal of Economics*, X (1896): 455–466.

10. On the league's program, see L. S. Rowe, "Public Accounting under the Proposed Municipal Program," *Proceedings of the Columbus Conference for Good City Government . . . , November . . . 1899* (Philadelphia: National Municipal League, 1899), pp. 104–123; Edward M. Hartwell, "The Financial Reports of Municipalities with Special Reference to the Requirement of Uniformity," ibid., pp. 124–135; and Samuel E. Sparling, "The Importance of Uniformity for Purposes of Comparison," ibid., pp. 136–147. For the congressional authorization, see U.S. Department of Labor, *Bulletin of the Department of Labor*, no. 24 (Sept. 1899), "Statistics of Cities," pp. 625–626.

11. U.S. Department of Labor, *Bulletin of the Department of Labor*, no. 24 (Sept. 1899), "Statistics of Cities," pp. 625–698; *Bulletin of the Department of Labor*, no. 30 (Sept. 1900), "Statistics of Cities," pp. 916–1014; *Bulletin of the Department of Labor*, no. 25 (Nov. 1899), "Statistics of Cities—Editorial Note," pp. 765–767; *Proceedings of the National Association of Officials of Bureaus of Labor Statistics in the United States, Fifteenth Annual Convention . . . , July . . . 1899* (Richmond: 1899), p. 44; G. W. W. Hanger, U.S. Department of Labor, "Present Condition of Municipal Statistics in the United States," *Proceedings of the Rochester Conference for Good City Government . . . , 1901* (Philadelphia: National Municipal League, 1901), pp. 264–265. For Wright's career and philosophy of statistics, see James Leiby, *Carroll Wright and Labor Reform: The Origin of Labor Statistics* (Cambridge, Mass.: Harvard University Press, 1960).

12. Milo R. Maltbie, review of Department of Labor, *Statistics of Cities: 1899*, in *Municipal Affairs* (1899), III: 747–748; S. N. D. North to Secretary of Commerce and Labor George B. Cortelyou, Oct. 5, 1903, Box 19, File 57869 (old File E 603), and North to Secretary of Commerce and Labor Oscar S. Straus, March 11, 1907, Box 37, File 65683, both in National

Archives Record Group no. 40, General Records of the Department of Commerce, Office of the Secretary, General Correspondence, (hereafter referred to as NARG no. 40, Correspondence of the Secretary of Commerce).

13. Bureau of the Census, *Bulletin 20, Statistics of Cities Having a Population of over 25,000: 1902 and 1903* (Washington, D.C.: 1905), pp. v, 1–6; for Bureau-League relations and North's report on the first year of the program, see Edward M. Hartwell, "Report of Committee on Uniform Accounting and Statistics," *Proceedings of the New York Conference for Good City Government . . . , April . . . 1905* (Philadelphia: National Municipal League, 1905), pp. 206–234. The National Association of Comptrollers and Auditing Officers was founded at a subsequent bureau conference for city fiscal officials in 1906. It has since changed its name and is now known as the Municipal Finance Officers' Association.

14. Census Bureau, *Circular of Information Concerning the Work of the Permanent Census Bureau: 1902–1913* (Washington, D.C.: March 1914), pp. 19–20.

15. Bureau of the Census, *Bulletin 20, Statistics of Cities: 1902 and 1903*, pp. 4–5, and following.

16. *Bulletin 20, Statistics of Cities: 1902 and 1903*, table 42, pp. 464–469, and textual discussion on pp. 21, 48–49.

17. Ibid., pp. 21–22, 49.

18. LeGrand Powers, "The Bureau of the Census as an Agent of Municipal Reform," *Proceedings of the Pittsburgh Conference for Good City Government . . . , November . . . 1908* (Philadelphia: National Municipal League, 1908), pp. 328–336.

19. S. N. D. North, "The Outlook for Statistical Science in the United States," *Publications of the American Statistical Association*, XI (1908–1909): 17–26.

20. Bureau of the Census, *Special Reports, Statistics of Cities Having a Population of over 30,000: 1907* (Washington, D.C.: 1910), p. 13.

21. W. F. Willoughby, "The Correlation of Financial and Physical Statistics of Cities," *Proceedings of the Buffalo Conference for Good City Government . . . , November . . . 1910* (Philadelphia: National Municipal League, 1910), pp. 203–213.

22. Ibid.

23. Bureau of the Census, *Special Reports, Statistics of Cities: 1907*, pp. 96–108 and accompanying tables; Bureau of the Census, *Special Reports, General Statistics of Cities: 1909* (Washington, D.C.: 1913). For the later development of municipal financial administration, see Mabel L. Walker, *Municipal Expenditures* (Baltimore: Johns Hopkins University Press, 1930).

24. Frank Goodnow, *City Government in the United States* (New York: Century, 1904); Frank Goodnow, *Municipal Government* (New York: Century, 1909); Horace Deming, *The Government of American Cities: A Program of Democracy* (New York: G. P. Putnam's Sons, 1909); Charles Beard, *American City Government: A Survey of Newer Tendencies* (New York: Century, 1912); William Bennett Munro, *The Government of American Cities* (New York: Macmillan, 1913).

25. Goodnow, *Municipal Government*, pp. 14, 42–44, 76–77, 85–95. The quotations are from pp. 14 and 42–44.

26. Deming, *Government of American Cities*, pp. 153–155; Beard, *American City Government*, ch. 1, "The People of the City," and p. 36 for the quotations from Deming.

27. Wallace Sayre and Nelson Polsby, "American Political Science and the Study of Urbanization," in Philip Hauser and Leo Schnore, eds., *The Study of Urbanization* (New York: John Wiley and Sons, 1965), p. 122; Leo S. Rowe, "City Government as It Should Be and May Become," *Proceedings of the National Conference for Good City Government . . . , January . . . 1894* (Philadelphia: The Municipal League, 1894), p. 121; John F. Dillon, *Commentaries on the Law of Municipal Corporations* (Boston: Little, Brown, 5th ed., 1911).

28. Goodnow, *Municipal Government*; Beard, *American City Government*.

29. Samuel P. Hays, "The Politics of Reform in Municipal Government in the Progressive Era," *Pacific Northwest Quarterly*, LV (Oct. 1964): 168.

30. Alfred Chandler, *Strategy and Structure, Chapters in the History of the American Industrial Enterprise* (Cambridge, Mass.: M.I.T. Press, 1962), Chapters 1 and 2; Joseph Litterer, "Systematic Management: Design for Organizational Recoupling in American Manufacturing Firms," *Business History Review*, XXXVII, 4, (Winter, 1963), pp. 369–391.

31. Hays, "Reform in Municipal Government," p. 168–169.

5. *Municipal Progress, 1904–1930*

1. Charles Zeublin, *American Municipal Progress* (New York: Macmillan, revised edition, 1916), pp. 8–9, 12.

2. The public library of the City of San Francisco has copies of city government reports for the 1890s. The city's own copies seem to have been destroyed in the earthquake. Merchants Association of San Francisco, *Report to the Merchants Association of San Francisco upon the Necessity of a Revision of the Accounting System of the City Government of San Francisco* (San Francisco: 1910); California State Tax Association, *The Problem of High Taxes in San Francisco: Being a Discussion of Some of the Avoidable Causes of Waste and Inefficiency in Transacting the City's Business* (San Francisco: 1915).

3. *Report on a Survey of the Government of the City and County of San Francisco*, prepared for the San Francisco Real Estate Board by the Bureau of Municipal Research, New York (San Francisco: 1916); San Francisco Board of Supervisors, *San Francisco Municipal Report for the Fiscal Year Ended June 30, 1915*. See also the reports for 1916 and 1917. In 1938, when the Municipal Finance Officers' Association required a model city to demonstrate good financial practices, they chose to describe San Francisco; see Municipal Finance Officers' Association, *Manual of Accounting and Financial Procedure, in the Office of the Controller of the City and County of San Francisco* (Chicago: July 1938).

4. Bureau of the Census, *Statistics of Cities . . . , 1906* (Washington, D.C.: 1908), pp. 35–41; Bureau of the Census, *Financial Statistics of Cities . . . , 1911* (Washington, D.C.: 1913), pp. 27–29.

5. Brazer's study also provides a good introduction to the objectives and methods of determinant analysis; see Harvey E. Brazer, *City Expenditures in the United States* (New York: National Bureau of Economic Research, 1959), Occasional Paper 66.

6. The 1904 constant dollar estimates were made by using the 1958 constant dollar GNP estimates in *Historical Statistics to 1970*, p. 224, as a standard. Details of these and other calculations are available on request from the author.

7. Ernest S. Griffith, the only historian to date to attempt to use per capita statistics of city expenditures before 1902, did his best to avoid having to contradict the prevailing hypothesis. Griffith argues in his text that the range of city services expanded remarkably in the late nineteenth century. He implies, without stating it directly, that the amount of service provided each city resident also increased. His statistics appear to show that per capita expenditures were declining in the 1880s and 1890s. They are not well presented, however. Griffith avoids any firm conclusions based on his statistics. See Ernest S. Griffith, *A History of American City Government: The Conspicuous Failure, 1870–1900* (New York: Praeger Publishers for the National Municipal League, 1974), pp. 160–163. The argument presented by Charles Glaab and Theodore Brown has been particularly badly constructed. "Needs," they argue, were "expanding" in the late nineteenth century. "Government," which presumably means the effectiveness of service production, was "deteriorating." Therefore, per capita expenditures were presumably increasing, probably quite rapidly. But because they have not examined estimates for many cities, Glaab and Brown cannot be certain. They indicate that expenditures in New York City rose from $6.53 per capita in 1850 to $27.31 in 1900, and leave their readers to draw their own conclusions about trends for all cities. See Charles N. Glaab and A. Theodore Brown, *A History of Urban America* (rev. ed.; New York: Macmillan, 1976), pp. 162–170.

8. Since some categories, and parts of categories, of expenditures have been excluded from the present analysis, the individual expenditure figures do not add up to the total shown under the heading "Total Expenditures." For descriptions of the Census Bureau categories, see *Bulletin 20, Statistics of Cities: 1902 and 1903*, pp. 30–33.

9. The standard for deflating the figures in Table 2 was obtained by splicing together an index of average annual earnings for federal government employees prepared by Paul Douglas, and a series of figures on average annual compensation for full-time employees in government prepared by Simon Kuznets. See *Historical Statistics: Colonial Times to 1957*, p. 91, for the Douglas series, and p. 95 for the Kuznets series. Current dollar values were multiplied by the following factors: 1912: 0.956; 1923: 0.657; and 1930: 0.556.

10. Census Bureau, *Bulletin 20, Statistics of Cities: 1902 and 1903*, p. 49. This aspect of the bureau's prescriptions is discussed in Chapter 4.

11. For an introduction to the complexities of analyzing the costs of providing city services, see Werner Z. Hirsch, "The Supply of Urban Public Services," in Harvey Perloff and Lowdon Wingo, eds., *Issues in Urban Economics* (Baltimore: Johns Hopkins University Press for Resources for the Future, 1968), pp. 477–525. Harvey Brazer also presents a good discussion of the problems of using population size as an independent variable in analyzing variations in expenditures from city to city; see *City Expenditures*, pp. 13–15, 18–19, 28, 66–68.

12. See Charles M. Tiebout and David B. Houston, "Metropolitan Finance Reconsidered: Budget Functions and Multi-level Governments," *The Review of Economics and Statistics* (Nov. 1962): 412–417.

13. Hirsch, "The Supply of Urban Public Services," pp. 504–509; L. R. Gabler, "Population Size as a Determinant of City Expenditures and Employment—Some Further Evidence," *Land Economics*, XLVII, no. 2 (May 1971): 130–138.

14. See Hirsch, "The Supply of Urban Public Services," and Brazer, *City Expenditures*, pp. 19–20, 29, 66–68.

15. Highway expenditures are an exception to the general trend. Highway costs should decline per capita with increasing residential density, as reflected in Brazer's −0.26 correlation for 1951. The Census statistics for highway expenditures are not appropriate for this kind of analysis because they do not properly account for the effects of state and federal highway programs.

16. Brazer, *City Expenditures*, pp. 4–5.

17. Brazer wrote in the introduction to his study of expenditures: "While the same dollar outlays do not, in any two instances, produce the same quality or quantity of public service, it is expenditures rather than performance or units of service that we are analyzing. Efficiency and quality of service contribute to variations in expenditure levels, but we are a long way from being able to measure either. They have been neglected only because it is not feasible to do otherwise." See *City Expenditures*, p. 2. Today we know a great deal more about the problems relating to the concept of "efficiency," but we are not much closer to being satisfied with our ability to measure it.

6. Dilemmas of Municipal Democracy

1. Frank Goodnow, *Municipal Home Rule: A Study in Administration* (New York: Macmillan, 1895), pp. 2–4.

2. Frank Goodnow, *Municipal Government* (New York: Century, 1909), p. 94.

3. Ibid., pp. 379–381.

4. Horace Deming, *The Government of American Cities: A Program of Democracy* (New York: G. P. Putnam's Sons, 1909), pp. 153–155.

5. Charles Beard, *American City Government: A Survey of Newer Tendencies* (New York: Century, 1912), pp. 36–40.

6. Delos F. Wilcox, "An Examination of the Proposed Municipal Program," pp. 225–239; and Horace Deming, "The Municipal Problem in the United States," pp. 36–58; both in National Municipal League, *A Municipal Program* (New York: Macmillan for the National Municipal League, 1900).

7. Leo S. Rowe, "A Summary of the Program," *A Municipal Program*, pp. 157–173.

8. Ibid., pp. 167–168.

9. Frank J. Goodnow, "The Place of the Council and of the Mayor in the Organization of Municipal Government—The Necessity of Distinguishing Legislation from Administration," in *A Municipal Program*, pp. 74–87.

10. Goodnow, *Municipal Government*, p. 382.

11. Ibid., p. 383. Delos Wilcox advocated ward representation for exactly the opposite reason from Goodnow's; Wilcox felt that the neighborhoods of a large city required ward councilmen to maintain their "local civic spirit." Wilcox personally preferred a mixed council, part ward-based and part at-large, the at-large members forming "an honorary class . . . for the purpose of intelligent leadership." See Delos F. Wilcox, *The American City: A Problem in Democracy* (New York: Macmillan, 1904), pp. 290–292.

12. Charles Beard, *American Government and Politics* (New York: Macmillan, 1910), pp. 587–588; Beard, *American City Government*, p. 145.

13. James Bryce, *The American Commonwealth* (1st ed., 2 vols.; London: Macmillan, 1889), I, 608; II, 67, 129–130, 459.

14. Frank Goodnow, "The Tweed Ring in New York City," in *American Commonwealth*, 1st ed., II, 334–353. For Bryce's moderating position, see II, 77. A. Oakey Hall, the man who had occupied the office of mayor when the Tweed Ring was in power, charged Goodnow with libel for the statements made in this chapter. Bryce withdrew it from later editions of the book and substituted his own description of the Tweed Ring. See Robert C. Brooks, ed., *Bryce's American Commonwealth, Fiftieth Anniversary* (New York: Macmillan, 1939), pp. 41–42, 160.

15. For Lieber's proposal, see above, Chapter 2. Among the reforms proposed by the Tilden Commission to prevent a recurrence of schemes resembling the notorious Tweed Ring was a recommendation that the city legislature consist of a board of aldermen elected by universal suffrage, and a board of finance elected by persons paying annual property taxes of $500 or rent of more than $250. Bryce may have had some sympathy for this scheme, calling it "most novel" and referring to its effectiveness in Australia, but he bowed to the judgment of "practical men" that no American electorate would approve it because it was "undemocratic." See *American Commonwealth*, 1st ed., I, 615–616. For Goodnow's proposal, see *Municipal Government*, pp. 384–385.

16. Lea, quoted by Bryce, *American Commonwealth*, II, 370; Lincoln Steffens, *The Shame of the Cities* (New York: McClure, Phillips, 1905), p. 193; Goodnow, *City Government in the United States* (New York: Century, 1904), p. 305.

17. Woodrow Wilson, "Bryce's American Commonwealth: A Review," *Political Science Quarterly*, vol. IV, no. 1 (March 1889); reprinted in Brooks, ed., *Bryce's American Commonwealth, Fiftieth Anniversary*, pp. 169–188.

18. Deming, "The Municipal Problem," pp. 57–58; Charles Beard and Birl E. Shultz, *Documents on the State-Wide Initiative, Referendum and Recall* (New York: Macmillan, 1912), pp. 12–13, 22–23, 32–35.

19. Clinton Rogers Woodruff, "American Municipal Tendencies," *National Municipal Review*, I (1912): 15. Beard made only a very minor reference to the role of women in *American City Government*, despite his claim that he was presenting a "survey of newer tendencies"; see pp. 84–87.

20. Leo S. Rowe, *Problems of City Government* (New York: D. Appleton, 1908), p. 52.

21. Ibid., pp. 204, 51–52, 123, 135, 94.

22. William H. Allen, *Efficient Democracy* (New York: Dodd, Mead, 1907), p. 264. On Allen himself, see Jane S. Dahlberg, *The New York Bureau of Municipal Research* (New York: New York University Press, 1966), pp. 7 and ff., 264–265.

23. Woodruff, "American Municipal Tendencies," pp. 13–15.

24. Why Beard's *An Economic Interpretation of the Constitution of the United States* (New York: Macmillan, 1913) became the most controversial book ever written about American history has been discussed at length by historians, but not in a way that provides a suitable explanation. For Beard on the commission system, see *American City Government*, pp. 96–97; and for the league committee's report: "City Government by Commission: A Report," *National Municipal Review*, I (1912): 40–49. The report recommended that for large cities the at-large commission should be replaced by either a ward-based "council of popular representatives" or by some plan of proportional representation; see pp. 41, 43.

25. Beard, *American City Government*, "The People of the City," pp. 3–30.

26. "Events and Personalia," compiled by Beard, *National Municipal Review*, I (1912): 500.

27. Beard resigned as a protest against a blatant violation of academic freedom by Columbia President Nicholas Murray Butler. Beard also resigned from the directorship of the bureau because of Butler. Beard believed that Butler had convinced Andrew Carnegie to cease contributing to the bureau while he was its director. See Richard Hofstadter, *The Progressive Historians* (New York: Alfred A. Knopf, 1968), pp. 285–286; Dahlberg, *New York Bureau of Municipal Research*, pp. 25–26, 30.

28. Beard, "Training for Efficient Public Service," *Annals of the American Association of Political and Social Science*, LXIV (March 1916): 215–226.

29. Ibid., pp. 217–218.

30. Ibid., p. 226.

31. Dahlberg, *New York Bureau of Municipal Research*, foreword by Luther Gulick, p. v.

7. *Metropolitan Problems and the Decline of Functional Innovation*

1. Kenneth T. Jackson, "Urban Deconcentration in the Nineteenth Century: A Statistical Inquiry," in Leo F. Schnore, ed., *The New Urban History* (Princeton: Princeton University Press, 1975), p. 120. Jackson reports that this density is higher even than densities reported in cities in India when the area compared is as large as the Tenth Ward.

2. The definitive study of deconcentration in American urban development is Amos Hawley's, *The Changing Shape of Metropolitan America: Deconcentration Since 1920* (Glencoe, Ill.: Free Press, 1956). See esp. pp. 12–16. Hawley demonstrated that when the trends of population growth and movement for the entire nation were analyzed, treating all metropolitan areas together, that it was not until after 1920 that the fastest rate of population growth occurred in the ring five to ten miles from the central focus. This was a very rigorous definition of deconcentrating urban growth and movement. Leo F. Schnore was the first to point out that the very largest cities showed a deconcentrating pattern of growth as early as 1850 and that the time at which a particular city's growth shifted from a concentrating to a deconcentrating pattern depended more on that city's own size and age than on factors relating to national urban development. See his "The Timing of Metropolitan Decentralization," first published in 1959, and "Metropolitan Growth and Decentralization," first published in 1957, both reprinted in Leo F. Schnore, *The Urban Scene: Human Ecology and Demography* (Glencoe, Ill.: Free Press, 1965). Kenneth Jackson has elaborated the kinds of insights presented by Schnore into a provocative challenge to the complacent belief that the "suburbs" are a phenomenon that first appeared in the 1920s; in addition to "Urban Deconcentration in the Nineteenth Century," see "The Crabgrass Frontier: 150 Years of Suburban Growth in America," in Raymond A. Mohl and James F. Richardson, eds., *The Urban Experience* (Belmont, Calif.: Wadsworth, 1973), pp. 196–221; and "Metropolitan Government Versus Suburban Autonomy: Politics on the Crabgrass Frontier," in Kenneth T. Jackson and Stanley K. Schultz, eds., *Cities in American History* (New York: Alfred A. Knopf, 1972), pp. 442–462. More analysis is needed, however. My use of the 1890s as the decade when deconcentration became the prevailing trend for cities of over 100,000, is an estimate based on the presently available information. It is meant to imply that deconcentration was taking place in more than half of such cities by 1900.

3. Charles N. Glaab and A. Theodore Brown, *A History of Urban America* (New York: Macmillan, 1967; 2nd ed., 1976), pp. 143–144, 153–154.

4. Census Office, *Tenth Census: 1880, Report on the Social Statistics of Cities*, George E. Waring, Jr., Expert and Special Agent (Washington, D.C.: 1886), I, 531–532.

5. Bureau of the Census, *Special Reports: Street and Electric Railways: 1902*, prepared by W. M. Steuart, Chief Statistician for Manufactures, (Washington, D.C.: 1905), pp. 4–5, 23ff. The "single urban center" was explained in an introduction written by Durand.

6. Geographer to the Director, memorandum on "Centers of Population and Manufactures," Sept. 23, 1905; National Archives Record Group no. 29, *Records of the Bureau of the Census*, "Alphabetical Subject File, 1899–1950" (Preliminary Inventory no. 161, entry 160), Box 71, folder on "Metropolitan Districts and Ten Mile Area, December 18, 1911."

7. Bureau of the Census, *Bulletin 101, Industrial Districts: 1905, Manufactures and Population* (Washington, D.C.: 1909), S. N. D. North, Letter of Transmittal, May 15, 1909, p. 7.

8. Clipping from the Boston *Herald*, Sept. 21, 1905, entitled "City Rank and Population"; NARG no. 29, Alphabetical Subject File, Box 71, "Metropolitan Districts and Ten Mile Area, December 18, 1911."

9. Ibid. The Boston Metropolitan District was created in the 1880s by the Massachusetts General Court as a park and sewage removal area administered by a special commission. The district included Boston and contiguous suburbs.

10. Ibid. The article in the bureau file is: New York *Sun*, Sept. 27, 1905, "The Metropolitan Area of New York." On New Orleans and San Francisco, see Geographer to Mr. Hunt, Population Division, Jan. 20, 1911, memorandum entitled "Industrial or Metropolitan Districts of New Orleans and San Francisco for 1890 and 1900." The article on the Greater London area concept for San Francisco in the bureau file is from San Francisco *Merchant's Association Review*, Feb. 1911. It is in Box 71, folder on "Metropolitan Districts: 1910. Density of Metropolitan Districts." The article expressed concern that geographic hinderances preventing annexations to San Francisco would soon create a situation in which its corporate population would be smaller than that of Los Angeles and Seattle, giving the false impression that they had surpassed San Francisco as the great city of the Pacific Coast.

11. See tracing maps and density tables in the folder "Metropolitan Districts: 1910, Density of Districts"; NARG no. 29, "Alphabetical Subject File," Box 71.

12. Ibid., envelope entitled "Metropolitan Districts—London and New York: Comparison and Growth"; draft of a press release for Oct. 29, 1911, E. Dana Durand, Director of the Census, to Managing Editor, Oct. 24, 1911.

13. Ibid., Rathom to Secretary of Commerce and Labor Nagel, Oct. 20, 1911; Durand to Rathom, October 23, 1911; Rathom to Durand, Oct. 24, 1911; Nagel to Durand, Oct. 27, 1911; Durand to Rathom, Oct. 30, 1911. Rathom apparently had an advance look at Durand's press release before Oct. 20.

14. The final report used a less exact minimum of "about 150 or 200" persons per square mile. For 1920 and after, the value of 150 persons per square mile was made the standard.

15. Ibid., folder on "Metropolitan Districts and Ten Mile Area, Dec. 18, 1911."

16. "Population of Metropolitan Districts," *Abstract of the Census, Thirteenth Census of the United States: 1910* (Washington, D.C.: 1913), pp. 61–62. The date of the letter of transmittal for this volume is Dec. 21, 1912.

17. The metropolitan district reports remained tentative until the census of 1930, when, probably at Durand's direction in his role as Assistant to the Secretary of Commerce, a special volume of 253 pages was compiled, indicating that the metropolitan district should now be considered a major facet of the Census Bureau's analysis of population and cities. The Chamber of Commerce of the United States, as part of a campaign to promote metropolitan area-wide provision of various functional services, had the chamber of commerce of each city of over 50,000 prepare, for the year 1927, a description of its metropolitan area based on functional economic criteria, such as telephone service, mail service, sewage systems, membership in voluntary associations, and operations of real estate companies. The chamber presented these descriptions to the bureau and proposed that the metropolitan district concept be revised along these lines. But the bureau decided that such functional economic criteria produced delineations of the "trade area" or "industrial area" of a large city, and that these were not the same as the "population center" mapped out by the density criteria of the metropolitan district concept. So the density criteria were retained. Also for the 1930 report, all districts, including those of cities of 100,000 to 200,000, were delineated to include "all adjacent and contiguous civil divisions having a density of 150 inhabitants or more per square mile," thereby putting all districts on a strict density basis. For the 1920 criteria see *Fourteenth Census of the United States: 1920, Abstract* (Washington, D.C.: 1923), p. 87; and for the 1930 volume, *Fifteenth Census of the United States: 1930, Metropolitan Districts*, prepared by Clarence Batschelet, Geographer (Washington, D.C.: 1932).

18. For an introduction to the analysis of national urban growth and to the growth of cities within the context of national "systems of cities," see Brian J. L. Berry, "Cities as Systems within Systems of Cities," in John Friedmann and William Alonso, eds., *Regional Development and Planning* (Cambridge, Mass.: MIT Press, 1964), pp. 116–137; and "City Size Distribution and Economic Development," *Economic Development and Cultural Change*, IX, no. 4 (July 1961): 573–588, which is also by Berry. For the use of this approach in a historical analysis of U.S. urban growth, see Eric E. Lampard, "The Evolving System of Cities in the United States: Urbanization and Economic Development," in Harvey Perloff and Lowdon Wingo, eds., *Issues in Urban Economics* (Baltimore: Johns Hopkins University Press for Resources for the Future, 1968), pp. 81–139.

19. If the central city had maintained its 1910 area of 99.2 square miles, the fringe area of 1920 would have been 1,200.2 square miles, but total fringe density would probably have been greater than the 402.4 persons per square mile of 1910 because of the high density of the area annexed to the central city.

20. Robert C. Brooks, "Metropolitan Free Cities," *Political Science Quarterly*, XXX, no. 2, (June 1915): 222–234. New York City's budget was already four times greater than that of New York's state government, while Chicago's was almost twice the size of Illinois's.

21. The San Francisco Chamber of Commerce founded the Greater San Francisco Association in 1907. When the 1910 census figures for cities and

towns in the San Francisco Metropolitan District became available, the Oakland Chamber of Commerce did some research and came up with the proposition that the city of "Greater" Oakland, on the eastern shore of the Bay, could have a larger population than San Francisco by 1920. See Oakland Chamber of Commerce *Bulletin*, May 1912.

22. Chester C. Maxey, "The Political Integration of Metropolitan Communities," *National Municipal Review*, XI, no. 8 (Aug. 1922): 229–253.

23. Frank Mann Stewart, *A Half-Century of Municipal Reform, The History of the National Municipal League* (Berkeley: University of California Press, 1950), pp. 76–78.

24. The textbook was an up-to-date version of functional theory for the students of 1927. William Bennet Munro, *Municipal Government and Administration* (2 vols.; New York: Macmillan, 1927), I, 436–438. Munro went on to add: "Such movements usually have an uphill road to travel, for small communities are traditionally averse to being swallowed up in larger aggregations, but the propulsive forces are also strong and in most cases some sort of metropolitan unity is only a matter of time."

25. National Municipal League, Committee on Metropolitan Government, *The Government of Metropolitan Areas in the United States*, prepared by Paul Studenski with the Assistance of the Committee (New York: National Municipal League, 1930), p. 386.

26. Ibid., pp. 95, 215, 254–255, 216, 315, 366, 386. Functional special districts were deemed undesirable because they were not "democratic," they contained no political structure capable of expressing the "will of the residents"; see p. 315.

27. Quoted in Stewart, *Half-Century of Reform*, p. 78.

28. Thomas H. Reed, "Metropolitan Government," in Roderick D. McKenzie, et al., *The Metropolitan Community* (New York: 1933; reprinted by Russell and Russell, New York, 1967), pp. 303–310.

29. Roderick D. McKenzie and Calvin Schmid, "Expansion of the Political Area of the City," in McKenzie, *Metropolitan Community*, pp. 191–198.

30. Reed, "Metropolitan Government," pp. 309–310.

31. McKenzie, *Metropolitan Community*, p. 316.

32. Studenski, *Government of Metropolitan Areas*, pp. 389–390.

8. *Urban Political Innovation and National Development*

1. Urbanism Committee, National Resources Committee, *Our Cities: Their Role in the National Economy* (Washington, D.C.: GPO, 1937). On the persistence of centralized metropolitan government see H. Paul Friesema, "The Metropolis and the Maze of Local Government," *Urban Affairs Quarterly*, II, no. 2 (Dec. 1966): 68–90. Functional innovation also persisted after the 1930s; it continued to be the leading approach to innovation in the field of professional municipal administration. By the mid-1950s, practitioners of the new approach began to object that municipal administration was dwelling in the past and that an overhaul of the municipal government textbooks was long overdue. Lawrence Herson argued that if Goodnow's

Municipal Government of 1909 were reissued in a new dustjacket in 1957, it "would be indistinguishable from today's publications." See Lawrence Herson, "The Lost World of Municipal Government," *American Political Science Review*, LI (1957): 330–345.

2. Roderick D. McKenzie et al., *The Metropolitan Community* (New York: 1933; reprinted by Russell and Russell, New York, 1967). For the origins of the Social Science Research Council and a concise discussion of the *Recent Social Trends* project, see Barry D. Karl, *Charles Merriam and the Study of Politics* (Chicago: University of Chicago Press, 1974), pp. 118–139. For the report, see President's Research Committee on Social Trends, *Recent Social Trends in the United States* (New York: McGraw-Hill, 1933), pp. xi, 1530.

3. On the founding of the Local Community Research Committee, see Karl, *Merriam*, pp. 149–152. Robert E. Park and Ernest W. Burgess, founders of the now famous "Chicago" school of urban sociology, were involved in the "research" aspect of the Committee's work. For a summary of accomplishments in the first five years and goals for the future, see T. V. Smith and Leonard D. White, *Chicago: An Experiment in Social Science Research* (Chicago: University of Chicago Press, 1929). The metropolitan government report is Charles E. Merriam, Spencer D. Parratt and Albert Lepawsky, *The Government of the Metropolitan Region of Chicago* (Chicago: University of Chicago Press, 1933), see pp. 19, 79–83, and passim.

4. Karl, *Merriam*, pp. 137, 226–250; National Resources Committee, *Regional Factors in National Planning and Development* (Washington, D.C.: GPO, 1935).

5. Urbanism Committee, *Our Cities*, p. vii.

6. Ibid., pp. 52 and 4.

7. Albert Lepawsky, "Development of Urban Government," in Urbanism Committee, National Resources Committee, *Urban Government*, vol. I of the Supplementary Report of the Urbanism Committee (Washington, D.C.: GPO, 1939), pp. 1–54, cf. pp. 3 and 54. Lepawsky gave a concise history of the development of functional municipal administration, which he described by the phrase "a rationalization of the whole inner administrative scheme along functional lines"; see p. 39. Modern urban social scientists have made the mistake of belittling the significance of the Urbanism Committee's work. Lloyd Rodwin, for example, claims that the *Our Cities* report represented no more than a reflection of "slight shifts in doctrinal currents," and included studies that were "no more than pulse-taking essays." See his *Nations and Cities, A Comparison of Strategies for Urban Growth* (Boston: Houghton Mifflin, 1970), p. 236.

8. *Our Cities*, pp. x–xii.

9. John Maynard Keynes, *The General Theory of Employment, Interest and Money* (New York: Harcourt, Brace and World, 1936).

10. For aid with Keynes' *General Theory* see Alvin H. Hansen's *A Guide to Keynes* (New York: McGraw-Hill, 1953). Hansen was the dean of American Keynesians, along with Paul Samuelson, who was his student. Klein was Samuelson's student and *The Keynesian Revolution* began as his doctoral dissertation, directed by Samuelson. After a flurry of opposition,

economists ceased disputing the claim that Keynes had revolutionized economic policy making. See Lawrence R. Klein, *The Keynesian Revolution* (New York: Macmillan, 1947, paperback, 1961), pp. 168–169.

11. The Keynesians' preferred form of federal spending was "investment" in the basic productive capacity of the economy, particularly "socially useful projects" that were insufficiently profitable to be undertaken by private enterprise. Klein's proposal for urban development in his 1947 book reflects the naive enthusiasm of early Keynesian reform: "For example, the slums in every metropolitan district of the United States should be cleared away and replaced with modern low-cost dwelling units. Cities should be redesigned to diminish the nuisance of smoke, provide better traffic arteries, allocate space more rationally between dwelling areas and recreation areas, etc. These investment projects have not been and are not being undertaken, yet they are certainly desirable. . . . It is well known that the magnitude of all such building programs that are socially desirable could insure full employment in the United States for several years, at least." See Klein, *Keynesian Revolution*, p. 170. The best short description of the evolution of federal urban policy is Lloyd Rodwin's essay "The Quest to Save the Central City: The Experience of the United States," ch. 7 of *Nations and Cities*, pp. 217–267. For a detailed history of the process by which modern federal urban policy developed, see Mark I. Gelfand, *A Nation of Cities: The Federal Government's Response to the Challenges of Urban America, 1933–1965* (New York: Oxford University Press, 1975).

12. Robert Dahl, *Who Governs?* (New Haven: Yale University Press, 1961); Wallace S. Sayre, and Herbert Kaufman, *Governing New York City, Politics in the Metropolis* (New York: Russell Sage Foundation, 1960; paperback edition, W. W. Norton, 1965); Robert C. Wood, *1400 Governments, The Political Economy of the New York Metropolitan Region* (Cambridge: Harvard University Press, 1961). An important abstraction of the results of the New Haven study and their significance for the new theory of city politics was published by Nelson Polsby, one of Dahl's associates on the project: *Community Power and Political Theory* (New Haven: Yale University Press, 1963).

13. Sayre and Kaufman, *Governing New York City*, p. 738; Dahl, *Who Governs?* pp. 276–310, quotation from p. 276.

14. Wood, *1400 Governments*, quotations, in order of appearance, from pp. 173, 113, and 198.

15. Samuel P. Hays' much quoted and reprinted article "The Politics of Reform in Municipal Government in the Progressive Era," *Pacific Northwest Quarterly*, LV (Oct. 1964): 157–169, for example, has been very influential in promoting the hypothesis that functionalist reform was largely a matter of internal struggles for political power within cities. Hays' proposed explanatory strategy tends to preclude the possibility that a national network of functionalist innovators played an important role. For a very detailed catalogue of many of the elements of the national functionalist network, see Urbanism Committee, *Urban Government*.

16. Sayre and Kaufman's study was used even before it appeared in print to facilitate the revision of New York City's Charter initiated by Mayor Robert F. Wagner, Jr. On pluralist contributions to the War on Poverty, see Daniel P. Moynihan, *Maximum Feasible Misunderstanding: Community Action in the War on Poverty* (New York: Free Press, 1969), and John C. Donovan, *The Politics of Poverty* (New York: Pegasus, 1967). On organized protest as a political strategy, see Michael Lipsky, *Protest in City Politics* (Chicago: Rand McNally, 1970). For a general discussion of pluralist models of urban reform see Peter Marris and Martin Rein, *Dilemmas of Social Reform, Poverty and Community Action in the United States* (New York: Atherton, 1967).

17. John C. Bollens and Henry J. Schmandt, for example, began the discussion of government in the metropolis in their pluralist textbook of metropolitan politics with the statement: "Government is of great importance to metropolitan areas, but it nevertheless shapes up as a complex and bewildering pattern." See *The Metropolis, Its People, Politics and Economic Life* (New York: Harper and Row, 1965), p. 141. For Wood on the circumstances of metropolitan structural change, see *1400 Governments*, pp. 173–199. For a pluralist-inspired school decentralization scheme see the so-called Bundy report: Mayor's Advisory Panel on Decentralization of the New York City Schools, McGeorge Bundy, chairman, *Reconnection For Learning* (New York: 1967).

18. See, for example, an editorial in the *Wall Street Journal* of Monday, January 31, 1977 entitled "Keynes Is Dead," as well as "Response to 'Keynes Is Dead,'" a selection of letters published in the *Journal* of Thursday, February 17, 1977, and a dissenting editorial in the *New York Times* of Monday, March 7, 1977 entitled "Old Soldier Keynes."

19. Wallace Sayre and Nelson Polsby, "American Political Science and the Study of Urbanization," in Philip Hauser and Leo Schnore, eds., *The Study of Urbanization* (New York: John Wiley and Sons, 1965), pp. 140 and 127.

Bibliographic Essay

It is probably unavoidable that the historiography of any period of American history must consist primarily of constant re-evaluations of the period's role in the evolution of the ideology of American politics, culture, and society. Even the new field of urban history has been inordinately concerned with American "urbanism," the ideas and beliefs that presumably shape life in American cities. Economic history has been relatively successful in avoiding this preoccupation by maintaining close ties with economics, especially the "institutional" school of economics associated with Thorstein Veblen, John R. Commons, Wesley Clair Mitchell and Joseph Dorfman, and the various economic development approaches pioneered by Simon Kuznets, Carter Goodrich, and the American heirs of the tradition of Joseph Schumpeter, among others.

I undertook the project that led to the writing of this book by approaching urban government in the late nineteenth and early twentieth centuries from the institutional and economic development perspectives of economic history. I was interested first in the large question of the role of cities in economic development, then in the evolution of urban governments as institutions, and finally in the specific topic of the book: the sources and character of innovations in urban government. The writings that were most important in helping to design and carry out the research can best be arranged under these three headings.

On the topic of innovation, there were no works that dealt directly with innovation in urban government. As I have explained in Chapter 5, urban historians have favored an evolutionary explanation for the appearance of the various services encompassed by the functionalist model of city government, arguing that as the "need" for new services emerged, cities responded by developing the capability to perform them. Charles Glaab and A. Theodore Brown, in their *A History of Urban America* (New York: Macmillan, revised edition, 1976), provide a good example of such an argument. The evolutionary approach is not an adequate explanation by any means, and I have only been able to propose one aspect of a more desirable replacement. We are still in need of histories of the national industrial-urban transformation that move beyond description of the new kinds of services undertaken by city governments to the formulation of a comprehensive political economy of cities and urban governments in the industrial capitalist system.

On the specific question of the origins of the functionalist model of city government, the prevailing hypothesis has been the argument of Samuel P. Hays that it was an attempt to transfer the centralized decision-making processes and administrative structures characteristic of large industrial corporations to the realm of city politics and government. I have discussed the inadequacies of this hypothesis in Chapter 4. Hays' argument had an important influence on my research, however, because it encouraged me to study innovation in business in great detail as a basis for developing a new hypothesis about urban political innovation. Five studies dealing wholly, or in part, with business innovation proved particularly valuable: H. J. Habakkuk, *American and British Technology in the Nineteenth Century* (Cambridge: Cambridge University Press, 1962), Paul Strassmann's *Risk and Technological Innovation: American Manufacturing Methods during the Nineteenth Century* (Ithaca: Cornell University Press, 1959), Joseph Litterer's "Systematic Management: Design for Organizational Recoupling in American Manufacturing Firms," *Business History Review*, XXXVII, no. 4 (Winter, 1963), 369–391, Thomas C. Cochran's *Railroad Leaders, 1845–1890* (Cambridge: Harvard University Press, 1953), and, most important of all, Alfred D. Chandler's *Strategy and Structure* (Cambridge: M.I.T. Press, 1962).

The evolution of urban governments as institutions was a topic that appealed to the functionalist political scientists, but has received little attention since the decline of functionalism. Ernest S. Griffith recently published a comprehensive history of city government in the late nineteenth century, but it was part of a multi-volume history in which the first volume, on the colonial period, appeared in 1927. Griffith was a participant in the functionalist enterprise, and his book, *A History of American City Government: The Conspicuous Failure, 1870–1900* (New York: Praeger for the National Municipal League, 1974), is of considerable interest. Another essentially functionalist treatment is Albert Lepawsky's long article "Development of Urban Government," in Urbanism Committee, National Resources Committee, *Urban Government*, Volume I of the Supplementary Report of the Urbanism Committee (Washington, D.C.: GPO, 1939), pp. 1–54. Until we develop an effective formulation of the role of urban governments in the industrial capitalist social system, it is not likely that any new comprehensive treatments of their institutional evolution will be attempted. There have been some excellent treatments of the evolution of government in individual cities. Bessie Louise Pierce's *A History of Chicago* (3 vols.; New York: A. A. Knopf, 1937–1957) includes portions on government that form an outstanding example. Wallace Sayre and Herbert Kaufman's *Governing New York City* (New York: W. W. Norton, 1965) covers the development of that government since the consolidation of 1898 quite effectively. Without an analytic framework for organizing the mountains of data about hundreds of individual cities, however, a comprehensive history of governments will remain an extremely difficult and relatively unrewarding enterprise.

The role of cities in national development is an area in which important theoretical advances have been achieved in recent years. Economic geographers and urban economists have led the way, and the "system of cities" hypothesis that they have formulated provided the underpinnings for my original hypothesis that functionalist innovation could have been initiated and guided by a national coalition that approached the urban government problem from a national perspective. The system of cities hypothesis argues that a nation's cities are highly interdependent units of a system that constitutes the urban sector of the national economy. Social and economic forces of national development, especially such major forces as urbanization and industrialization, act upon the system of cities as a whole, while equilibrating forces within the system distribute population and economic activities in such a way as to maintain a remarkably stable pattern of relative population sizes and economic functions among the cities of the system. Individual cities may change their relative population size and functional role vis-à-vis the system of cities over long periods of time, but the overall pattern of distribution of population and economic activities among all cities tends to remain stable. Three articles that will introduce the hypothesis and present its most complete application, to date, to American urban development are: Brian J. L. Berry, "Cities as Systems within Systems of Cities," and "City Size Distributions and Economic Development," both reprinted in John Friedmann and William Alonso, eds., *Regional Development and Planning: A Reader* (Cambridge: M.I.T. Press, 1964), pp. 116–137 and 138–152; and Eric E. Lampard, "The Evolving System of Cities in the United States: Urbanization and Economic Development," in Harvey Perloff and Lowdon Wingo, eds., *Issues in Urban Economics* (Baltimore: Johns Hopkins Press for Resources for the Future, 1968), pp. 81–139. A pathbreaking application of a related form of systemic approach to the history of the origins of a single city is Eugene Smolensky and Donald Ratajczak, "The Conception of Cities," *Explorations in Entrepreneurial History*, Second ser., II (Winter, 1965), 90–131. The city is San Diego.

Defining the issues that eventually became the specific concerns of my research also involved an open-ended search along various paths. The more important stopping points are worth noting. Seymour J. Mandelbaum's *Boss Tweed's New York* (New York: John Wiley, 1965), for example, portrays Tweed as a master innovator, considerably more ingenious at creating administrative structures and organizing ambitious ventures than the private entrepreneurs of his day. More importantly, however, Mandelbaum points out that Tweed did no more than make the most of what was possible, given the state of national development and the character of the economic and social system in the 1860s. It was an era of almost anarchic market conditions, and "the mechanisms of the market place, which gave every commodity and every man a price, dominated society" (p. 5). Tweed "united the elements in a divided society," Mandelbaum argues, "in the only manner in which they could be united: by paying them off" (p. 67). This approach to Tweed's manner of coping with the urban government problem suggested that as the industrial capitalist social and economic system acquired a more rigid structure, in the 1880s and 1890s, more effective forms of urban government became possible. It also suggested that something more than indigenous trial-and-error in the cities was required to determine how more effective urban government should be structured and administered.

Reading Thomas Kuhn's *The Structure of Scientific Revolutions* (Chicago: University of Chicago Press, 1962) was an experience of singular importance. Kuhn's method is essentially the same as the currently popular social, economic, and intellectual approaches by which the major political revolutions are studied, but their application to the history of science produces reflections back upon the method itself in ways that stimulate re-examination of the reader's own relationship to his or her chosen historical methodology. An older book that sparks similar reactions in its readers is Carl Becker's *The Heavenly City of the Eighteenth-Century Philosophers* (New Haven: Yale University Press, 1932).

Two collections of essays were especially important in expanding my conception of what "cities" are, and of what the term "urban" should encompass. They are: Melvin Webber et al., *Explorations into Urban Structure* (Philadelphia: University of Pennsylvania Press, 1964), and Lowdon Wingo et al., *Cities and Space: The Future Uses of Urban Land* (Baltimore: Johns Hopkins Press for Resources for the Future, 1963). Two indispensable readers on urban and regional economics are Harvey Perloff and Lowdon Wingo, eds., *Issues in Urban Economics* (Baltimore: Johns Hopkins Press for Resources for the Future, 1968), and John Friedmann and William Alonso, eds., *Regional Development and Planning: A Reader* (Cambridge: M.I.T. Press, 1964).

Working out a clear position on the relationship between urban governments as entities with definite and only infrequently changing geographic boundaries, and cities and metropoli as continually fluctuating and changing conglomerations of population, required many, many hours of pondering over various historical studies of urban population data. Four of these were particularly useful: Leo Schnore, *The Urban Scene* (New York: Free Press, 1965); Warren S. Thompson, *Population: The Growth of Metropolitan Districts in the United States, 1900–1940* (Washington, D.C.: GPO, 1947); Amos Hawley, *The Changing Shape of Metropolitan America: Deconcentration since 1920* (Glencoe: Free Press, 1956); and Donald Bogue, *Population Growth in Standard Metropolitan Areas, 1900–1950* (Washington, D.C.: Housing and Home Finance Agency, 1953).

Once I had decided that it was necessary to research the role of the Census Bureau, two documents became essential: the "preliminary" inventory to Bureau records in the National Archives, which is available in most libraries, U.S. National Archives and Records Service, *Records of the Bureau of the Census, National Archives Preliminary Inventory Number 161* (Washington, D.C.: 1964), prepared by Katherine H. Davidson and Charlotte M. Ashby; and Bureau of the Census, *Circular of Information Concerning the Work of the Permanent Census Bureau: 1902–1913* (Washington, D.C.: March, 1914). Neither of the two books about the Bureau was of much direct assistance, but they are worth mentioning if only to brighten the obscurity into which they have fallen. They are: Carroll D. Wright, *The History and Growth of the United States Census* (Washington, D.C.: 1900), prepared for the Senate Committee on the Census with the assistance of William C. Hunt; and William Stull Holt, *The Bureau of the Census: Its History, Activities and Organization* (Washington, D.C.: Brookings, 1929).

The relationship between professionalized social science and reform activism requires much more attention than it has received. An excellent recent social history that focuses primarily on the emergence of professionalized economics is Mary O. Furner's *Advocacy and Objectivity: A Crisis in the Professionalization of American Social Science, 1865–1905* (Lexington: University Press of Kentucky, 1975). A good source of information on the development of statistics in the late nineteenth century is James Leiby's *Carroll Wright and Labor Reform: The Origins of Labor Statistics* (Cambridge: Harvard University Press, 1960). Sidney Fine's *Laissez Faire and the General Welfare State: A Study of Conflict in American Thought, 1865–1901* (Ann Arbor: University of Michigan Press, 1956), remains the best general description of social science and reform in the period, to be supplemented by Joseph Dorfman's *The Economic Mind in American Civilization* (5 vols.; New York: Viking, 1946–1959), on economic thought and economic reform proposals.

The decline of functionalism and the emergence of what I have called Keynesian-pluralist innovation have been roughly sketched in Wallace Sayre and Nelson Polsby's "American Political Science and the Study of Urbanization," in Philip Hauser and Leo Schnore, eds., *The Study of Urbanization* (New York: John Wiley, 1965), pp.

115–156. Lloyd Rodwin's *Nations and Cities: A Comparison of Strategies for Urban Growth* (Boston: Houghton Mifflin, 1970) contains one of the few discussions of the strategy of urban development in the United States since the 1930s to give explicit recognition to the importance of Keynesian theory. For a straightforward history of the evolution of federal participation in urban development, see Mark I. Gelfand, *A Nation of Cities: The Federal Government and Urban America, 1933–1965* (New York: Oxford University Press, 1975). For a fascinating example of modern theorizing about metropolitan government, see Vincent Ostrom, Charles M. Tiebout, and Robert Warren, "The Organization of Government in Metropolitan Areas: A Theoretical Inquiry," *American Political Science Review*, LV (December, 1961), 831–842.

The recent appearance of a school of urban development analysis employing an explicitly Marxist methodology has generated considerable excitement and presents the possibility that a major new framework for considering the role of cities and urban governments in national development is taking shape. Insightful examples of the new analysis include: Manuel Castells, "The Wild City," Richard Child Hill, "Fiscal Crisis and Political Struggle in the Decaying U.S. Central City," and Ann R. Markusen, "Class and Urban Social Expenditures: A Local Theory of the State," all in *Kapitalistate*, No. 4–5 (Summer, 1976), pp. 2–30, 31–49, and 50–65; also Matthew Edel, "The New York Crisis as Economic History," and David Gordon, "Capitalism and the Roots of Urban Crisis," both in Roger Alcaly and David Mermelstein, eds., *The Fiscal Crisis of American Cities* (New York: Random House, 1977), pp. 228–245 and 82–112, and David Harvey, "The Political Economy of Urbanization in Advanced Capitalist Societies: The Case of the United States," in Gary Gappert and Harold M. Rose, eds., *The Social Economy of Cities* (Beverly Hills: Sage Publications, 1975), pp. 119–163.

Finally, I want to acknowledge my debt to Robert Wiebe, whose *The Search for Order, 1877–1920* (New York: Hill and Wang, 1967), took the first step toward supplanting the dominance of the "conservative" liberal mode of analysis over the historiography of the late nineteenth and early twentieth centuries. There is no question that Richard Hofstadter, the dean of this school, was a brilliant historian. But the ideological uses to which he turned the history of the period in his published writings in order to influence the political and intellectual situation of the 1940s and 1950s, first with *Social Darwinism in American Thought, 1860–1915* (Philadelphia: University of Pennsylvania Press, 1944), and then with *The Age of Reform, from Bryan to F.D.R.* (New York: A. A. Knopf, 1955), the Pulitzer Prize winner in history for 1956, mean that we are not likely to make rapid progress toward a more desirable understanding of the late nineteenth and early twentieth centuries until we develop an entirely new framework for designing our research.

Index